HOUSES OF THE PRESIDENTS

OTHER BOOKS BY HUGH HOWARD

Mr. and Mrs. Madison's War

Houses of the Founding Fathers

The Painter's Chair

Dr. Kimball and Mr. Jefferson

Writers of the American South

Natchez

Colonial Houses

Thomas Jefferson, Architect

House-Dreams

Wright for Wright

The Preservationist's Progress

How Old Is This House?

OTHER BOOKS BY ROGER STRAUS III

Houses of the Founding Fathers

America's Great Railroad Stations (with Hugh Van Dusen and Ed Breslin)

Writers of the American South

Natchez

Thomas Jefferson, Architect

Wright for Wright

Modernism Reborn: Mid-Century American Houses (with Michael Webb)

U.S. 1: America's Original Main Street (with Andrew H. Malcolm)

Mississippi Currents (with Andrew H. Malcolm)

HOUSES OF THE PRESIDENTS

CHILDHOOD HOMES, FAMILY DWELLINGS, PRIVATE ESCAPES, AND GRAND ESTATES

by

HUGH HOWARD

Original Photography by

ROGER STRAUS III

Little, Brown and Company
New York | Boston | London

A nation must believe in three things.

It must believe in the past.

It must believe in the future.

It must, above all, believe in the capacity

of its own people so to learn from the past

that they can gain in judgment

in creating their own future.

FRANKLIN DELANO ROOSEVELT,

JUNE 31, 1941

CONTENTS

The ghost of Chester Arthur might well recognize this home—but he never actually lived in it. Re-created from a photograph in 1953, the tiny parsonage in Fairfield, Vermont, has two rooms downstairs with a sleeping loft above. *President Chester A. Arthur State Historic Site/Vermont Division for Historic Preservation*

INTRODUCTION

A CONSTITUTIONAL MATTER

As the eighteenth century drew to a close, the American experiment was regarded by European monarchs as little more than a worrisome aberration, and the new nation's impact on the world stage appeared to extend no further than the capacity of its farmers to produce grain and its merchant ships to carry goods to market. To Europe's surprise, no doubt, the United States survived and its role in the world evolved, guided by a series of men chosen under the auspices of a legal instrument that codified American governance.

The Constitution, promulgated in 1787 by fifty-five delegates and ratified by the states, superseded the Articles of Confederation. An election conducted under its terms in 1788 meant that the former commander in chief of the Continental Army, the man who had chaired the "Grand Convention," became the first head of the new republican state at his inauguration in 1789. As president (from the Latin *praesident,* literally "sitting before"), he would preside over a body of consenting citizens, not as its king but as its chief executive.

George Washington created a cabinet, calling upon the best available men to serve and freely delegating responsibilities to the likes of Secretary of State Thomas Jefferson and Secretary of the Treasury Alexander Hamilton. For the most part, Washington resisted the trappings of aristocracy. He listened more often than he spoke and, in his characteristically measured manner, he made the best decisions he could for the country he helped found. He set countless precedents that, to this day, guide the conduct of the nation's president. When his second term in office neared an end, he set perhaps the most important precedent of all when he retired willingly to his home, Mount Vernon, enabling the crucial mechanism of succession to advance the democratic experiment to its next stage.

Each of the men who followed him would, in his own way, build upon Washington's foundation. If kings and queens in our time are not yet an antiquarian curiosity, then, thanks in no small measure to those who have served as the nation's president, the most important American export has proved to be democracy, as constitutional governments have become the rule (with notable exceptions) around the globe.

HOME SWEET HOME

Houses of the Presidents sets out to examine the nation's chief executives in their domestic circumstances—that is, in their homes. Once again, George Washington is the paradigm: to understand the general, truly one must see him in his favorite place, Mount Vernon.

The forty-three men who have served (Grover Cleveland was elected to nonconsecutive terms, making him the twenty-second and twenty-fourth president of the United States) are survived by a great miscellany of dwellings that represent a range of social classes. The Virginia estate that Washington occupied for his entire adult life was a great plantation of some eight thousand acres, with its aptly

Major General Zachary Taylor shortly before his 1849 election to the office of the president, in an N. Currier (later to be Currier & Ives) colored lithograph.
Library of Congress / Prints and Photographs

named Mansion House overlooking the Potomac River. Though quite apart in time and place, the Roosevelt family home, Springwood, in Hyde Park, New York, offered its most famous occupant, Franklin Delano Roosevelt, a similarly majestic view of the mighty Hudson River throughout his life.

Other presidential houses are more modest, such as the birthplaces occupied briefly by presidents-to-be John F. Kennedy and Richard M. Nixon. Kennedy was born on a middle-class street in a trolley-car suburb of Boston, while Nixon entered the world at the opposite edge of the country in a plain bungalow-style cottage his father purchased as a kit from the pages of a catalog.

To travel to such landscapes, to visit these homes, is to learn something of each president, to gain a more intimate acquaintance with the men who occupied the nation's highest office. Just as the houses are varied, so are the life stages of the principal inhabitants of these birthplaces, boyhood homes, midlife dwellings, or, in later

life, retirement homes, such as Woodrow Wilson's row house in Washington, D.C., or Martin Van Buren's upstate New York country home, Lindenwald.

In the course of our survey, we witness men engaged in renovating or even designing their houses. Having studied the architectural volumes in his vast library, Thomas Jefferson spent more than half a century building and rebuilding Monticello outside Charlottesville, Virginia, and in doing so helped nudge the nation's architectural taste toward classicism. Abraham Lincoln took a different approach, as the roof was raised on his Quaker brown dwelling in Springfield while he was elsewhere in Illinois, as a country attorney traveling the court circuit.

There are houses closely associated with the office of the presidency. Lyndon Johnson's "Texas White House" near Johnson City and Theodore Roosevelt's "Summer White House" in Oyster Bay, New York, were longtime homes that entered the public domain during their owners' time in the presidency. The Hermitage, Andrew Jackson's plantation house outside Nashville, Tennessee, was nearly destroyed by fire while its owner occupied the President's house in Washington, D.C., which had only recently come to be called the White House.

One building in this volume remains home to a living ex-president and his wife, that of Jimmy and Rosalynn Carter, in Plains, Georgia, the town where both of them were born. In some cases, more than one house is associated with an individual president; there are, for example, four linked to Woodrow Wilson and three each with Franklin Delano Roosevelt and Ulysses S. Grant. But not all the men who occupied the office of the president are survived by sites that are open to the public, as there is no restored dwelling associated with Zachary Taylor (1849–1850) or Gerald Ford (1974–1977). The handsome brick home that Barack Obama (2009–) shares with Michelle Obama and their two daughters in the Kenwood section of Chicago remains a private dwelling, and none of his other domiciles, which included a rental in a '60s-era apartment building in Honolulu where he spent much of his childhood, has yet become a museum.

Gerald Ford's birthplace on Woolworth Avenue in Omaha, Nebraska. He and his mother lived here just sixteen days, after which his parents separated, and mother and child made their way to Michigan, where she would subsequently remarry.
Gerald R. Ford Library

Between 1971 and his school graduation in 1979, Barack Obama lived with his grandmother on the tenth floor of the Punahou Circle Apartments in Honolulu's Makiki neighborhood.
Luci Pemoni

The task in creating this book involved identifying not only the essential sites but also the means of telling stories that would locate each president in what had been, at some point in his life, his personal place. Thus, assembling this book has necessitated choices, such as the one to focus upon Grant's Cottage in upstate New York, where the dying Grant, with the financial support of Mark Twain, raced to complete his memoirs. Included here is the Lincoln Cottage at the Soldiers' Home in Washington, D.C., where one can almost envision Lincoln, just returned from a day of managing the war between the states from his White House office, standing on the porch at the cottage and watching the burials in a nearby graveyard, where the men he sent to war are laid to rest.

Looking at the presidents at home can sometimes explicate aspects that examining their political careers cannot. While in office both Calvin Coolidge and Ronald Reagan were the objects of strong personal affection among much of the electorate (admittedly to the puzzlement, in both instances, of many in opposition). But for admirer and doubter alike, to revisit them at work on their acreage in Vermont or California is to gain a broader apprehension of both "Silent Cal" and the actor-turned-politician, respectively, in the context of their rugged landscapes.

None of these men lived alone; to visit their homes is to meet the women with whom they shared their private lives. Even the only lifelong bachelor in the mix, James Buchanan, had an orphaned niece, Miss Harriet Lane, to greet his guests, and widowers Thomas Jefferson and Benjamin Harrison deployed their daughters. These women, along with memorable spouses (Dolley Madison, Mary Todd Lincoln, Eleanor Roosevelt, and many others) and influential mothers (among them Sara Delano Roosevelt, Rose Kennedy, and Hannah Milhous Nixon), occupied these homes and thus walk through these pages. There are also sons and daughters, grandchildren, valets, slaves, secretaries, and others.

Thomas Woodrow Wilson is one president proudly remembered by more than one community. In addition to his retirement home in Washington, D.C. (see page 116), his birthplace in Staunton, Virginia (*left*), has been restored as part of the Woodrow Wilson Presidential Library and Museum; and, in Augusta, Georgia, the Boyhood Home (*right*) revisits the eleven years "Tommy" Wilson spent there during the Civil War era.
Woodrow Wilson Presidential Library and Museum, and Historic Augusta, Inc.

Perhaps most important of all are the life histories of the presidents themselves. Even the least remembered presidents played essential roles in United States history, so in assembling *Houses of the Presidents* there was an implicit charge to locate these men in the public as well as the private context. To accomplish this, the chapters include brief presidential biographies that incorporate important story lines that, when woven together, amount to a larger national narrative.

THE AMERICAN WAY

Houses of the Presidents is organized chronologically by presidential years in office. At the core of the book are twenty-two chapters that

focus upon the houses of twenty-four presidents (two dwellings were home to father-and-son presidents, namely the Old House in Quincy, Massachusetts, home of John and John Quincy Adams, and the George W. Bush Childhood Home in Midland, Texas, once owned by George H. W. Bush). Another fifteen presidential residences that have been conserved are described in briefer fashion at the close of the book (see *Other Presidential Homes,* page 224).

In learning of these places, one encounters more than a little of the drama that is the story of the United States in the theater of world politics. An early move toward international influence was engendered by the man who lived at Montpelier, James Madison. His reluctant declaration of war on Great Britain in 1812 led to something less than a resounding victory for his nation, but during the conflict the U.S. Navy gained international respect, having more than held its own against the seemingly invincible Royal Navy. After Madison retired to Montpelier, President James Monroe, aided by the pen of his secretary of state, John Quincy Adams, articulated what came to be known as the Monroe Doctrine, which warned the powers of Europe to leave the Americas well enough alone. Later in the century Theodore Roosevelt left his Sagamore Hill home to lead his Rough Riders to Cuba, where he memorably confronted Spanish forces in 1898; during his presidency, he won the 1906 Nobel Peace Prize after his diplomatic efforts ended the Russo-Japanese War.

In what Henry Luce described as the "American Century," Woodrow Wilson set a new tone in his address to Congress in 1917, asserting that "the world must be made safe for democracy." Having made the case for United States participation in the Great War, he became the first American to be regarded by the heads of state in Europe as a statesman of international significance; his Washington home is filled with memorabilia that attests to the respect shown him by monarchs and even the pope, when Wilson traveled to Europe to present his plan for the League of Nations.

Together with Churchill, Franklin Delano Roosevelt led the Allies in World War II, while a future president, Dwight D. Eisenhower, masterminded the military victory in Europe. The later outcomes of Asian conflicts—in Korea and Vietnam—and those in the Middle East (Iraq and Afghanistan) are more complex, but the American role is central. One cannot visit Eisenhower's farm, Reagan's ranch, or Jimmy Carter's suburban home without recalling the owner's role in international affairs.

The vagaries of domestic politics are also writ between the lines on every page of this book. We see the evolution of the process of campaigning. While the early presidents limited their efforts to writing letters—they gave no speeches, shook no hands, kissed no babies—the election of William Henry Harrison saw him traveling widely to deliver speeches in a campaign during which sloganeering emerged as a political tool (Harrison and running mate John Tyler were carried into office to the lyrics of "Tippecanoe and Tyler Too").

Lincoln's great rhetorical gifts as both a speaker and a debater helped him win office, just as the radio proved an effective tool for Calvin Coolidge and, in particular, for Franklin Roosevelt, as he took to the airwaves for his "Fireside Chats." The advent of television made possible electrifying moments such as the Kennedy-Nixon debates in 1960 and *The Man from Hope,* the film profile of Bill Clinton broadcast from the 1992 Democratic National Convention.

In the researching and writing of this book, the attempt has been to take the political equivalent of a nondenominational approach to matters of party. Thus the reader will find no sharp judgments offered in these pages, as the assessments are based upon broad historical consensus rather than a particular point of view. The aim is to offer a fresh perspective for regarding the presidents within the continuum of the nation's history.

Some presidents have been virtually lost in the mists of time; thus, another goal of *Houses of the Presidents* is to dispel to some degree reductive thinking such as that of Thomas Wolfe, who once described Ulysses S. Grant, Benjamin Harrison, and other presidents of their era as men of "gravely vacant and bewhiskered faces." In truth, there is much to admire in the lives of presidents Grant, Harrison, and the rest.

The presidential perspective is hardly all-encompassing, but it does offer glimpses of the nation's most essential moments. Standing at their posts along the timeline of American history, inhabiting places fancy and plain, these presidents all played parts in the pursuit of our national destiny. By recollecting them—as boys or elder statesmen, as officers and presidents, as sons and husbands and heroes—perhaps we may reach a richer appreciation of both the nation's dramatic past and the potential for its future.

MOUNT VERNON

GEORGE WASHINGTON
(1789 – 1797)

MOUNT VERNON, VIRGINIA

"I can religiously aver that no man was
ever more tired of public life,
or more devoutly wished for retirement,
than I do."

**GEORGE WASHINGTON TO EDMUND PENDLETON,
JANUARY 22, 1795**

◇◇◇◇◇◇◇◇◇◇◇

A FINAL RETIREMENT

T he year 1799 began with a happy occasion. As it had for each of the last forty years, the close of the holiday season at Twelfth Night coincided with a marital milestone: George and Martha's nuptial day had been January 6, 1759.

The next month brought a birthday to honor, as the aging general, just two years retired from the office of the president, celebrated his sixty-seventh birthday. If he showed his years, that was unsurprising, given that over the decades he had survived two wars as well as attacks of dysentery, smallpox, pneumonia, skin cancer, arthritis, continual dental problems, and recurring bouts with malaria, most recently during the summer of 1798, when he took to his bed for a month. Yet, as one visitor reported that February, George Washington (1732–1799) had a "healthy look" in spite of his "rough, weather beaten countenance." He was the first to say that he was also delighted to be home, having returned to what he called "my long forsaken residence at Mount Vernon."

The arrival of the birthday brought a double dose of good spirits to the Mount Vernon household, compliments of Nelly. "Beautiful Nelly," as some called her, was her stepgrandfather's favorite. She had been put in the care of her grandmother as a baby, and had been George and Martha's ward since the death of her father when Nelly was two. But this day the lively young woman would add another marital bond between the Washington and Custis families.

The talk after their return to Mount Vernon had been that Nelly was in love with George Washington Lafayette, the Marquis's son, who had been in the care of the Washingtons during his father's imprisonment in France in the wake of the French Revolution. But Nelly had dismissed the rumors. Since then young Lafayette had returned to France, and an unlikely suitor had won her hand. Washington's nephew, Lawrence Lewis, son of George's sister Betty, was a widower twelve years Nelly's senior. Though staid and less ambitious than the general might have wished, he won Nelly's heart ("Cupid," she wrote to a friend, ". . . slyly called in Lawrence Lewis to his aid, & transfixed me with a Dart"). In honor of the general's birthday, Nelly descended the stair in the main passage at Mount Vernon, her arm resting on his, with magnificent feathers in her hair, as the candles were lit on February 22, 1799.

The revelry lasted for more than a week, and even the slaves took part (many years later, one recollected "how olde Mistis [Mistress

---

Previous page: Washington's most significant contribution to American architecture was the piazza that runs the full ninety-six-foot length of the East Front; its piers support a roof eighteen feet above. It's a social space for coffee and conversation where the family relaxed and guests were welcomed.

Opposite: The devoted grandfather ordered this harpsichord for Nelly Custis from London in 1793. Although the instrument departed with Nelly to her nearby home at Woodlawn after the general's death, descendants returned it to Mount Vernon, where it is now installed in the Little Parlor.

The hall, or passage, is the house's internal crossroads, running the depth of the home, allowing for breezes in the warm Virginia climate, and accessing both the upper floors and four principal downstairs rooms. Visible through the open doorway to the left is the Small Dining Room; even at a distance, its verdigris green glazing is striking.

Washington] let all the servants come in and see it & gave them such good things to eat"). Mr. and Mrs. Lewis embarked on a traditional bridal tour to the homes of friends and family, and didn't return until late October. When they did, Nelly was large with child, and she and Martha set about making preparations for the arrival of the "sweet stranger." George had gifted the couple two thousand acres of land adjacent to Mount Vernon on which to build a house. Until construction was completed, however, the Lewises would remain at Mount Vernon, Nelly in the bosom of her family.

Frances Parke Lewis, a baby girl to be known as "Parke," arrived on November 27. As Nelly regained her strength, nursed by her doting grandmother, life had a happy domesticity for the multigenerational family in residence at Mount Vernon. But that would come to a sudden end when George Washington succumbed to an ague (fever and chills) complicated by swelling in his throat and excessive bloodletting treatments prescribed by his well-intentioned doctors. Shortly after ten o'clock on the evening of December 14, 1799, George Washington's breathing seemed to ease and, after taking his own pulse, Washington uttered his last words. He said simply, "'Tis well."

The ritual passages of life—birth, marriage, and death—were all enacted at Mount Vernon in the closing year of the eighteenth century.

Above: More than a dozen dependencies for a mix of agricultural purposes dotted the landscape around the Mansion House, which is visible to the left in this image. The smaller structures in the foreground here on the North Lane include the Salt House and the Gardener's House.

Right: Like so many enlightened eighteenth-century gentlemen, the squire of Mount Vernon was influenced by the Palladian Revival, an architectural wave inspired by the work of sixteenth-century architect Andrea Palladio. Like many of Palladio's villas, Mount Vernon consisted of a main block flanked by dependencies and linked by structures such as curved arcades (or "colonnades," as they were known). The covered way pictured here protected the Washingtons and the house slaves passing to and from the Servants' Hall; the mirror-image colonnade on the other side of the mansion protected people as they went between the kitchen and the door leading to the Butler's Pantry and the Small Dining Room.

A VISIT TO MOUNT VERNON

Seeking the company of the great and the good, Joshua Brookes pointed his horse westward, turning from the main thoroughfare onto a private wooded road. Two miles on, the twenty-six-year-old Englishman, together with two traveling companions, ascended a hill, passed through a white gate, and approached the Mansion House. They carried a letter of introduction to the man who was already well known as the father of his country, but it is Brookes's own jottings—he kept a detailed journal of his travels—that even today breathe life into his visit on February 4, 1799, barely a fortnight before Nelly's wedding.

As its owner hoped it would, the wide white building with the tall red roof fooled the eye of the approaching visitor. "The house is of stone," noted Brookes in his diary—although the general's home was actually a wood-framed structure, sided with pine boards. Washington had instructed his carpenters to cut and chamfer matched planks to give the exterior the look of rusticated stone, an effect that was enhanced when fine sand was dashed onto still-tacky paint.

Brookes looked upon a proud house, one that Washington in his years of ownership had twice enlarged and improved. At the time of his marriage, Colonel Washington—he had earned his rank serving in the Virginia militia (1754–1758) and fighting for the British in the French and Indian War—had welcomed Martha and her two children to a home where the roof had just been raised to include a full second story and garret rooms on the third floor; later, as he emerged as a national figure during the Revolution (1775–

Above: The home that young George Washington inherited in 1754 after his half brother Lawrence's death didn't look like this. In two separate campaigns he raised the roof (to provide a third story) and added two bays to each end of the home, roughly tripling the size of Mount Vernon.

Left: Edward Savage's *The West Front of Mount Vernon* portrays Washington's world as the first president envisioned it, with the Palladian mansion he designed at its center, his family in the foreground.
Courtesy of the Mount Vernon Ladies' Association

1783), *General* Washington had added rooms at each end of the house and a tall cupola to the roof. A pair of flanking support buildings ("dependencies"—one a servants' hall, the other a kitchen) were, observed Brookes, connected to the main house by "a covered curved passage of arches in front." The symmetrical arrangement added a welcoming grandeur, embracing the paved carriageway and the elliptical plot of grass that Washington called his "bolling green."

When Brookes viewed Mount Vernon from the opposite elevation, with its "commanding prospect" of the Potomac, his observations were closer to the mark: "The back of the house is a deep piazza about ten feet [deep]." Unlike many of the house's traditional details, this was of Washington's own imagining, and his two-story-tall covered porch would come to be widely copied by subsequent generations.

Arriving at noon, Brookes found the general had ridden out, as was his habit, to survey his farm properties. In 1754, Washington had inherited 2,126 acres after the death of his half brother Lawrence. He had since expanded his holdings to some 8,000 acres, organized into five separate farms; with the aid of more than 300 slaves, 3,000 acres were in tillage. Farmer Washington had long since abandoned the cultivation of tobacco, substituting grains such as wheat and corn, which he rotated from year to year in his clay soils.

In Washington's absence, Tobias Lear greeted the visitors and showed them into a small parlor. Their arrival surprised no one at Mount Vernon, since strangers were forever appearing, expecting a meal and even accommodations. Washington himself had once ruefully compared his house to "a well resorted tavern, as scarcely any strangers who are going from north to south, or from south to north, do not spend a day or two at it."

Having been served a glass of wine from a "globular decanter," Brookes found himself "much charmed with the portrait of Miss Custis" that hung on a nearby wall. The young woman herself soon arrived to greet them. He thought her "modest, well bred, intelligent and sensible." But it was Washington he had come to see, and at half past two, the general returned.

Presented with the letter of introduction, the aging Washington donned his spectacles, read the note, and bowed to his guests. He prevailed upon them to stay to dinner, which was shortly served. "He appeared a reserved man," Brookes confided in his journal, "[but] became pleasant, free and sociable at dinner, [and] seems naturally austere and reflective." Martha, dressed in "a Mazareen blue satin gown," sat at the head of the table. The visitor thought her "cheerful, about 70 years of age, [with] mildness and affability."

Joshua Brookes would take his leave after dinner, when, fortified by three postprandial glasses of wine, he and his companions mounted their horses as the general and Lear watched from the doorway. As one of thousands of visitors to Mount Vernon in the general's time of habitation, he cast his appraising eye on the man and his house. In his diary, he recorded much that he had seen during his brief

From high in the house—note the capital atop one of the columns that support the piazza roof—the visitor can look down upon the broad Potomac River and across to the Maryland hills.

When the Washingtons entertained a large number of guests, the grandest room in the house, the Large Dining Room, was prepared for company. Sometimes called the New Room, it was the last completed and the most fashionable of Mount Vernon's rooms. Its decorations, inspired by the work of Scotsman Robert Adam, included delicate applied plaster details.

The Washingtons used the Small Dining Room in cold weather and when the room could accommodate the number of guests at hand. The man of the house liked the color green—he once said he found it "grateful to the eye."

The West Parlor was the center of Mount Vernon's social life, where card games were played and tea served.

visit, remarking upon the London-made harpsichord that Nelly played; oil portraits of the general, Martha, Lafayette, and Benjamin Franklin; prints of Revolutionary War scenes; and a fine marble mantelpiece in the house's grandest room, the "New Room," as it was sometimes called, being among the last of the spaces completed in the long building campaign. Remarkably, all those objects remain at Mount Vernon today and can be seen in situ at General Washington's house.

LOOKING AT THE LEGACY

Three generations of Washington descendants owned the house after Martha's 1802 death, but in 1860 Mount Vernon became one of the nation's first historic sites. Since the Mount Vernon Ladies' Association opened the house to the public, almost *eighty million* people have followed in Joshua Brookes's footsteps, visiting a home restored to look as it did in 1799.

The house, the plantation, and a museum of Washington artifacts offer an immersion in things Washington. The oversize bedstead

in which he died remains in the chamber he shared with Martha. On the piazza, there is a sense of leisure, with a panoramic view of the Potomac. The original terra-cotta bust of Washington, made by French sculptor Jean-Antoine Houdon at Mount Vernon in 1785, is also on view, offering perhaps the best available glimpse of what the man himself looked like in life.

This home was a collaborative enterprise. The general and the wife he cherished did much together; if theirs was not a passionate union, certainly it was characterized by warmth, interdependence, respect, and great courtesy. Martha brought something else to the marriage as well: money. In 1759, the groom was a minor planter with substantial indebtedness; George's bride, Martha Dandridge Custis, brought him solvency as well as social status.

Objects in the Mount Vernon collections illuminate not only his time in residence but the years away commanding the Continental Army to victory during the Revolution; chairing the 1787 meetings in Philadelphia now known as the Constitutional Convention; and presiding over the nation after his unanimous election to the presidency in 1789, as he put his unmistakable stamp on the office. Martha's family—they became George's family too—is amply represented in miniatures, canvases, and objects. And Mount Vernon is more than a house. A dozen other buildings portray life in what was, in effect, a self-sufficient village. There's a salt house and spinning house, for preserving fish and producing fabric, respectively, and a smokehouse, storehouse, washhouse, and stable.

At Mount Vernon, much of the dramatic narrative of the nation's founding, in which Washington played so prominent a role, is recounted. But that story is accompanied by the discordant notes of slavery. Mount Vernon respects that long-muted piece of the past, interpreting the lives of the men, women, and children who worked the dependencies and tended the gardens and surrounding landscape. There are restored slaves' houses where they lived; there is a slave cemetery where many were buried.

Washington himself in his last year faced the paradox of a newly free people enslaving others, declaring in his last will and testament, "It is my Will & desire that all the Slaves which I hold in my *own*

THE WASHINGTON FAMILY

Despite having fathered no children of his own, George Washington would come to be known as the *Patriæ Pater* (Latin for "father of his country"), the "Great Father" (as the Creek Indians called him), and *Des Landes Vater* ("Founding Father" in German). Washington also had distinctly paternal relationships with a number of men, including the Marquis de Lafayette, Alexander Hamilton, and Tobias Lear.

As a functional parent, Washington, after his marriage to Martha in 1759, had welcomed to Mount Vernon her son, John Parke Custis (known as "Jacky"), and her daughter, Patsy, both of whom he raised as his own. When Jacky died at just twenty-six, Martha and George became parents again, taking as their wards Jacky's two youngest children, George Washington Parke Custis and Eleanor Parke Custis.

On the president's birthday in 1796, a life-size painting called *The Washington Family* went on exhibition in Philadelphia. It is large—nine and a half feet wide, seven tall—and features Nelly and her younger brother, Wash. The patriarch is in uniform. Martha points with her fan at the map of the city named after her husband. It's a domestic scene, featuring the Washington family unit, but it's a family image in another way too, offering as it does a hint of the larger Washington household—note the slave in livery standing at the ready.

Above: This bedchamber was occupied by many guests at Mount Vernon, possibly including the general's surrogate son, the Marquis de Lafayette. That's a Charles Willson Peale portrait of the French volunteer to the American cause on the far wall.

Right: Painted by Edward Savage, *The Washington Family* was reproduced as a copperplate engraving as well as a large canvas. The general himself purchased four prints directly from Edward Savage; this is one of those copies, and it hangs today over the mantel in the Small Dining Room at Mount Vernon. *Courtesy of the Mount Vernon Ladies' Association*

right, shall receive their freedom." Of his slave-owning peers among the Founding Fathers, he was nearly alone in freeing his chattel; in fact, even in his own household, he could not free all the slaves at Mount Vernon, as more than half were "dower" slaves and thus remained the property of the estate of Martha's first husband, Daniel Parke Custis.

The visitor at Mount Vernon is invited to imagine this man, seated in his presidential chair in his study, a portrait of his brother Lawrence over his shoulder, writing letters as he did daily throughout his years there, not merely grappling with the events of the day but shaping the presidency itself.

THE OLD HOUSE

JOHN ADAMS
(1797 – 1801)

AND

JOHN QUINCY ADAMS
(1825 – 1829)

QUINCY, MASSACHUSETTS

"I was not fully sensible of the change

till I entered his bed-chamber,

the place where I had last taken leave

of him. . . . That moment was inexpressibly

painful, and struck me as if it had been

an arrow to the heart."

JOHN QUINCY ADAMS, *DIARIES*, JULY 13, 1826

FATHER AND SON

O n August 25, 1823, John Quincy Adams (1767–1848) returned to the Old House from his duties as secretary of state in Washington City. Though he found the family home in Quincy little altered, he was struck by how the man of the house had aged. Widower, stalwart farmer, and John Quincy's father, John Adams (1735–1826) approached his eighty-eighth birthday, and time had begun to tell.

"I was deeply affected at meeting him," John Quincy confided in his diary. "Within the two last years, since I had seen him, his eye-sight has grown dim; his limbs stiff and feeble. He is bowed with age, and scarcely can walk across a room without assistance."

Confronted with this vision of decline, the son summoned Gilbert Stuart. The Rhode Island–born painter had trained in London but returned some thirty years earlier to record the worthies of the Revolutionary generation and, in particular, General Washington (very much later, Stuart's Washington would become the face of the one-dollar bill). Stuart had recorded John Adams once before in a painting begun in the waning days of the

Adams presidency. Now the son wanted the man he called the "first Painter in this Country" to once again make a likeness of the second president.

Though almost twenty years younger than his sitter, Stuart looked to be his contemporary. He was a snuff user, and as Adams's grandson, Charles Francis, remarked after observing a sitting, "Stuart is a singular man . . . said to be habitually intemperate and his appearance confirms it." Whatever Stuart's bad habits, however, the eldest Adams found his company stimulating. As he observed to a neighbor, Stuart, unlike other portraitists for whom he had sat, "keeps me constantly amused by his conversation."

John Adams himself was a voluble man whose independent bent had led him to early prominence in 1770 when, as a young lawyer, he defended British soldiers accused of firing upon innocent

---

Previous page: The Old House, as seen on approach in autumn, along the main axis of the garden that parallels Adams Street. The stone library is the building to the left.

Left: A copy of Gilbert Stuart's last portrait of John Adams hangs at the Old House today. Painted by the artist's daughter, Jane Stuart, who became a portraitist in her own right, it captures something of the surviving intensity of the aging but determined patriarch.
Adams National Historical Park / National Park Service

Opposite: Half hidden behind the vine-covered trellis is the face of the Adams house. The 1799–1800 addition to the earlier 1730 house included the three bays on the right.

colonists at what his cousin Sam would dub the "Boston Massacre." Though very much a Patriot himself, John had won acquittals for six of the eight grenadiers. Six years later he had been Thomas Jefferson's second in Philadelphia at the Continental Congress, where he helped write the Declaration of Independence. A man possessed of strong opinions, thin skin, and penetrating intellect, he had been Washington's vice president before serving as chief magistrate himself. Even in his declining years, according to the American minister to Britain, Richard Rush, Adams's insights "had the smack of rich and old wine."

Adams had assumed a seat on a comfortable red sofa in the paneled room at the Old House; Stuart reached for his brush, and a memorable portrait slowly emerged. The frail former president, his body as one with the couch, extends an arthritic hand that rests on the head of his cane. But the face of the man compels the viewer's interest. His skin is lined, his pate bald, the cottony swirls of his gray hair hang over his ears. Mr. Stuart did not merely draw the face; he painted an impression of it in colors that blend into facial features. The elder Mr. Adams lives on Stuart's canvas, the rheumy eyes fixed upon the viewer, the mouth set. As Boston mayor Josiah Quincy remarked on seeing the finished painting, "Stuart caught a glimpse of the living spirit shining through the feeble and decrepit body . . . at one of those happy moments when the intelligence lights up the wasted envelope."

PEACEFIELD

The house at what is today designated 135 Adams Street represented a step up in status for John and Abigail Adams when they purchased it in 1787. They had birthed their children in a saltbox house nearby, but that cramped and low-ceilinged structure seemed plain and unadorned compared to what had been the summer home of a wealthy sugar planter, Leonard Vassall. Needing a larger residence that better suited his rising station, John remembered the Vassall house, which was a short walk from his birthplace in Braintree. From London, where John was in service to his country as minister to the Court of Saint James's, he acquired title to the house and its parcel of seventy-five acres for £600.

Freshly graduated from Harvard and reading law in Newburyport, John Quincy inspected their new home before his parents did. He wasn't impressed. He reported that he saw the house "in a very unfavorable light." It had been alternately rented and empty since its Tory owners fled Boston in 1775 and now needed, thought John Quincy, many repairs.

On Abigail's orders, work was soon under way. A kitchen ell was added and other work begun, but upon her return in the summer of 1788, she thought the house in a "shocking state"; it was, she observed, "a swarm of carpenters, masons, and farmers." John set to work reestablishing his cattle herd while she unpacked their furni-

ture, saw to papering and painting, and ordered two new windows opened in the west wall, the better to view the garden.

During the Adamses' years abroad, the convention in Philadelphia had promulgated the Constitution; after its ratification in September 1788, states chose electors who, in turn, selected the president. That Washington would be awarded the office was a foregone conclusion (his election would be unanimous), and Adams appeared the most likely choice for vice president.

Within hours of learning that the electoral college had made his election official, the nation's first vice president left Quincy, bound for the temporary capital at New York. Abigail would soon follow, and though they returned home as often as they could, two vice presidential terms and John Adams's four years as president would pass before the property they referred to as Peacefield would truly become their home.

◇◇◇◇◇◇◇◇◇◇

In his last year in office, John and Abigail Adams, along with the rest of the government, moved to the new Federal City. The first couple took up residence in the new President's house, to be known later as the White House. The unfinished state of the mansion — the

master chamber had yet to be plastered — echoed the state of their own home. They had decided upon a renovation back in what had become the town of Quincy.

A cellar had been dug and a stone foundation laid in 1799 for the large addition at the east end of the Vassall house. A wood frame was rising, making the symmetrical, center-entrance Georgian house, originally constructed in 1731, half again as long. Its façade was to feature a second doorway and two new pairs of windows, upstairs and down. Although only two new living spaces were added, the addition almost doubled the original footprint.

The timing proved fortuitous, as Quincy would once again become the official full-time address for John Adams as of March 4, 1801. Before dawn that day he boarded the early stage for Baltimore, departing Washington City at four in the morning. He chose not to attend the inauguration, and thus did not hear his opponent and former friend Thomas Jefferson utter the words "We are all Republicans, we are all Federalists." To him, the words would undoubtedly have had all the flavor of a mouthful of ashes.

The man who returned to Quincy was embittered by his electoral loss after just one term, which he regarded as a rejection by

Opposite, left: A plaster bust of John Quincy Adams by Vermont-born sculptor Hiram Powers rests on a bracket high on the wall in the Long Hall, adjacent to the main entrance to the home. Near at hand for an exiting Adams is a collection of canes. They belonged not only to various of the four generations of Adams men but to at least one of the women, Abigail Brooks Adams (Mrs. Charles Francis Adams).

Opposite, right: In the dining room hang the two pendant portraits that John Adams commissioned of Massachusetts-born artist Edward Savage during Adams's service as Washington's vice president. In 1790 he paid Savage "forty Six Dollars & 2-3rds for a portrait of The President of the United States & His Lady."

Above: The desk in the upstairs study came from Paris, where Henry Adams used it in his apartment; the ormolu clock on the mantel belonged to his grandfather John Quincy Adams. But it was John Adams who spent many of his later years in this room, his body enfeebled but his mind clear.

Right: Gilbert Stuart, the most gifted American painter of his generation, made likenesses of most of the rich and powerful people in Federal America. His last sitter would be John Quincy Adams, whom he painted in 1828. The likeness of the younger Adams was unfinished at Stuart's death later that year but was completed by Thomas Sully, who left Stuart's treatment of the head untouched.

Adams National Historical Park / National Park Service

the nation he helped found and tirelessly served for three decades. His spirits were further burdened by the loss of his thirty-year-old son Charles, who had succumbed barely three months before. Charles had died of drink; as his mother observed, "He was no mans Enemy but his own."

At age sixty-five, John Adams arrived at his newly renovated home. He was nearly toothless, wounded by a political campaign full of poisonous insults, his long political journey seemingly at an end. But the home to which he returned was grander than it had been, more comfortable, and spacious enough to accommodate the expected influx of grandchildren. The visitors who would inevitably arrive seeking the company and counsel of the former president would be greeted in the "Long Hall,"

which ran the full depth of the wing, conveying on entry a sense of a new, more generous scale, its staircase an elegant contrast to the dogleg stairway squeezed behind the narrow entrance of the original house. Those fortunate enough to be invited in were to be entertained in the richly furnished parlor, or "Long Room," on the first floor.

For the next quarter century, when he needed moments of privacy and solitude, the bookish Adams would climb the stairs to his study and library. He often rose at five and began the day by reading; when the light of the day faded, Abigail often read to him. At the desk he had purchased in 1783 in France, he wrote a letter of reconciliation on New Year's Day 1812. The addressee was Thomas Jefferson, Adams's old ally, sometime friend, and rival, but most essentially his fellow Founding Father. For the next fourteen years, the two men put on paper a unique epistolary dialogue about their lives and times, both for each other and for posterity.

Just down the hall, daughter Nabby would be treated for cancer (doctors performed a mastectomy there, without the aid of anesthetics). The surgery prolonged her life, but she would die two years

Above: The Long Hall is lined with portraits and busts—including one of the proud patriarch, the stout and studious John himself in the foreground.

Below: John's great-grandson, historian Henry Adams (1838–1918), on his 1858 graduation from Harvard.
Harvard Art Museums / Fogg Museum

HENRY ADAMS

Rather than *presidential*, the adjective *magisterial* seems most often to come up in reference to Henry Adams—and it's usually when other historians are acknowledging his nine-volume *History of the United States During the Administrations of Thomas Jefferson and James Madison* (1889–1891). A great-grandson of John, grandson of John Quincy, and brother of Brooks, Henry produced books of vivid detail, strong narrative, and thorough scholarship.

Though he never held elective office, Adams as a young man functioned as his father's secretary when Charles Francis served in Congress and as minister to the Court of Saint James's. Henry would later be a journalist, a professor of medieval history at Harvard, a novelist, and

the author of *The Education of Henry Adams,* a memoir and portrait of his times that remains a staple of American studies programs. Henry Adams's circle of acquaintances extended to scientists Charles Lyell and Clarence King, artist John La Farge, public men John Hay (McKinley's secretary of state) and Theodore Roosevelt, writer Edith Wharton, and aesthete Bernard Berenson.

Henry Adams was erudite, inquisitive, and vastly well traveled (he saw most of Europe as well as the South Seas, the American West, and Japan), and he left a rich trove of correspondence. He's been called America's "first cosmopolite," and his histories remain invaluable references for presidential scholars today.

Above: John and Abigail Adams both died here—he in 1826 (of old age) and she in 1818 (of typhus); the bed came from Holland, after John's diplomatic service in the 1780s.

Below: John Adams returned from his ministry abroad with this Louis XVI secretary desk. While seated at it, he maintained a voluminous correspondence, not least with Thomas Jefferson. The secretary was also a specific bequest, left to the then-sitting president John Quincy Adams.

later, in 1813. With the passage of another five years, John would bury Abigail too, after fifty-four years of partnership. A widower, John Adams, his mind active and his spirit strong, lived on surrounded by family (at times, there were as many as twenty dependents in the house, including his son Thomas with his wife and six children). Adams entertained friends and visitors as varied as Lafayette and a young visionary from Harvard named Emerson. All too infrequently, his namesake son returned.

THE DUKE AND DAUPHIN OF BRAINTREE

In those years, many in the North complained of the *Virginia dynasty.* Jefferson's eight years in office had been succeeded by two terms each for his Central Virginia neighbors James Madison (1809–1817) and James Monroe (1817–1825). But it would be the Adams family

Along with countless other Adams possessions at Quincy were books and papers from two presidencies and beyond. In John Adams's will, he specified that "all my manuscript letter-books and account books, letters, journals, and manuscripts books" were to go to his son John Quincy; by 1870, what had become a twelve-thousand-volume library and priceless collection of papers required a new home, and grandson Charles Francis built a stone structure on the property. Note that the patriarch of the dynasty oversees matters in a standing portrait by William Winstanley that dates from the elder Adams's presidency.

that would produce the nation's first father-and-son tandem: in March 1825, John Quincy Adams was sworn in as the nation's sixth president, having finally prevailed in an election decided in the House of Representatives.

John Quincy Adams was the most experienced diplomat in the country's history. At age eleven, he had accompanied his father to France in 1778; at fourteen, he became secretary to the U.S. mission in Russia. After John Quincy's Harvard years, President Washington appointed him U.S. minister to the Hague (Adams was twenty-six). As president, his father dispatched him to the Prussian court at Berlin. That same year (it was 1797) John Quincy married Louisa Catherine Johnson, daughter of another American diplomat.

The younger Adams had won elective offices too, serving terms in the legislature of his native state and as its representative in the U.S. Senate. President James Madison named him minister to the Russian court at St. Petersburg, then detailed him to negotiate the Treaty of Ghent, which ended the War of 1812. After a tour of duty as minister to Great Britain, he became James Monroe's secretary of state in 1817. In the latter office he shaped the famous "Monroe Doctrine," the brusque warning issued to the European powers to stay out of the affairs of the Western Hemisphere. It would prove to be a fixed principle of American foreign policy, though it bore the name not of its chief author but of his superior.

In the autumn of his first year as president, John Quincy returned home for a brief visit; the several days he and his father spent under the same roof would be their last together. By the time John Quincy returned on July 12, 1826, it was to hear memorial sermons for his father, dead a week earlier, on the nation's birthday. The elder Adams's will stipulated that the sitting president would inherit the house, some 103 acres, and his Louis XVI secretary desk, a proud reminder of the elder Adams's diplomatic service.

⬥⬥⬥⬥⬥⬥⬥⬥⬥⬥

President John Quincy Adams met the same electoral fate his father had, retiring to Quincy after one term, having been soundly defeated by Andrew Jackson. He too had lost a son, George Washington Adams, a suicide. And he arrived at Quincy alone, his wife in Washington mourning the loss of their son.

Like his father, he worked the surrounding acres, tending to a generous vegetable garden, his orchards, and his chickens. He remodeled the kitchen. John Quincy was sixty-three and suffered from rheumatism and a persistent catarrh that produced coughing spells every morning. Yet his retirement proved much briefer than his father's: within two years, he was back in the political fray, this time as a candidate for Congress.

Above: The Old House, as it appeared in a mid-nineteenth-century daguerreotype.
Adams National Historical Park / National Park Service

Top right and right: John Adams's birthplace, a classic "saltbox" design, in nearby Braintree.

The former president was sworn in as a member of the U.S. House of Representatives in March of 1831. In the years that followed, he chaired the committee that created the Smithsonian Institution, but more important still, his voice was often heard from the floor of the House on the subject of slavery. He repeatedly presented petitions in the face of Southern opposition to any discussion of the topic whatsoever. Though he was no abolitionist, he foresaw the long-term risks to the Union. If his presidency had lacked distinction, he proved an effective, influential, and respected parliamentarian until he suffered a stroke at his desk in the Capitol in 1848. He died two days later.

The Old House remained in the Adams family for a total of four generations, and the evolution of the structure reflects each of the men who lived there. John Quincy added a rear passage to connect the two existing ells; his son Charles Francis took over management of the property during his father's congressional tenure (after John

Quincy's death, Charles Francis would serve his country as a Massachusetts congressman until Abraham Lincoln appointed him British ambassador). He constructed a freestanding stone library, and the last Adams to inherit the house, John's great-grandson Brooks, began the process of conserving the place as a museum. At his death in 1927, the property passed into the possession of the Adams Memorial Society, then to the National Park Service as a national historic site in 1946. Far from the "abandoned ruin" that Brooks Adams inherited, the Old House today is rich in recollections of a two-generation presidential family.

MONTICELLO AND POPLAR FOREST

THOMAS JEFFERSON
(1801 – 1809)

CHARLOTTESVILLE AND FOREST, VIRGINIA

"Directly or indirectly American classicism

traces its ancestry to Jefferson,

who may truly be called

the father of our national architecture."

FISKE KIMBALL, *THOMAS JEFFERSON,*
***ARCHITECT* (1916)**

THOMAS JEFFERSON, ARCHITECT

Alone among American presidents, Thomas Jefferson (1743–1826) has a place in the pantheon of great American architects. He didn't merely inhabit his remarkable house, Monticello (*Mon-ti-CHELLO*) — he also dreamt it, drew it, and supervised its construction. As he rethought and refined its design for some *fifty-four* years, the redheaded idealist who helped launch an unstoppable wave of democratic change gradually aged into a gray and stooped elder statesman. Today, the impact of his restless intelligence over that entire span is on display in Monticello's classical details, eclectic furnishings, art, and other collections.

Jefferson's architectural reputation rests on more than Monticello. As he prepared to leave the presidency, he began construction on a home away from home, Poplar Forest. A three-day ride from Charlottesville, the villa near Lynchburg, Virginia, is almost the antithesis of Monticello; it's smaller and simpler, a more idealized, isolated, and introverted dwelling. Unlike Monticello, which has the feeling of an unfolding experiment, Poplar Forest is a place with the clarity of an architectural epiphany. Thomas Jefferson, architect, also masterminded the design of a college and a Capitol, played a notable role in endowing the new Federal City with its essential classical character, and offered designs and guidance to friends. His enthusiasm and encouragement directly influenced two generations of American architects and builders.

The private Jefferson can be best understood in the context of his domestic environs. To visit Monticello and Poplar Forest is to gain fleeting glimpses of Jefferson, refracted and reflected in a looking glass of his making, and to see the evolution of this complex man's enthusiasms and ideals in three dimensions.

Previous page: In the parlor at Monticello a Campeachy chair (named for the mahogany from Campeche, Mexico, sometimes used in their manufacture) sits before the mantelpiece. Such Siesta chairs, as they were also known, were popular among Jefferson and his friends, and some were made by John Hemmings in the Monticello joinery. Commissioned by the subject himself in Paris, the terra-cotta bust of Jefferson was the work of Jean-Antoine Houdon, perhaps the greatest sculptor of his generation.

Left: Jefferson sat for Gilbert Stuart in 1805, and this portrait was one of several that resulted. It belonged to Jefferson and descended in his family, hanging for generations at Edgehill, the home of his favorite grandson, Thomas Jefferson Randolph.
Courtesy of the National Portrait Gallery, Smithsonian Institution, and the Thomas Jefferson Foundation, Inc. / Monticello

Opposite: Neoclassical architecture became popular in the United States, in no small measure because of Jefferson's efforts to persuade people of its beauty. Certainly the front façade and portico at Monticello reinforced his argument.

MAKING MONTICELLO

Born in Charlottesville in 1743, Thomas Jefferson attended William and Mary College for two years, graduating in 1762. He remained in Williamsburg to read law but returned to Charlottesville to practice and, in 1772, married Martha Wayles Skelton. She bore him six children, two of whom would survive to adulthood. Before the Revolution Jefferson was elected to the Virginia Assembly; during the war, he became Virginia's governor. Martha died in 1782, and her husband would never remarry.

From 1785 to 1789, Jefferson served as minister to France and, upon returning home, accepted newly elected George Washington's appointment as the first secretary of state, a job he performed until 1793. He was elected vice president in 1797, then president

(1801–1809). After leaving office, he was bent upon creating an "Academical Village" for his fellow Virginians; in 1825, the University of Virginia welcomed its first students.

The home he began on the top of a mountain was never conceived as a simple dwelling. The bookish Jefferson wished to raise the tastes of his region. He studied architectural texts, chief among them Andrea Palladio's *The Four Books on Architecture* (1570). In the plates of the villas that Palladio designed for his native Veneto, Jefferson recognized both beauty and practicality in designs that aligned with his own desire for a grand country house that would double as the administrative center for his plantation. The Virginian and the Renaissance designer shared a passion for carefully proportioned, symmetrical, and balanced buildings. Jefferson based his first plan for Monticello on Palladio's Villa Cornaro.

perimeter roof railing, gave the structure the look of a gracious one-story house, but one with living space on the ground floor, mezzanine, and attic levels. The new plan enlarged upon the first, as eight rooms became twenty-one, not including the kitchen, stables, and other dependencies that were to be largely hidden in a pair of flanking service wings below grade.

Jefferson needed a larger home to accommodate both a growing, multigenerational family and his collections, as Monticello became an immense curio cabinet packed with evidence of his varied enthusiasms. He was a natural philosopher (*scientist* in the parlance of the day); his most private room, his "Cabinet," was chockablock with scientific instruments, including a theodolite and microscope. He trusted the printed word beyond any man's, and in his eighty-three years, he accumulated three distinct libraries, totaling some ten thousand volumes, many in foreign tongues (he had a reading knowledge of six languages, including Latin and Greek, in addition to English). He was an inveterate tinkerer, always on the search for new devices. One that he adopted and helped perfect was the polygraph, a mechanical contraption that made file copies of his letters as he wrote them.

Jefferson brought back more than architectural ideas from France; he shipped some eighty crates of objects to Virginia. A lifelong shopper, he found goods to acquire in the United States too, and as a result the public spaces in his house were decorated with copies of old master paintings along with portraits and busts of worthies who ranged from Enlightenment thinkers (including Locke and Newton) to friends and contemporaries he admired (Franklin, Lafayette, and Washington). The entrance hall became a museum of American artifacts, including maps, antlers, and Native American objects.

Jefferson also had an appetite for food and wine, and regarded himself as a farmer above all. Monticello's acres are a mix of ornamental landscape garden and agricultural workplace, where foodstuffs for the table were grown even as Jefferson conducted botanical experiments.

Monticello has been restored to its postpresidential appearance, when it was home to the former president and his extended family,

Jefferson's initial vision of Monticello was never fully realized, since the slow building process was interrupted by his wife's death. By the time construction resumed more than a decade later, Jefferson had a new design. He returned from his five-year ministerial sojourn in Paris, where he had practiced his architectural skills, dispatching back to Richmond renderings for a new Virginia Capitol, one based on an ancient Roman temple, the Maison Carrée in Nîmes. The new plan he had conceived for Monticello drew upon modern precedents, one in particular. Certainly the house would be classical, with a temple front (meaning its façade featured columns supporting a triangular pediment). However, having become "violently smitten" with a grand mansion he saw under construction in Paris, the Hôtel de Salm, he borrowed its dome (thereby making Monticello the first residence in America to be capped by a dome) and, by lowering the second-floor windows and adding a

Opposite: Research into Jefferson's life at Monticello continues, and a recent paint analysis determined that the dining room was repainted around 1815 using a newly available pigment, chrome yellow. In an age when nighttime illumination provided well less than the equivalent of a mere five watts of light, bright colors were fashionable and enhanced the atmosphere.

Above: Jefferson's Tea Room is an intimate space, as the semi-octagonal end wall seems to embrace the table at the center of the high-ceilinged but small (eleven-by-fifteen-foot) room. Looking down from cornice level are four busts, all copies of the work of French sculptor Jean-Antoine Houdon. From left are Lafayette, Benjamin Franklin, George Washington, and naval hero John Paul Jones.

Left: On Jefferson's return from his Paris years, he employed the French convention of the built-in, or alcove, bed. In this image the view is from his bedchamber through to his study, or Cabinet.

Top: Jefferson created a suite of private rooms for himself at the south end of Monticello. Known as the Cabinet, or study, this was perhaps the most private space of all. It has been called his inner sanctum and even his architectural thinking cap. Whatever term one applies, this was the space where the philosopher Jefferson was alone with his thoughts, his books, and his correspondence (of which he made copies with the polygraph, the device on the table at center).

Bottom: The "Dome Room" at Monticello is, as its name suggests, the grand space beneath the dome.

which included his daughter Martha Jefferson Randolph and her children. But the plantation that surrounded his mansion was inhabited by a larger and more diverse community of people.

"A VERY EXTRA WORKMAN"

A boy child was born at Monticello in 1776, the year Jefferson wrote the Declaration of Independence. The father, an itinerant carpenter named Joseph Neilson, soon drifted to points unknown, but the boy would spend his life on Jefferson's "little mountain." He became a woodworker of surpassing skill and, half a century after his birth, turned his hand to a store of special stock set aside in Monticello's joinery. The task of making "old Master's coffin" fell to Johnny Hemmings on July 4, 1826.

When the former president died, roughly a third of the 130 enslaved people at the Albemarle County estate were members of Monticello's second family. They were descendants of John's enslaved mother, Elizabeth (Betty) Hemings, whom Jefferson's wife inherited when her father died in 1773. (Although the more usual spelling of the family name contains a single *m,* John signed his name *Hemmings.*) Betty bore fourteen children, six probably the offspring of Jefferson's father-in-law, John Wayles, including Betty's youngest daughter, Sarah, called Sally. In turn, Sally delivered six babies almost certainly fathered by Thomas Jefferson, the widower husband of her half sister.

In the two centuries since, the stormy debate that swirled around Jefferson's relationship with Sally has made her the most discussed member of the Hemings clan. Yet a look at the life of her half brother, given his enduring role in Jefferson's architectural and decorative musings, offers a means of taking a more measured view of the intermingling of the black and white branches of the Monticello family tree.

⬦⬦⬦⬦⬦⬦

At fourteen, John Hemmings joined the crew of Jefferson's "out-carpenters." These men and boys spent their days felling trees

Above: The garden façade of Monticello is an architectural essay in classicism; it was also the first domestic structure in America to be capped with a dome.

Below: Almost no built fabric survives from the structures the enslaved inhabited at Monticello, but this chimney stack does. It is a remnant of the joinery, which was one of the first buildings to be constructed on Mulberry Row, where there once stood as many as twenty-one buildings, including workshops, storage sheds, and dwellings for both white and enslaved workers.

for fences, structural timbers, and firewood, but John's training began in earnest in 1798. A new arrival, Irish immigrant James Dinsmore, brought sophisticated skills, and, as a team, house joiner Dinsmore and apprentice Hemmings completed Monticello's interior. The quality of their work was such that Jefferson boasted, "There is nothing superior in the US."

Dinsmore departed in 1809, traveling a few miles north to work at Montpelier, the plantation of Jefferson's old friend Madison (see *Montpelier*, page 40). That left Hemmings in charge of Monticello's joinery. Without his presidential salary, Jefferson's finances were more than a little strained. When the desire struck him for a new contrivance or piece of furniture, his request, sometimes accompanied by a drawing in his own hand, went to the joinery on Mulberry Row, a collection of perhaps twenty trade buildings, sheds, and

"THE ACADEMICAL VILLAGE"

The great passion of Mr. Jefferson's retirement years was the creation of the University of Virginia. Today, his vision has become a twenty-eight-acre oasis at the center of one of the world's great research universities. His "Academical Village" also happens to be perhaps the most remarkable architectural experience in America.

The Lawn, as the Jefferson precinct is known, consists of a central building, the Rotunda, which dominates the landscape. Jefferson wanted a library rather than a church to be the armature of his college, and he chose to build as his "temple of knowledge" a half-scale copy of the Pantheon in Rome. Flanking the Rotunda are two facing rows of pavilions, a total of ten that were domiciles for professors and also contained classrooms. Linking the pavilions are dormitory rooms, each with its own fireplace, all fronted with columns. Behind the pavilions and dormitory rooms are dining rooms, known as *hotels* in the parlance of the place.

The University of Virginia was to educate the young men of the Commonwealth, both in the classroom and by exposure to their classical surroundings. Jefferson personally chose the books for the library, hired the professors, and planned the curriculum. He saw education as an essential building block in ensuring that the democratic republic he helped build would continue to stand.

Above, left: At Jefferson's university, the pediments, arcades, Chippendale railings, and sea of columns all coalesce into a visual expression of the classical past.

Above, right: The parlor windows at Poplar Forest overlook the sunken lawn. In Jefferson's time, according to archaeology conducted at the site, it was defined by elaborate plantings of lilacs, roses, and other shrubs.

dwellings on the Monticello hillside that were manned by white workers as well as free blacks and the enslaved.

Hemmings's woodworking talents were much in evidence at Monticello. The architectural elements he executed included arches, Chinese railings that decorate the exterior, interior moldings, and shutters. As a furniture maker, his skills were on display in "dumb-waiters" (tiered shelves, on casters, for the dining room), presses for storing papers, cases for books, and "Campeachy chairs," the slung-back design that suited the rheumatic Jefferson in later years.

More than a resident craftsman, Hemmings was almost a part of the Jefferson family. He was an avuncular presence for several of Jefferson's granddaughters; his wife, Priscilla, belonged to Jefferson's daughter and cared for the grandchildren. The enslaved at Monticello were not routinely taught to read and write, but Hemmings was lettered, and one of Martha's daughters, Cornelia, provided him with a dictionary. More than a dozen of his letters survive, most to his master but one to the youngest of Jefferson's granddaughters,

Poplar Forest was never elaborately furnished, but in 1809 Jefferson purchased three dozen basic Windsor chairs like this one, which he specified were to be painted black with yellow bands.

Septemia. John Hemmings was referred to as "Daddy Hemmings" in the girls' correspondence, and the childless Hemmings clearly reciprocated the children's affection. He made another of Jefferson's granddaughters, Ellen, an elegantly crafted lap desk on the occasion of her marriage to Bostonian Joseph Coolidge. When her baggage was lost at sea, Hemmings took the news hard. "He was au desespoir!" Jefferson wrote Ellen Randolph Coolidge.

Hemmings was one of two slaves to receive an annual gratuity (Jefferson's butler, Burwell, Hemmings's nephew, was the other). In a codicil to his will, Jefferson gave five members of the Hemings clan their freedom. They included John; John's cousins Joseph

Fossett and Burwell (who took the surname Colbert on his manumission); and two nephews, Madison and Eston Hemings, Sally's sons, who had been apprenticed to Hemmings in the joinery shop.

When he registered as a freeman, Hemmings was entered in the rolls as being five feet, five and a half inches tall and of "light complection." Although no images of him survive, it is tempting to imagine him standing in a tableau with two taller men with whom he shared essential connections. One would be Jefferson, his eyes bright and his mind engaged, perhaps talking of his newest pet project. The other would be the taller of the two Hemings apprentices. Perhaps, were we privileged to glimpse Jefferson and the tall apprentice together, we would be struck, as some of their contemporaries were, that the two of them, one master, one slave, bore a remarkable resemblance in frame and face to each other.

Left: Poplar Forest's portico fronts what appears to be a one-story building, with its tall Tuscan columns, made of brick that has been parged with mortar to the color of the local stone.

Right: When one views the garden façade of Jefferson's Bedford County house, a fuller understanding of the building can be reached—it isn't simply a one-story cottage. The portico on the main floor is supported by an arcade that offers access to the service room in the raised basement.

A JOURNEY TO POPLAR FOREST

One of John Hemmings's projects was a carriage, a landau he built to Jefferson's specifications. Hemmings, who had trained as a wheelwright, constructed the vehicle with facing seats. Joseph Fossett, a blacksmith, fabricated the ironwork, and Burwell painted it.

In the summer of 1816, Jefferson and two favored granddaughters climbed aboard and, pulled by four horses guided by two postilions, headed for Bedford County. Burwell rode alongside on a fifth horse.

Jefferson kept his young companions amused on the long journey. "His cheerful conversation, so agreeable and instructive, [and] his singing . . . made the time pass pleasantly." Another distraction was a favorite new contrivance of Jefferson's, an odometer affixed to the wheel of the carriage. With a face like a clock, it had a bell mechanism that rang each time the hand on its dial made a full circuit, indicating another ten miles traveled. Jefferson noted the ring of the chime and, on arrival, calculated the journey covered at ninety-three miles.

The distance was important. Since the plantation property in Bedford County was a reliable source of income, Jefferson's presence there to supervise planting and harvest made good business sense. But his visits to Poplar Forest offered the now-famous "philosopher" an opportunity to escape, as he himself put it, the "stream of strangers" who came to Charlottesville. Countless uninvited visitors wanted an audience with the Sage of Monticello (and, typically, dinner and accommodations too). Tired of such intrusions, Jefferson wished for "a tranquility and retirement much adapted to my age."

The seventy-three-year-old former president and his granddaughters arrived at a house that, after ten years of construction, was habitable but hardly finished. Plaster was still to be applied to the walls—during at least one later stay, the girls took refuge in their chamber to avoid the dust and mess of the plastering process. But on their first visit, the nineteen-year-old Ellen and her sister Cornelia, sixteen, walked into a space that was an exercise in pure geometry.

A narrow, low entrance hall opened into a bright twenty-foot cube lit by a sixteen-foot skylight. The square dining room stood at the center of the house's octagonal footprint, which Jefferson described as being "50 f. in *diameter* [italics added]." The drawing room beyond overlooked a sunken lawn; two bedchambers flanked the central space.

The house was sited at the center of a larger circle, a five-acre plat enclosed by a road some 540 yards in circumference. That circle was bisected by two symmetrical rows of trees that extended from the house to two matching earthen mounds 100 feet to each side. Beyond the conical earthworks were octagonal privies. Jefferson was consciously echoing a favorite Palladio configuration, with the house at the center as the main block, the trees as connective hyphens, the hillocks standing in for Palladian pavilions, and the outhouses adding symmetrical emphasis.

While their grandfather spent time with his books and correspondence (a second polygraph was at hand), the young ladies devoted themselves to their studies. The trio dined together, and Cornelia and Ellen accompanied Jefferson on walks and excursions. It wasn't all recreation, as the patriarch required his granddaughters to catalog the nearly one thousand books in his Poplar Forest library.

Over the years, the symmetry at Poplar Forest would be compromised by practical considerations. Jefferson added a wing, which, like Monticello's dependencies, was partly built into grade. From the entrance façade, only a low wall is visible, but the kitchen, laundry, smokehouse, and storage spaces made the house a more practical place for Jefferson, his family, and his servants to reside for sustained periods.

For more than a decade, Jefferson found the quietude he wanted at Poplar Forest, making regular visits, typically accompanied by pairs of his grandchildren (over the years, seven of Martha's eleven children visited there). Over a construction span of fourteen years, he saw the progress that Johnny Hemmings made as he executed the classical trim on the interior, employing the Tuscan, Doric, and Ionic orders that Jefferson specified. Even after Jefferson's health prevented him from making the long journey—by then, Poplar Forest was home to a married grandchild and his young family— he was still issuing instructions to John Hemmings to install decorative ornamentation. Part of the pleasure of architecture for Jefferson was in shaping a mental image of a building in his capacious mind.

In Jefferson's time, Monticello and Poplar Forest complemented each other. The first was the official home of a world-renowned political philosopher, the second a place of escape where, as Jefferson described it, he found the "solitude of a hermit" to enjoy his books, cherish his family, and think uninterrupted thoughts. Shortly after Jefferson's death, however, financial problems forced the sale of both houses—for a president who prided himself on managing the national debt, he proved an unreconstructed spendthrift at home, leaving his heirs with debts that required two generations to clear. While Monticello was preserved, after a fashion, by thoughtful care-takers, Poplar Forest's history would be forever altered by a disastrous fire in 1845. The conflagration left the house a roofless masonry hulk, its fine woodwork reduced to ash.

Both homes are now operated as historic sites, and the contrast between the two is illuminating. In the public domain since 1923, Monticello represents Jefferson's aspirations fulfilled. It is a fine museum, rich in collections and period rooms, surrounded by a manicured landscape. In contrast, Poplar Forest was described by scholars as recently as the 1950s as no longer in existence; only recently has its owner peeled away later remodelings. The site remains a work in progress, as a restoration team mimes Jefferson's own construction sequence, adding plaster surfaces, molding treatments, and other finishes. The workmen today use the same building methods and hand tools that Hemmings and the rest of Jefferson's crew did. Visitors watch as a facsimile of the original reemerges one brick and one length of molding at a time.

To visit both these homes is to gain new understandings of Jefferson's domestic dream as he attempted to impose a sense of order and reason in the architectural realm, just as he sought to do in the larger world.

MONTPELIER

JAMES MADISON
(1809 – 1817)

ORANGE, VIRGINIA

"Hospitality is the presiding genius of this house."

MARGARET BAYARD SMITH, AUGUST 4, 1809

◇◇◇◇◇◇◇◇◇◇◇

AUGUST 1828

etirement had not been easy for the Madisons. Money was tight. James's health was unpredictable. Dolley complained that she felt "fixed" at Montpelier—seventeen years younger than her husband, she thought life in Central Virginia rather isolated after her sixteen years as the nation's first hostess. But both Mr. and Mrs. Madison could always rise to the occasion when old friends came calling.

They used the brass telescope on the front portico to monitor the mile-long approach to the house. One day in early August 1828, a carriage emerged from the wooded perimeter of the Montpelier estate. For Margaret Bayard Smith; her husband, Samuel; and Anna, the youngest of their four children, the sight of the Madison mansion was a relief in the drenching rain. As their horses plodded along, they watched as the broad façade of Montpelier loomed up before them.

Mr. Madison himself met them on the sheltering space of the tall portico. The four immense Tuscan columns dwarfed the former president. Never a large man—perhaps five foot, four inches in height and very slight of build—he had assumed the wizened and brittle look of a man of seventy-seven years. But he was delighted to welcome his old political ally, the man who had founded the *National Intelligencer,* a Washington newspaper sympathetic to the Democratic-Republican Party that Madison and Thomas Jefferson had established.

"In the Hall Mrs. Madison received me with open arms," Mrs. Smith soon wrote to her sister, "and all that overflowing kindness and affection which seems a part of her nature." At sixty, Mrs. Madison appeared to have aged surprisingly little in the decade since moving permanently from Washington City to Montpelier. She remained every bit the woman the American storyteller Washington Irving had described as "a fine, portly buxom dame, who has a smile and a pleasant word for everybody." Even her wardrobe remained the same.

The party moved into the drawing room, the central space in the sprawling house, with its view of the yard to the rear. Sixteen-year-old Anna was given books to peruse, as Mrs. Smith examined some of the portraits that lined the walls, along with the busts that rested on the mantelpiece, tables, and corner brackets. Many of the faces were known to the party, as there were likenesses of George Washington, James Monroe, John Adams, Benjamin Franklin, and other worthies of the era, including Mr. Madison's now lamented friend Jefferson, dead just two years earlier.

Previous page: The main block at Montpelier and its two matching wings, when taken together, are 157 1/2 feet across.

Opposite: The domed temple that Madison had built in 1811 served as an ornament to the gardens at Montpelier. But the classically detailed structure was also more than it seems—beneath its floor was a twenty-three-foot-deep well for the storage of ice. Insulated by the earth, the densely packed slabs, cut in winter and packed in straw, would last to midsummer and beyond for household use.

Above: The drawing room was the social center of the house, the place where the Smiths and other guests were greeted. Madison was known to play chess here, and guests gathered before dinner.

The ladies went upstairs to change their damp clothes. The men very likely retired to Mr. Madison's study, a room lined with his books and packed with his papers. James and Dolley had spent much of his retirement editing and organizing correspondence, memorandums, and his other writings. One lot had already been sold, but perhaps the most valuable document of all, his "Notes of the Debates in the Federal Convention of 1787," remained closely held. Although he resisted the characterization "Father of the Constitution," insisting that the founding charter could hardly have been "the off-spring of a single brain" but rather "the work of many heads and hands," he understood how unique, valuable, and possibly controversial were his detailed notes from the 1787 gathering we now call the Constitutional Convention.

The Madisons and their guests dined at four o'clock, and Mrs. Smith reported Mr. Madison to be in excellent form. Almost twenty years before, she had been in attendance when he rose to read his address at his first inauguration; then Mrs. Smith had thought him "extremely pale . . . scarcely able to stand [as,] with a tremulous and inaudible voice, he read what none except a few nearest to him could hear." Today was a different matter.

"Mr. Madison was the chief speaker," Mrs. Smith reported, "and his conversation was so enlivened by anecdotes and epigrammatic remarks . . . that it had an interest and charm, which the conversation of few men now living, could have. He spoke of scenes in which he himself had acted a conspicuous part and of great men, who had been actors in the same theatre."

The last of the most essential Founding Fathers, holding court for old friends, Madison kept his audience enthralled until ten o'clock. "Every sentence he spoke, was worthy of being written down," concluded Margaret Bayard Smith. "It was living history!"

REMAKING MONTPELIER

No antique house remains unchanged over a period of centuries —but few houses have seen the radical transformations that Montpelier has.

In 1763, James Madison Sr. built a symmetrical, two-story brick house, topped by a hip roof. It was the largest dwelling in Orange County, Virginia. Standing atop a raised basement, the house featured two pairs of rooms on the main floor that flanked a central passage, with five rooms on the upper level. One of the public rooms was a dining room for formal meals and entertainments, a recent innovation among the Virginia gentry. On moving-in day, James Jr. was an early adolescent, the eldest of a brood that would expand to twelve children, seven of whom would live to maturity.

Though Montpelier would remain his home for his entire life, the younger James spent long periods far from his father's plantation. For five years, he lived in tidewater Virginia at boarding school; he spent another three in Princeton at what was then known as the College of New Jersey (1769–1772). Thereafter a career in public service was launched, with successive offices as a delegate to the Virginia Convention in Williamsburg in 1776, where he helped draft the Virginia

Constitution, and then to the Continental Congress in Philadelphia in 1780. At age twenty-nine, he was the youngest delegate.

Although he served four sessions in the Virginia House of Delegates in Richmond after the Revolution (1784 and after), Madison's chief labor of the mid-1780s was a self-assigned research project. Closeted in the second-floor library in his father's house, he spent countless hours reading widely on the topic of government (one year he read four hundred books). His syllabus, which included many volumes sent to him by Jefferson from Paris, approached the subject from a mix of historical and theoretical perspectives, covering both modern and ancient models. But Madison's investigations were more than an intellectual exercise. As a son of the Enlight-

---

Below, left: The careful architectural restoration has been succeeded by a time of equally thoughtful refurnishing. Since the house's contents were sold and no detailed inventory exists, the curatorial approach is to reintroduce objects only when the evidence makes it clear what was there in the Madison years. In the dining room, some objects have been added, including a banquet table and sideboards.

Below, right: James Madison's library is the principal room in the north wing, the place where he spent his retirement years at work editing his papers and maintaining his correspondence (for several years after Madison left office, his successor, James Monroe, forwarded diplomatic dispatches to Montpelier).

Above: The drawing room was also a gallery of worthies; among those represented were Madison's fellow presidents: Washington (*top*); Adams, Monroe, and Jefferson (*left to right*).

Opposite: In these pendant portraits painted by Joseph Wood around 1816, Dolley looks delighted to have served as Washington City's leading lady; James, like most presidents toward the end of their terms, looks weary and worried. *Virginia Historical Society*

enment, Madison believed such a disciplined study might produce a plan whereby man could control his destiny. He was looking, in short, for political solutions to self-government.

A plan was required, he believed, because of what he termed the "imbecility" of the Articles of Confederation, which, having granted the central government few powers, left the nation unable to levy taxes, negotiate with foreign powers, or manage its economy. Madison was readying himself for a gathering of states for a "Grand Convention." He and fifty-four other delegates from twelve states would spend seventeen weeks in Philadelphia in 1787, hammering out the nation's governing document, the U.S. Constitution.

After its 1788 ratification—which Madison helped accomplish, as a cowriter (with Alexander Hamilton and John Jay) of the essays collectively known as *The Federalist Papers*—Madison was elected to the House of Representatives. There, as President George Washington's most trusted ally in Congress, Congressman Madison guided the passage of the first ten amendments to the Constitution, now known as the Bill of Rights. During his four terms in Congress, the unmarried Madison, at forty-three, met a young widow, Dolley Payne Todd, who, in 1794, became his wife.

Upon leaving Congress in 1797, Madison retired to Montpelier, together with Dolley, her five-year-old son, John Payne Todd, and her younger sister, Anna. To accommodate his new family, he set about constructing a large addition to his father's house. The new section would serve as James and Dolley's quarters, complete with its own entry, since both Madison's parents, James and Nelly, still resided in the existing house. The younger Madison also added the imposing portico, and the house gained the name Montpelier.

Shortly after the addition was finished, Thomas Jefferson, newly elected the nation's third president, named Madison as his secretary of state. As James and Dolley prepared to move to the new Federal City in February 1801, his father died. His mother, Nelly Conway Madison, would remain a fixture at Montpelier until 1829, when she died at age ninety-eight.

In 1809, having succeeded his friend as president, James Madison commenced once more to reinvent Montpelier in a manner in keeping with his elevated status. During the next four years, Madison's workers unified the central block of the house with a center entrance (previously, there had been no interior access between Nelly's quarters and James and Dolley's on the first floor). A colonnaded porch was added across the rear, as well as one-story wings at each end of the house, one for James's library, the other for his mother. Significant changes were made not only to the house but to the gardens, support buildings, and even the landscape, which became an open park. To this house the Madisons retired in April 1817, and here James Madison died in 1836, never again having left the Commonwealth of Virginia.

Much later, Montpelier would house another notable family. After James's death, financial difficulties forced Dolley to sell the house in 1844; seven owners later, William duPont acquired the property. William and, after his death, his daughter, Marion, owned the house for more than eight decades. The wealthy duPonts made the place their own, enveloping the Madison dwelling with additions that nearly tripled its size (the Madisons inhabited twenty-two rooms; the duPont house enclosed fifty-five, plus twelve

tigation is required to establish how each room was used. Documentary materials, archaeological studies, and contemporary recollections (such as Margaret Bayard Smith's, recorded in a letter to her sister) are enabling the curatorial staff to put in place prints, china, maps, and pieces of furniture that match those the Madisons owned. Slave quarters and other outbuildings are also being investigated, as the house and all its inhabitants, masters and enslaved, are studied and remembered.

bathrooms) A steeplechase course was added to its grounds. The property that Dolley and James knew was difficult to discern within the sprawling country estate it became.

REDISCOVERING MONTPELIER

In her will Marion duPont Scott left the Montpelier estate to the National Trust for Historic Preservation; it was her stated hope that the house might be restored to Madison's "architectural patterns." With the turn of the twenty-first century, the Montpelier Foundation was established, and a twenty-million-dollar grant from the estate of philanthropist Paul Mellon made possible an extraordinary adventure in architectural restoration.

After a comprehensive study established that sufficient architectural evidence survived to re-create the Madison-era mansion, later additions were carefully recorded before being dismantled; in the process, many clues were found to the Madison-era structures, since wooden elements had been reused. After the building had been stripped back to what survived of its original mass and surfaces, inside and out, the restoration began. Using the array of data assembled from surviving original paint, nail holes, the ghosts of molding profiles, and thousands of fragments of physical evidence, the restorers aimed for the look of James Madison's retirement years, 1817–1836. By 2008, the walls were replastered and painted, and the structure of the house was deemed complete.

Yet the restoration process continues. With no comprehensive household inventory and few Madison objects at hand, further inves-

James Madison played a principal role in the early years of the nation, perhaps most memorably as an essential voice at the 1787 Philadelphia convention. But he was also the nation's fourth chief magistrate; he was the first president to declare war, as the War of 1812 was fought during his administration. When he retired to Montpelier, his preoccupation remained the public life of his nation, but by then he was content to be an observer, worrying at the future and, in particular, what he called the "dreadful calamity" of slavery.

But to understand James, one must also appreciate Dolley. Theirs was a complementary partnership. When the public eye was trained upon her, she seemed to generate light and warmth; for James, such attention had precisely the opposite effect, and people perceived him as cold and withdrawn. She was undoubtedly her best self in public, while he served his country quietly, trusting the counsel of a few, working harder and longer than anyone else.

Their marriage was clearly more than the sum of its parts. As his Federalist opponent grumbled after the election of 1808, "I was beaten by Mr. and Mrs. Madison. I might have had a better chance if I had faced Mr. Madison alone." While James Madison's remarkable contributions to his country are well known, this candid admission by the defeated Charles Cotesworth Pinckney suggests the outsize role Dolley Payne Todd Madison played not only in the political sphere of Washington but in the life and times of James Madison. Though the house was James's home from childhood, Montpelier today reflects both President Madison and the woman many in her time called the "Presidentess."

ROXBURY.1ST JULY.MDCCCXXIII

THE HERMITAGE

ANDREW JACKSON
(1829 – 1837)

HERMITAGE, TENNESSEE

"Could I with honor . . . I would fly to
[The Hermitage], there to bury myself
from the corruption and treachery of this
wicked world."

ANDREW JACKSON TO **JOHN COFFEE**

OCTOBER 13, 1834

With the four o'clock sun settling low in the sky, an enslaved servant laid a fire in the family sitting room. Andrew Jackson Jr. had yet to return from the fields; his wife, Sarah, had just come home from her afternoon ride.

Intended to ease the chill of the autumn afternoon, the hungry flames did not remain confined to the stone hearth but soon ignited an accumulation of soot and unburned creosote. Sparks issued from the mouth of the chimney, some of which fell to the roof. The dry wood shingling was soon afire; fanned by a sharp northwest wind, the flames spread.

Squire, a trusted slave who manned the plantation's cotton gin, was the first to spot the smoke rising from the main section of The Hermitage. When Squire raised the alarm, men working nearby, both white and enslaved, came quickly to fight the blaze, but the roof was steep and the quenching water could be delivered only one bucket at a time. Inside the house, Sarah took charge, directing the removal of furniture, papers, and heirlooms. Though much was saved, more was lost. Larger, heavier pieces such as wardrobes and bedsteads had to be abandoned along with much else.

The elder Andrew Jackson (1767–1845) was not present. A month earlier he had returned to Washington City, where he was midway through his second term as president. He heard the news via the U.S. Mail, learning "the perticulars of the unfortunate burning of the Hermitage House" from Nashville's postmaster. He also got a letter from Andrew Jr., his adoptive son and his wife's nephew, whom they had raised from birth as their own. The father was philosophical ("I suppose all the wines in the cellar have been destroyed," he wrote) and quick to absolve his son and daughter-in-law of any blame. "No neglect is imputed to any one, and…[the fire] an act of providence. Tell Sarah [to] cease to mourn its loss."

For the sixty-seven-year-old Jackson, the fire was a shock, but nothing compared with the sudden and unexpected loss of his wife, Rachel, six years earlier. After almost forty years of marriage, he had been inconsolable at her death. The Hermitage had been her place too, a property he purchased after their marriage with a house they had planned and completed together.

The very hour he learned his home had burned, he vowed it would rise again. "I will have it rebuilt," he wrote to his son. Portions of the roof had collapsed, and much of the upper story was destroyed. The damage was extensive on the first level (only the dining room wing remained largely intact), but in the end The Hermitage would

Previous page: The elliptical curve of the stair adds to the drama of the central hall, but then so does the wallpaper. Rachel Jackson originally chose the papers for the house; after the 1834 fire, Andrew's replacement was the same paper his late wife chose (it cost $120). Made in France by the firm of Dufour, the paper tells a story that appealed to Jackson, depicting the wanderings of Ulysses's son Telemachus.

Opposite: The six gargantuan columns with Greek Corinthian capitals stand tall across The Hermitage façade, linked by a second-story porch.

be rebuilt, updated, and improved. "Was it not on the site selected by my dear departed wife I would build it higher up the hill," Jackson mused. "But I will have it repaired."

A SELF-MADE MAN

Andrew Jackson arrived in the world under less than auspicious circumstances. He was born on the frontier in a log cabin built by his father, a hardscrabble farmer who had cleared a few acres in the western Carolinas. But he never knew the Scots-Irish emigrant whose death left Elizabeth Hutchinson Jackson a widow with two young sons and a third in her belly. Born March 15, 1767, the boy was given his father's name.

Andrew grew up in the company of his brothers and cousins at a time of revolutionary ferment. He learned his letters and how to cast accounts at two local academies, but by age thirteen he was in service to the Continental Army. His military experience fostered a hatred of the British, most famously when, captured by the king's dragoons, the lad was ordered to clean an officer's jackboots. When Jackson refused, the officer struck him with his sword, leaving the boy with gashes on his head and left hand. The memory and the scars would remain with Jackson for life.

Orphaned by the war—his mother died of "ship fever" (probably typhus) contracted on a prison ship while caring for Americans imprisoned by the British—Jackson tried out the saddler's trade before clerking in a North Carolina law office. By age twenty, he had passed the bar and earned a reputation as a man with a taste for drink, cardplaying, horse racing, and practical jokes (a favorite prank was relocating a "necessary house" to a distant field). But in 1788, the red-haired, blue-eyed Jackson, rugged and rangy at six foot one, accepted an appointment as a public prosecutor in North Carolina's western district.

Arriving in Nashville, he lived at a boardinghouse. Within three years he married the proprietor's daughter, Rachel Stockley Donelson, who was on the rebound from an unsuccessful first marriage. His own considerable presence, his wife's small inheritance, and the

Opposite, top: One of the less appealing aspects of a great estate like The Hermitage is its history of slavery. This double-pen log structure, an 1840s slave dwelling known as Alfred's Cabin, was within sight of the mansion.

Opposite, bottom: The Hermitage is the name of Jackson's plantation, not his mansion; and the big house wasn't always the principal domicile on the property. For seventeen years, Andrew and Rachel Jackson lived in a set of well-appointed but more modest log structures. These two cabins were then the Jackson farmhouse and kitchen; later, much modified, they served as slave cabins.

Above: The dining room may seem large, but the Jacksons rarely dined alone, as both family and people passing through were welcomed at The Hermitage.

Right: By the time this glass-plate image was made in 1892, The Hermitage had fallen into disrepair. The following year, the last Jackson family member moved out and the Ladies' Hermitage Association assumed responsibility for the care and restoration of the property.
The Ladies' Hermitage Association

connections of the Donelson clan enabled him to gain influence in Middle Tennessee. He was a delegate to the new state's constitutional convention (Tennessee joined the Union in 1796), then its first congressman and subsequently a senator. With mixed success, he bought and sold farms and stores, and purchased The Hermitage in 1804. It was a less impressive place than a previous property he had been forced to sell; its dwelling was but a two-story log house. But the plantation would be his principal home for the rest of his life.

Jackson was elected a major general in the Tennessee militia during these years, and with the outbreak of the War of 1812, he would achieve his first national fame. On a five-hundred-mile march in 1813 from Mississippi to Tennessee, his sheer toughness inspired his own men to nickname him "Old Hickory." With widespread tension between land-hungry settlers and Native Americans, he became a hero to Westerners for vanquishing the Creeks at the Battle of Horseshoe Bend in 1814. The Battle of New Orleans in January 1815 would be remembered as the war's high point, a total victory over the much-vaunted forces of the British that gained the American military new respect. After peace with Great Britain, Jackson had continued to enhance his reputation as an Indian fighter, defeating the Seminoles in Georgia before seizing Pensacola, Florida, a key step in the acquisition of Florida by the United States.

REMAKING THE HERMITAGE

Upon returning from the wars in 1819, Andrew Jackson set about transforming The Hermitage. Over the years, he had added to his holdings—his land approached a thousand acres—and his family was outgrowing the log house, with Andrew Jr., adopted in 1809, nearing adolescence. Andrew and Rachel decided upon an entirely new structure, one that would be more in keeping with the general's prosperity, fame, and growing political influence.

They chose to build in the Federal style, using brick molded and fired on the site by slave labor. Although the most impressive house in the vicinity of Nashville, the new home, completed in 1821, was slightly outmoded by the standards of the coastal states,

where the new Grecian taste had come into vogue. The Hermitage had a symmetrical floor plan with two pairs of rooms flanking a central hall on each of the two principal stories; as one contemporary described it, "It was just a square brick house with no embellishments or architectural pretentions." The single decorative flourish was the entry door, with sidelights and an elliptical fanlight.

Almost a decade later, the house underwent a considerable remodeling. Jackson had been elected president in 1828 and had returned to Middle Tennessee for more than two months in the summer of 1830 (during his eight years as chief magistrate, he came home just four times, since the arduous journey to and from the capital required almost two months). While at The Hermitage, the president found he was host to an unending series of guests; as at Mount Vernon, Monticello, and Montpelier, friends and strangers alike were always knocking on the door. Work commenced in 1831 to build a west wing with a larger dining room (together with a new kitchen and pantry), along with a new east wing that would contain Jackson's library and an overseer's office. The main façade was updated too, with a line of ten Doric columns that defined a one-story porch topped with a turned balustrade. A second-story portico helped transform the house into a classical statement—one fitting the great man and president who resided there. The enlarged home would also meet the needs of Andrew Jackson Jr. and his new bride, who moved there in 1832. It was this basic configuration that burned in 1834.

The house that survives today is the third incarnation, as rethought and reconstructed after the fire. As president, Jackson had grown fond of the White House, with its temple front and white-painted exterior; at Jackson's request, a portico of colossal columns was applied to The Hermitage façade, updating the place in the fashionable Greek Revival style. The expense was considerable, with construction costs totaling $6,288, twice the original estimate. Replacement furnishings proved dear too. Shipped from Philadelphia by steamboat, new dressers, wardrobes, tables, chairs, carpets, drapes, and sundry other items priced out at $2,303.77. But before they could be brought ashore, the ship carrying the goods, the SS *John Randolph,*

Above, left and right: In his last years, Jackson was increasingly infirm, as age and an accumulation of old wounds caught up with him. He spent most of his time in this, his bedchamber, and in the adjacent library, both on the first floor.

burned at a Nashville wharf. In the end Jackson had to pay twice to refurnish his majestic home.

RETIREMENT AND REMEMBRANCE

Eighteen months were required to rebuild The Hermitage, but upon Jackson's return to Nashville on March 25, 1837, he saw that his wishes had been honored. The exterior of his house had an evident new grandeur; once inside, Jackson found that his personal library, heated by its own iron stove, was "a good room to which I can retire." He had come home for good, succeeded by his trusted vice president, Martin Van Buren, and though Jackson was aging and his health uncertain, he confided in a friend, "I live in hopes of regaining my strength so that I can amuse myself in riding over my farm and visiting my good neighbors."

At age seventy, his carriage remained erect, and Jackson was still striking with his rising shock of white hair. Though a widower, a man exhausted by long military service and more recently by the burden of moving his country in what he regarded as a distinctly different direction, he remained formidable. He had been buoyed by the journey home, punctuated as it had been by what Jackson termed the "patriots reward." He wrote to Van Buren just days after his return, "I have been every where cheered."

Jackson was a man of parts. His political enemies dismissed him as "King Mob" (after a near riot at his inauguration) and "King Andrew" (for his imperious ways). He was thin-skinned, ever conscious of his reputation. His temperament could be mercurial; his

THE AGE OF JACKSON

Like General Washington, the president with whom he was often compared, Jackson owed his early fame to success in battle. Unlike all the other men who had held the nation's first office, however, Jackson had not been endowed at birth with inherited lands or even reputation. He owed no allegiance to what he called the "aristocracy of the union." He had little formal education but abundant confidence in his own instincts and experience—and in the wisdom of the common man.

His standing as a hero had enabled him to run for the presidency, but essential to his electoral success was his innate grasp of what average people cared about. When he took the oath of office in 1829, the growing Union consisted of twenty-four states, including Missouri, Alabama, Illinois, Mississippi, and Indiana. The electorate had greatly expanded, and not just because of population growth. Some states had done it earlier and others did it later (Delaware in 1792, Massachusetts and New York in 1821, Virginia in 1850), but property requirements for suffrage were gradually being eliminated. One result was that *four times* the votes were cast in the 1828 election than four years earlier. Jackson's popularity with the masses was such that an immense crowd overwhelmed the White House reception on Inauguration Day ("Lank, lean, famished forms, from fen and forest," quoth Henry Clay).

Jackson's sheer presence and political power, as well as his confidence in himself and what would come to be referred to as his nation's "Manifest Destiny," were such that he gave his name to his time: historians have long since labeled the era the "Age of Jackson."

fierce sense of honor cultivated earlier in life had driven him to fisticuffs in the streets and even to kill a man in a duel (though he did so only after he himself took a bullet to the chest, which remained lodged near his heart for the rest of his life). On the softer side, friends and family knew him as a man of great loyalty and generosity, as he saw to the care and education of several nieces and nephews (during his retirement, The Hermitage was home to six children, including five boys under the age of twelve).

From a twenty-first-century perspective, his is a case study in paradox. It is difficult not to admire his hardheaded fiscal policies (for one year during his presidency, the nation had no debt for the only time in its history, before or since). On the other hand, when Jackson the frontiersman expanded white settlements westward, he did so at the expense of Native Americans (his policy of Indian removal led to relocation of most Southern tribes to territories west of the Mississippi). He was a populist with an abiding confidence in the "virtue and power of the sovereign people," although, as a man of his time, he saw no need to extend "the great body of the democracy of our Country" to African Americans. As a major slaveholder in his region, he owned well over a hundred slaves and freed none of them in his will.

The Hermitage held a precious place in the president's heart, and he lived out his years within its acres. Every day he visited Rachel's grave, a site marked with a domed temple that he had commissioned while in the White House. At his own death on June 8, 1845, he would be interred beside Rachel in The Hermitage family cemetery.

Opposite: Painter Ralph Earl arrived in Nashville as a young man. His alliance with the family made official by his marriage to one of Rachel Jackson's nieces, he became almost a court painter to Andrew Jackson, even living in the White House during Jackson's presidency. This image was taken around 1833, one of thirty-four known Earl likenesses of "Old Hickory."
The Ladies' Hermitage Association

Above: The Hermitage library reflects the retired Jackson. There's a traveling liquor chest on the table, great volumes of bound newspapers in the foreground (he subscribed to fifteen papers in retirement), and a mechanical "invalid" chair, upholstered in red wool, which had been presented to him by the Mechanics Association of Nashville.

Right: The two parlors, front and rear, were formal rooms, filled with furniture in the latest taste from Philadelphia.

LINDENWALD

MARTIN VAN BUREN
(1837 – 1841)

KINDERHOOK, NEW YORK

"I never acted with a more frank and candid man than Mr. Van Buren. It is said that he is a great magician. I believe it, but his only wand is good common sense which he used for the benefit of the country."

ANDREW JACKSON

THE MAGICIAN IN RETIREMENT

Some years retired from the presidency—though not out of politics—Martin Van Buren had new worries. As he wrote to a friend in the winter of 1848, "Don't think me deranged when I say to you that my quiet & . . . comfortable establishment is to be turned topsy-turvy, . . . drowned in the harsh sounds of the ax, the saw, & the trowel." A promise he had made to his son and daughter-in-law, Smith and Ellen Van Buren, was about to change his daily life: if they would move their family into his home (as a doting grandfather, he very much desired they do so), the former president had agreed that his son would "be permitted to add sufficient to my house to make as many rooms as he may want."

In short, the "Little Magician," as he was known to both detractors and admirers for his political conjuring, faced the drawn-out torment of a home renovation.

Architect Richard Upjohn's plans were soon completed and the workmen hired. The $10,000 estimated cost of construction was another source of consternation to Martin Van Buren, but as fate would have it, the irritations of the building process would come to seem minor indeed when a shocking loss befell the family. The work at Lindenwald was in the early stages when Ellen James Van Buren died suddenly, leaving behind her husband, Smith; four children, including an infant daughter; and a father-in-law who knew all too well the pain experienced by his widower son. He himself had buried his wife of twelve years in 1819, and assumed the task of raising his four sons. He had never remarried.

AN UNLIKELY PRESIDENT

Martin Van Buren (1782–1862) was the first American president not born a British subject, as his birth postdated not only the signing of the Declaration of Independence but even General Washington's victory at Yorktown, Virginia, in the deciding battle of the Revo-

Previous page: During the 1849 renovation, new marble mantels and Brussels carpeting were installed, though the earlier woodwork remained little changed. In the Green Room, as this parlor is known, Martin Van Buren's son John looks down from his portrait upon the elegant Empire-style furnishings. Like his father, John served as New York's attorney general.

Left: Although out of government during his years at Lindenwald, Martin Van Buren maintained an active political life for many years. This photograph was taken circa 1850.
Martin Van Buren National Historic Site / National Park Service

Opposite: Van Buren's Lindenwald is a Federal house restyled as a Victorian: the austere, balanced form of the original mass gained Italianate brackets and a Gothic front porch that transformed the front façade.

AN ARCHITECTURAL ASIDE

The architectural plan for the remodeled Lindenwald had come from the drawing board of Richard Upjohn, a British-born architect much ballyhooed in New York for his Trinity Church in Lower Manhattan (years later, Upjohn would be cofounder of the American Institute of Architects).

Though he termed it merely an "architectural aside," Upjohn reinvented the old-fashioned Federal structure in the newly popular Italianate style. Dormers sprouted from the roof, along with a center gable. A new wing was added and a reconfigured basement gained the family ten new rooms of living space. And that was not all.

A four-and-a-half-story tower rose over the rooftop. In a more practical era, the builders of the original 1797 house had been happy with their vantage and easy access to the Albany Post Road out front. But the new campanile-like structure at the rear of the house was capped by an open porch, or belvedere, from which the Van Burens and their guests might take in the full panorama of the surrounding Hudson Valley.

lution. Nor was Van Buren's ancestry British. When the boy entered school at age eight, he spoke Dutch, as did most of the townspeople in his native village of Kinderhook, New York, about 130 miles north of Manhattan.

Nevertheless, his childhood home had been a place of politics. Though little more than a farmhouse, Abraham Van Buren's one-and-a-half-story tavern accommodated his family of eight children, along with a mix of travelers, many of whom were making their way between New York's capital at Albany and New York City. As an innkeeper's son, the ingratiating young Martin shared both his father's political preferences—he was a Jeffersonian Republican—and his access to lively conversation about the events of the day.

At fourteen, he was a clerk in a lawyer's office; just shy of his twenty-first birthday, Martin Van Buren was admitted to the New York bar. His careful preparations, superior memory, and gift for rhetoric brought him rapid success in the courtroom, but he was soon drawn to the business of governing. At age twenty-nine he was elected a state senator and, at thirty-two, became attorney general of the State of New York. Six years later he was elected to the U.S. Senate, then served briefly as governor in his home state before resigning to become secretary of state for the newly elected Andrew Jackson in 1829. After his appointment to minister to the Court of Saint James's was rejected by the Senate, he was chosen as Jackson's running mate and served as vice president from 1833–1837.

Red-haired and of small stature (Van Buren stood barely five foot five), the "Red Fox" had proved a consummate politician. In New York he played an essential role in persuading the legislature to authorize construction of the Erie Canal; that waterway had proved of enormous importance to trade and industrial development in the Empire State. As a delegate to New York's constitutional convention of 1821–1822, he put his influence behind a proposal to extend the franchise beyond property holders to every white male who had paid taxes or served in the militia. That expansion of the franchise in what had become the most populous state helped initiate a larger wave throughout the nation. One beneficiary had been candidate Jackson, who, as a military hero and man

President Van Buren—artist Hiram Powers executed this likeness during Van Buren's term in office—portrayed as an heir to the classical tradition of Greek democracy and the Roman republic, dressed in a toga.

of Tippecanoe in 1811, was memorialized for his military exploits, along with his running mate, John Tyler, in the song "Tippecanoe and Tyler Too." The ditty also belittled his opponent as "Little Van ...a used-up man." Harrison was the first presidential candidate to travel the country, giving speeches on his own behalf. The tradition until 1840 had been to remain at home as if a disinterested bystander.

In anticipation of his eventual retirement, Van Buren in 1839 had purchased an imposing brick house back in his hometown of Kinderhook; when he lost his bid for a second term, he retired to his country home and set about making it his own.

LINDENWALD

For Martin Van Buren, the house represented more than a comfortable domicile. He had known the place in childhood, and carried with him a recollection of a day when the haughty owner had refused to acknowledge young Van Buren's presence. It was with a sense of having truly climbed to the top of the social hierarchy that Van Buren purchased the estate for $14,000 and renamed it *Lindenwald,* after a grove of linden trees on the property.

The property had deteriorated, and Van Buren found its fields filled with weeds, its acreage lined with rotting fences. Having visited Jefferson's Monticello and Andrew Jackson's Hermitage, Van Buren set about making his estate suitable for a presidential retirement. Insofar as he wished to maintain an impressive mansion in order to convey his own standing to other powerful and important men, Van Buren's vision for Lindenwald matched those of the third and seventh presidents. Yet in a region where the slaves had been emancipated, his could not be a sprawling plantation. Even after adding land to his original purchase, he held title to a bit more than two hundred acres, compared to the thousands owned by Washington, Madison, and his presidential predecessors from the South.

Van Buren planted orchards of apples, pears, and plums, and drained nearby acreage to create meadows of timothy. He would keep about a dozen cows, a pair of oxen, a few pigs and goats, perhaps a hundred sheep, and a mix of fowl. His fields would produce

of humble origins, promised to obey "the will of people," which swept him into the White House.

Van Buren became Jackson's chosen successor, and in 1836 he defeated four opposing candidates, including Daniel Webster and William Henry Harrison. Just weeks after he took office, however, the nation's banking system, shaken by failed harvests and a fall in cotton prices, showed signs of collapse. Banks closed their doors in what came to be known as the "Panic of 1837," and Van Buren's presidency never recovered from the nation's first major economic depression. Four years later, an ever-enlarging voting public replaced him in what has often been described as the first modern election campaign, in which slogans played as big a part as the issues. Eventual winner General William Henry Harrison, who had come to national notice with his victory over the Shawnee at the Battle

Once two rooms, the central passageway became this grand entertaining space where Van Buren held court. His original mahogany dining table (this is a precise copy) probably came from the shop of New York maker Duncan Phyfe. It has an accordion-like mechanism that, when fully extended, seats thirty people; when closed it is a mere twenty-six inches long.

hay, rye, and potatoes, but he knew full well they would never make him rich. Still, with the orchards, the meadows, an existing allée of black locusts that lined the approach to the house, an elaborate garden he added, and two ponds he had made and stocked with trout, pickerel, and perch, he created a verdant landscape suitable for a country gentleman. He repainted the brick house a fashionable pale yellow with brown trim.

For the interior, he rearranged the center hall, moving the stair in order to create a grand dining room. From Lindenwald, he would manage two more campaigns for president, losing again in 1844 and 1848. His life with his sons and grandchildren gradually became more important than his political past, and by all accounts he was a doting grandfather who played often with the growing brood of grandchildren, including Martin Van Buren III, born in 1844 and known as "Marty."

A VISITOR FROM KENTUCKY

By August 1849, the remodeling was complete: the house now had thirty-six rooms, a water closet, and a bath. Van Buren was looking for company and good political conversation—and Henry Clay was in the neighborhood.

To some, they seemed an odd pair. For decades they shared the national political stage, but more often as adversaries than allies. Once upon a time Henry Clay, a brilliant orator, had seemed almost certain to take up residence in the White House, but despite five attempts, thrice in opposition to Van Buren, he had never won the office of chief magistrate. Regardless of their combative history, the two old warhorses had long since demonstrated "an unfailing readiness," as Van Buren put it, to set aside their many political disagreements in favor of "friendly personal relations."

Their political identities strangely mirrored each other. Clay was a Southern man with Northern principles (he favored the National Bank, for example, as well as infrastructure investments in roads and canals, and tariffs to protect American manufacturers). Van Buren was a Northerner with a Southern orientation (his party affiliations had been with the Jeffersonian Republicans and Jackson's Democrats, both of which were pro-slavery with slave-holding leaders). When Clay, his health failing, arrived to immerse himself in the health-giving mineral waters at nearby Saratoga Springs, Van Buren issued an invitation to the former senator, Speaker of the House, and secretary of state. Clay agreed to visit a fortnight later, after a stop at Newport, Rhode Island, where he wished to test the efficacy of the "bracing Sea air."

At age seventy-two, dogged by a racking cough but feeling better than he had in months, Clay arrived at Lindenwald. For four days and four nights, the two aging political wizards engaged in "unrestricted and family chats," as Van Buren noted in his *Autobiography*. "The feuds of the past and the asperities caused by them were as completely ignored in their conversations as if they had never existed." Yet one subject Van Buren left unmentioned in his memoir (though the two men no doubt touched upon it) perhaps best highlights the paradoxes of their relationship and, in a larger sense, the complexities of their times.

While Clay was in Newport, his personal body slave, Levi, had fled to Boston. Writing home to Kentucky from Lindenwald, Clay confided in his wife that Levi had been "carried or enticed away by Abolitionists" who gifted him the very handsome sum of three hundred dollars. Upon reaching the Massachusetts capital, however, Levi had "become distrustful" of those who had abetted his escape and, after returning the money given him, rejoined his master. Clay wasn't unsympathetic (he would later remark that "it is probable that in a reversal of our conditions I would have done the same thing"), but he was still a slave owner from a slaveholding state.

The arrival of the enslaved Levi at Lindenwald was a reminder to both Clay and Van Buren of a long-evolving national disagreement, one with unresolved implications for the future that both men feared. Van Buren himself owned no slaves, though his father had owned six; certainly he relied upon servants to run his household, but they were almost exclusively Irish, many recent arrivals from Ireland, and almost none remained in his employ for more than a few years. More important, they were free and could come

In the corner of his bedchamber, at the ready for his morning ablutions, is Van Buren's shaving stand.

and go as they wished. In contrast, slavery had been a fact of life to Clay from birth. He had often expressed antislavery sentiments (he called slavery the "deepest stain upon the character of the country" and supported the American Colonization Society's efforts to transport African Americans back to Africa). The abolitionists still denounced him as a slaveholder even though many of his regional brethren proclaimed him an abolitionist.

Both Clay and Van Buren had tread tricky political paths with respect to slavery. Clay had secured passage of the Missouri Compromise, taking an eye-for-an-eye approach to the admission of new states, allowing Maine to join the Union in tandem with slave state Missouri in 1820. During his tenure as attorney general of New York, Van Buren had played a role in the 1817 passage of a statute that would free virtually all slaves in the state a decade later (ironically, in 1841 a section of that law had been repealed, allowing travelers to the state, like Clay, to keep their slaves). A national debate in 1844 over the annexation of Texas as a slave state had harmed both men's electoral prospects. It was apparent to observers as thoughtful as Clay and Van Buren that the South, the dominion of slavery, which had been the source of most of the nation's presidents, was increasingly at odds with the North, where a growing abolitionist movement was taking hold. The seemingly unresolvable disagreement had fostered the birth of the new Free Soil Party, with which Van Buren himself had been affiliated in the election of 1848, with its platform calling for the end of Southern domination of the national government in order to stop the expansion of slavery.

How much of this history these two pragmatic men revisited in their time together that September 1849 is unknowable; very likely, as public men who had sought solutions to their nation's problems with the same passionate conviction they had shown in seeking public office, they wondered aloud as to the prospects of a future they knew to be clouded. Certainly they had no easy answers, and neither man had ever found a fixed position to take on the issue of slavery.

Before Clay departed, neighbors stopped by to shake his hand. Despite suffering from an attack of gout that made it difficult for him to put his boots on, Van Buren escorted the Kentuckian to the train station. As Van Buren noted, "We parted never to see each other again." Clay would die three years later at Ashland, his home in Lexington, Kentucky—but only after having helped craft a set of compromise bills in 1850 that, once again, provided a short-term solution to sectional differences.

Martin Van Buren outlived Clay by a decade, surrounded by two generations of family. The eighth president died at Lindenwald on July 24, 1862, well after shots were fired at Fort Sumter and only weeks before the sixteenth president delivered the Emancipation Proclamation.

The Van Buren family at Lindenwald was served by a staff of domestics. The servants typically consisted of four young Irishwomen—a cook, a table server, a chambermaid, and, at different times, a laundress or nurse for the children. They ate here in the servants' dining room, along with the Lindenwald coachman.

WHEATLAND

JAMES BUCHANAN
(1857 – 1861)

LANCASTER, PENNSYLVANIA

"I have always felt and still feel that
I discharged every public duty imposed on me
conscientiously. I have no regrets for any
public act of my life, and history
will vindicate my memory."

JAMES BUCHANAN, FROM HIS DEATHBED,
WHEATLAND, MAY 31, 1868

DEPARTING WHEATLAND, WINTER 1857

Though James Buchanan was no longer young, he wore his advancing years well. "He is a fine looking personage," wrote one reporter in early 1857. "He has a large head and massive forehead, denoting great intellect. His hair is thin and is as white as driven snow." The writer had come to see firsthand the man of whom all America wished to know more: Buchanan (1791–1868) had just been elected president.

To visit him required a trip to Lancaster, Pennsylvania, ten miles north of the Mason-Dixon Line, where Buchanan had lived since 1809. Having graduated from Dickinson College in nearby Carlisle, the young man had arrived to study law, then began to practice his new profession in 1812. Within two years he held elective office in Pennsylvania; by 1820, he was on his way to Washington. Prior to his election as president, he had served five terms in the

House, portions of three in the Senate, and four years as secretary of state in President James Polk's administration (1845–1849). His twenty-six-year span of service in Washington had been broken only by his nineteen months as Andrew Jackson's minister to Russia and, most recently, by a tour of duty as minister to Great Britain in the administration of President Franklin Pierce (1853–1857).

In the inaugural winter of 1857, another journalist, this one a worldly New Yorker, remarked upon Buchanan's home, known as Wheatland (the Lancaster banker who built the house in 1828 gave it the name in honor of its setting amid amber fields of grain). Though the writer thought the place "not imposing, or indeed of any architectural beauty," he allowed that Buchanan's brick house possessed "an air of comfort, respectability and repose." Located a mile and a half from downtown Lancaster, the two-story home sat on a gently rising slope, looking down upon Franklin and Marshall College, of which Buchanan served as chairman of the board of trustees. Though he had no guard at hand to ensure his security, Buchanan shared his twenty-two acres with his large and devoted Newfoundland dog, Lara, along with a pair of eagles sent by a

Previous page: During the 1856 campaign, a lithograph of Wheatland's imposing front façade was widely distributed. Particularly in the South, the tacit message was that, though a Pennsylvanian, Buchanan lived a life not so dissimilar from plantation owners in their gracious homes in that region.

Left: President James Buchanan in the White House, as photographed by Mathew Brady circa 1857.
LancasterHistory.org

Opposite: The center of Buchanan's campaign activity was his study. The cast-iron parlor stove kept the library warm on cold winter days, when Buchanan was often to be found reading in his leather barrel chair.

friend from California's Sierra Madre range. According to another reporter, the birds "show[ed] no disposition to wing their flight from Wheatland."

As for Buchanan, his preferred habitat was his study. When then secretary of state James Buchanan purchased the property in 1848 for $6,750, he had acquired for an additional $75 the bookcases in the library, which were now lined with his books. A marbleized slate mantelpiece anchored the end wall, and a writing desk occupied the center of the room. According to another observer, this one from *Frank Leslie's Illustrated Newspaper,* every available surface was covered with books, papers, letters, and newspapers, including the mahogany sofa with its damask pillows.

In this room the president-elect received guests, political and otherwise, often with a cigar in his mouth and slippers on his feet. They came from near and far. The most optimistic in the land hoped that Buchanan might offer a solution to the sectional strife that gripped the country, but according to James Gordon Bennett of the

New York Herald, the geographic differences were to be observed in even the smallest details. He noted that men from the South were more likely to pronounce their host's name as *Jeems Buck-an-an,* while to his Northern neighbors he was *Jimmy Bewchanan.* As events unfolded during the next four years, the nation's inability to agree upon so small a linguistic matter proved symptomatic of the immense challenges facing the man some called simply "Old Buck."

BUCHANAN'S WAR

In a rhetorical sense—that is to say, when judged by the speeches he gave—James Buchanan's presidency is bracketed by his inaugural address and his final State of the Union Message. Therein lies the tale of a presidency that has consistently been ranked among the worst by historians.

On March 4, 1857, the day of his swearing in, President Buchanan offered his assessment of the unavoidable debate concerning

President-elect Buchanan greeted journalists and others in the Wheatland library, including a representative from the newly founded *Frank Leslie's Illustrated Newspaper,* in which this engraving of Buchanan (*left*) appeared. LancasterHistory.org

when—or whether—the inhabitants of a territory might decide to join the Union with or without slavery. Having often said of himself, "I acknowledge no master but the law," Buchanan regarded the matter as of "little practical importance . . . [and] a judicial question, which legitimately belongs to the Supreme Court of the United States, before whom it is now pending, and will, it is understood, be speedily and finally settled."

He referred to the case of *Dred Scott v. Sanford.* The facts were that Scott, though born into slavery, had for a time resided in the state of Illinois and the territory of Wisconsin, where slavery was prohibited, before returning to Missouri, a slave state. Scott sued for his freedom, and his case had worked its way up to the docket of the Supreme Court (Scott's argument was, in brief, to borrow a phrase from one lower-court ruling in the case, "once free, always free"). Three days after Buchanan's inauguration, however, the highest court in the land issued a broad ruling, asserting that Scott, because he was black, was not a citizen and had no legal standing to sue. The stark finding pleased many slaveholders; equally it outraged abolitionists. Far from offering the speedy and final settlement to the disagreement that Buchanan had promised, the Court served only to further exacerbate sectional antagonisms.

Four years later, Buchanan's presidency neared its end (true to a promise made at his inaugural, he had not sought a second term). Abraham Lincoln had been elected to succeed him, and disunion seemed nearly inevitable. But in his Fourth Annual Message to Congress, delivered December 3, 1860, Buchanan again argued that the rule of law would offer a solution. On the one hand, Buchanan asserted, the Southern states had no right to secede from the Union. On the other, he saw the principal cause of the crisis as the "intemperate interference of the Northern people with the question of slavery in the Southern States." His solution was "to obtain 'an explanatory amendment' of the Constitution of the subject of slavery." Once again, his confidence that a legalistic formulation would resolve the issue of slavery proved unrealistic; as the *Cincinnati Enquirer* observed, "Seldom have we known so strong an argument come to so lame and impotent a conclusion." Few in either the North or the South were satisfied, and seventeen days later, South

The scale of the house is evident in this shot of the garden façade. After his retirement Buchanan established a fine garden; in the winter he liked to take his horses for a trot, riding in his sleigh.

Wheatland was certainly James Buchanan's home, but when a popular publication of the day, *Frank Leslie's Illustrated Newspaper,* described the house as in "perfect good taste," it was Harriet Lane they had in mind. "The whole arrangement reflects the highest credit upon the young lady, Mr. Buchanan's niece, who has so long presided over the hospitalities of Wheatland." The portrait of James Buchanan was painted by William E. McMaster in 1856, the year of his election to the presidency.

Carolina seceded from the Union, followed shortly by six other slave states.

Some historians place substantial blame for what has been termed "Buchanan's War" on the Pennsylvanian. A contrary case has also been made by Buchanan's more sympathetic biographers that, in a less fratricidal time, his long experience in government and diplomacy might have served his nation to great advantage. Certainly there is little reason to believe that anyone else could have found a means of achieving national reconciliation. Circumstances being what they were, and Buchanan's legalistic mind-set being what it was, his efforts to prevent the conflict that became the Civil War proved insufficient, if not misguided. In the eyes of history, the consensus seems to be that his old boss James Polk had it

about right when he confided in his diary years earlier, "Mr. Buchanan is an able man, but . . . sometimes acts like an old maid."

As the bewildered and exhausted Buchanan prepared to retire to Wheatland in March 1861, the Confederate States of America had been formed, and military preparations were under way on both sides. Buchanan's successor faced every prospect of war, and the outgoing president revealed his feelings upon greeting Abraham Lincoln at the White House. "If you are as happy, my dear sir, on entering this house, as I am in leaving it and returning home, you are the happiest man in this Country." Barely a month later, the Civil War began with the Confederate attack on Fort Sumter, but by then James Buchanan had retired to Wheatland.

MISS HARRIET LANE

To understand either Wheatland or James Buchanan, one must make the acquaintance of Miss Harriet Rebecca Lane.

James Buchanan was the only bachelor president of the United States. The White House had been occupied by single men, among them the widowers Thomas Jefferson and John Tyler (the latter's first wife died during his term). Later in the century, Grover Cleveland would marry while in office. Though "Old Buck" was the only chief executive who never married, there had been a woman at his side in London who also filled the role of first lady both in Washington and at Wheatland.

Miss Harriet Lane had been orphaned at age ten when both her parents died within a year of each other. She became a ward of her mother's brother; to the tomboyish Harriet, her uncle, then a U.S. senator, became "Nunc." He, in turn, called her "Hal." After attending several boarding schools, she joined her uncle in Washington in 1848 during his tenure as secretary of state. He gave her wise advice about life in the Capital City: "Be on your guard against flattery; & should you receive it, let it pass into one ear gracefully & out the other."

The attractive young woman with the lustrous hair was much admired. During Buchanan's days as minister to the Court of Saint James's, Harriet was presented to Queen Victoria. The young woman so impressed the monarch that she ordered Miss Lane be accorded the respect due an ambassador's wife. Later, as Buchanan's official hostess at the White House, she and her uncle received the first royal visit to the United States with the arrival of the prince of Wales (subsequently King Edward VII) in 1860.

She postponed marrying until after Buchanan left the White House. Following her marriage in 1866, she bore two children and

outlived not only her uncle but her husband and both her sons. Following Buchanan's philanthropic pattern (he contributed to Franklin and Marshall and to Dickinson, and set up a trust in Lancaster for widows and orphans), she helped establish a school in Washington (St. Albans School) and donated the art she had begun collecting in England

Above: Upstairs in the master chamber is the equipment Buchanan used for his ablutions—including the washtub.

Below, left: The bachelor Buchanan relied upon his ward (and niece) Harriet Lane to be his hostess. She was a great hit in Washington, where, at Buchanan's inauguration, dressed in a white gown and strands of pearls, she was hailed as "Our Democratic Queen."
LancasterHistory.org

to the Smithsonian in the hopes that a national art gallery would be established. A bequest from her husband led to the establishment of the Harriet Lane Home for Invalid Children at The Johns Hopkins University in Baltimore.

Another role she played until her death in 1903 was as a vigorous defender of her uncle's political legacy.

∞∞∞∞∞∞∞∞∞

Wheatland was the place where the only Pennsylvanian to be elected president nurtured his ambitions for the nation's first office.

When he "retired" to Lancaster in 1849, he wrote to a Washington colleague, "I am now residing at this place, which is an agreeable country residence. . . . I can say in all sincerity that I am contented & even happy in my retirement." To all outward appearances, he

The elegant stair, with its curvilinear railing and balusters of figured maple; on the facing wall is a gilt convex mirror topped by an American eagle.

lived the life of a country gentleman for the next four years. But those first four years at Wheatland were hardly apolitical.

Though he assiduously avoided what he called "the Capital City...the great theatre of President making," his voluminous correspondence indicated he was very much in the running for the nation's first office in 1852. Although he did not win that year, after he and Miss Harriet returned from Great Britain in 1856, he was again a candidate but once more chose not to travel in pursuit of the presidency. His was a so-called front-porch candidacy: politicians, job-seekers, and journalists alike came to him at Wheatland.

Today's visitors to Wheatland get a glimpse of antebellum life in the North. The furniture, fabrics, and elegant interiors speak for the tastes and cosmopolitan experience of James Buchanan and his niece Harriet Lane.

LINCOLN HOME
AND
PRESIDENT LINCOLN'S
COTTAGE

ABRAHAM LINCOLN
(1861 – 1865)

SPRINGFIELD, ILLINOIS
WASHINGTON, D.C.

"Mr. Lincoln may not be

as handsome a figure [as Stephen Douglas]

but the people are perhaps not aware

that his heart is as large as his arms are long."

MARY TODD LINCOLN

◇◇◇◇◇◇◇◇◇

THE RAIL-SPLITTER

The tall man stood on the street corner. After long weeks of traveling the midstate Illinois court circuit, he was happy to be home—but the house before him was not as it had been on his departure. The one-story Grecian-style house had been transformed, gaining an upper floor and a new roof.

Turning to a passerby, he asked in an accent that revealed his Kentucky origins, "Stranger, do you know where Lincoln lives?" He paused, then added, "He used to live here."

As his listener knew full well, the speaker was Abraham Lincoln himself, a man whose sober countenance then, and in the images that have come down to us, belied the presence of his wry and mischievous wit.

The Lincolns acquired the house on Eighth Street in Springfield on May 2, 1844, for the sum of $1,500. It had been built five years earlier for the Reverend Charles Dresser, the man who conducted the wedding ceremony in November 1842 at which the charming, well-educated, and dainty Mary Ann Todd had married her gangly suitor, Abraham Lincoln (1809–

1865). The groom was a struggling lawyer, described by one contemporary as "the rawest, most primitive looking specimen of humanity I ever saw."

Their well-made house had floors of random-width oak boards and siding of native walnut. With three rooms on the main floor, the house had been comfortable enough for a time (certainly it compared favorably to the rented rooms in the Globe Tavern in downtown Springfield, where the Lincolns resided for the first year of their marriage). But the years had brought children, and with three boys in the house—twelve-year-old Robert Todd; William Wallace, age five; and the baby of the family, Thomas, just three—the

---

Previous page: The meandering appearance of the sometime presidential home in Washington, D.C., Lincoln's Cottage, bespeaks both its style—Gothic Revival is typically asymmetrical—and the presence of two additions made to the original structure.

Left: This well-remembered 1860 photograph—Lincoln called it his "shadow"—was taken by Mathew Brady in his New York City studio. On that day Lincoln, not yet a candidate for president, made his famous speech at Cooper Union, intoning, "Let us have faith that right makes might, and in that faith, let us, to the end, dare to do our duty as we understand it."
Library of Congress / Prints and Photographs

Opposite: The Lincolns used their front and back parlors for entertaining; on occasion, Abraham would greet a client there too. "An air of quiet refinement pervaded the place," reported one visitor to the Lincoln home in 1860. "You would have known instantly that she who presided over that modest household was a true type of American lady." Rocking chairs like this mahogany one (*left*) came to be known in the later nineteenth century as "Lincoln rockers."

attic sleeping spaces, one of which was occupied by a servant girl, had begun to seem cramped. By 1856, the Lincolns had money in hand to pay the $1,300 cost of the renovation, both from Abe's growing law practice and from the sale of a parcel of land Mary inherited from her father.

With the completion of the renovation later that year, Abraham and Mary gained adjoining upstairs bedrooms. There was a small maid's room, a bedroom for the boys, and a well-furnished and comfortable guest chamber. Downstairs the old master bedroom became the rear parlor. The exterior of the house was painted the colors Lincoln specified, Quaker brown with shutter green trim.

Enlarged as it was, the homestead remained a middling dwelling, described by one Eastern visitor as "a plain, two-story wooden building, . . . looking like the residence of a man neither poor nor rich." In contrast, just as the Lincolns finished their remodeled home, adding wallpaper to its walls, Illinois governor Joel Aldrich Matteson commissioned a fine brick mansion for himself. A few blocks away, the governor's Italianate house, with its four-and-a-half-story tower (Mary Todd termed it "a palace"), cost $93,000 to construct.

The Lincolns' home on the corner would be the site of a great many events in the seventeen years they were in residence. Abraham and Mary suffered the anguish of losing a child, when Edward "Eddie"

Baker Lincoln died of "chronic consumption" in 1850, a month short of his fourth birthday. Their enlarged home permitted the hospitable Lincolns—she was a capable cook, he a gifted raconteur—to entertain, and they were known to invite hundreds of people for berry-and-cream parties in season. Robert Todd went off to preparatory school in the East; Abraham gained local fame and, over time, national recognition for his position on the expansion of slavery to the Western territories.

Yet even after his victory in the 1860 presidential election, his Springfield neighbors found the householder Lincoln little changed. One reported that he continued to carry his own shopping basket each morning to the butcher's and baker's a few streets away. When one acquaintance addressed him as "Mr. President," Lincoln remained his unpretentious self. "Well, yes, I suppose so," he responded with an air of reluctance upon hearing his new title, then added, "I will have to go and leave you before long. You must call and see me when I am living in the big house."

LAWYER LINCOLN

The Abraham Lincoln whom the citizens of Springfield first knew had arrived in town with an untidy list of accomplishments. He had built and sailed a flatboat to carry goods to New Orleans, operated a general store, been a postmaster and county surveyor, and served in the Illinois Militia in a war against the Black Hawk Indians in 1832. Altogether he had accumulated fewer than two years of formal education, but after his local popularity in the frontier town of New Salem won him a seat in the Illinois General Assembly in 1834, Lincoln decided to read law. As he put it, he "studied with nobody" but gained admission to the bar two years later. In 1837, he moved to the new Illinois capital to establish a law practice, arriving with all his worldly goods stowed in two saddlebags.

He was a general practitioner. He drafted wills, represented criminal defendants, and worked for railroads and steamboat companies; he practiced divorce, property, and corporate law at all levels, once pleading before the U.S. Supreme Court. He argued cases for and against slaveholders. Though he also served four terms in the Illinois legislature, the law was his livelihood.

His courtroom skills gained him a wider reputation, but as he honed his ability to persuade juries and judges, his larger visibility in Illinois grew too, thanks in part to spending several months a year traveling the Eighth Judicial Circuit, which gained him the acquaintance of many townspeople in rural Illinois. In 1846, he was elected to the U.S. Congress but served just one term in Washington, retiring from politics to return to his family life in Springfield. The practice of "Honest Old Abe" grew once again, thanks in part to his reputation for hard work and truthfulness. "If, in your own judgment, you can not be an honest lawyer," he once wrote, "resolve to be honest without being a lawyer."

Though he had made antislavery statements earlier, he was prompted to reenter politics when, in 1854, the Kansas–Nebraska Act was passed by Congress, permitting the expansion of slavery to states entering the Union. Joining the newly formed Republican Party in 1858, Lincoln ran against Illinois senator Stephen A.

Opposite: Although Mary had grown up in a slaveholding family in Kentucky, she prided herself in cooking meals and tending to her family's needs.

Above: A less formal space than the parlors, the Lincoln sitting room on the other side of the entry hall was a family place. According to family remembrances, however, Lincoln did not find the chairs comfortable, so he often settled himself on the floor.

As was customary in families of a certain means, the Lincolns maintained separate bedrooms. That suited Abraham and Mary's differing schedules: an insomniac, he often worked late; as the chief cook in the house, she usually rose early. Note the chamber pot beneath his four-poster bed.

Douglas, the sponsor of the Kansas-Nebraska Act. Though Lincoln lost the election, his campaign debates with Douglas brought him to the nation's attention. A memorable speech delivered at the Republican convention, held in Springfield, defined in biblical terms the nation's largest disagreement. Lincoln quoted Jesus—"A house divided against itself cannot stand"—then explained what those words in the gospel meant in a new context. "I believe this government cannot endure," he warned, "permanently half slave and half free."

On May 19, 1860, a delegation of men from his party arrived in Springfield from Chicago. Lincoln was expecting them and, in the rear parlor of the house on Eighth Street, offered his guests ice water (he and Mary had argued whether to offer them whiskey; Abraham decided not, aware of the political power of the temperance movement). The notice of nomination was read: Lincoln had been chosen as the party's candidate for president on the third ballot at the just-completed Republican convention. Lincoln asked for

time to consider the party platform, but four days later he accepted.

On Election Day, November 6, 1860, the candidate himself brought the news home. The telegraph machine had delivered the polling results, and Abraham Lincoln, returning late to his brown house, called out to his wife, "Mary, we're elected!"

WASHINGTON CITY AT WAR, 1864

Disregarding the warnings of his friends and the lateness of the hour, the president rode alone. His favorite mount, *Old Abe,* had carried him some three miles from the War Department. His destination was the Soldiers' Home, where—as President Buchanan had done before him—Mr. Lincoln, along with his wife, Mary, and their son Tad, took summer refuge from the bustle downtown.

As Lincoln recalled later, "I was jogging along at a slow gait, immersed in deep thought contemplating what was next to happen in the unsettled state of affairs."

A shot rang out.

Before the man could react to the report of the rifle, his horse bucked. Though the rider's inordinately long legs helped him retain his seat in the saddle, his tall hat fell from its perch on his head. "At

In 1852, an act of Congress had established a "military asylum for the relief and support of invalid and disabled soldiers of the army of the United States." The site of the Riggs property was deemed appropriate for such an installation, and Riggs, together with an adjoining landowner, conveyed 463 acres and the existing dwellings to the federal government. A large building of marble with a castellated tower was constructed to house the soldiers, and the Riggs cottage was put to a variety of uses. Though President Buchanan had summered in a smaller cottage on the property, Lincoln was the first chief executive to occupy the generous home that had belonged to Riggs.

The Lincolns arrived with more than the clothes on their backs. In late June or early July of 1862, 1863, and 1864, their White House servants transported household goods and Lincoln belongings, including furniture and Tad's toys. They would remain until

Above: The house at the corner of Eighth and Jackson Streets in Springfield, Illinois—the only home the Lincolns ever owned.

Below: From the high eminence on which it was built—the third-highest hill in the federal district—the cottage afforded Lincoln clear views of the military cemetery near at hand and of the Capitol in the distance.

a break-neck speed," Lincoln told a friend the next day, "we soon arrived in a haven of safety."

After inquiring of the hatless president what had happened, members of Lincoln's presidential guard at the gate of the Soldiers' Home precinct descended the hill to investigate. They found Lincoln's eight-dollar silk hat in the road—with a bullet hole through the crown. Though Lincoln refused to believe "that any one has shot or will deliberately shoot at me with the purpose of killing me," he was thereafter accompanied by a military escort on his trips to and from Washington City.

⬦⬦⬦⬦⬦⬦⬦⬦

The comfortable cottage the Lincolns inhabited had been constructed in 1842–1843 for banker George Washington Riggs. It was hardly a cottage in today's sense of the word (including generous hallways, there were thirty-four rooms), but, in the manner of Andrew Jackson Downing, author of *Cottage Residences* and a leading tastemaker of the day, it was "a sensible, solid, unpretending country house, with an air of substantial comfort and refinement, not overpowered by architectural style, but indicating intelligent, domestic life in the country."

Constructed to take advantage of the vistas and breezes of its hilltop site, the Lincoln Cottage had been built in the Gothic Revival style. Its structure of brick was covered with roughcast stucco, and gingerbread verge boards lined the gables. Terra-cotta pots topped the chimney flues; there was a broad porch with flattened pointed arches.

MARY TODD LINCOLN

The house on the hill granted Lincoln a fleeting sense of distance from the day-to-day details of administering the war, but for his wife, Mary Todd Lincoln, its very unfamiliarity was a much-needed relief. During their first summer at the Soldiers' Home, she was, as she herself said, "in need of quiet," still devastated by the loss of her eleven-year-old son, Willie, who had died of typhoid at the White House on February 20, 1862.

Throughout their marriage, the high-strung Mary Todd Lincoln often needed time to recover herself despite the fact that hers was a cheerful and lively temperament. Delighting in company, she was renowned as a cultured, talkative, and social neighbor in Springfield. A woman capable of great kindnesses—once she was wet nurse to a neighbor's child, feeding the baby even as she nursed her own—Mrs. Lincoln became subject to repeated periods of emotional fragility.

Her Springfield neighbors told tales of her temper; she was known to berate tradesmen and even to strike her husband in anger. She suffered intense headaches. Having been raised in comfortable circumstances on a Kentucky plantation, waited on by slaves and educated in private schools, she found that the demands of running a household, often on her own, exacted a great toll and left her enervated; her husband's regular absences left her lonely. He would fulfill the ambitious plans they shared for his future, but his loss and that of three sons became almost too much to bear.

Ten years after her husband's assassination, Mary Todd Lincoln was temporarily institutionalized by order of the court in a proceeding initiated by her only surviving son, Robert Todd Lincoln; he told the jury, "She has been of unsound mind since the death of Father." That she was released less than four months later and subsequently declared mentally competent only begins to suggest why Mary Lincoln's complex character remains a subject of debate and speculation among historians.

the chill of the fall, typically the end of October. Altogether, Lincoln would spend about thirteen months of his forty-nine-month presidency in residence at the Soldiers' Home.

At the cottage, President Lincoln could sometimes indulge himself in matters other than the tribulations of war. He played with his young son Tad. He rode his horse about the scenic estate—and cemetery. As a man who had long recognized the power of poetry (he found verse moving, and committed to memory many lines and even entire poems), he revisited favorite works. His personal secretary noted in his diary that the president "was fond of reading aloud. . . . He passed many of the summer evenings in this way . . . at the Soldiers' Home." One or another of Shakespeare's plays was often his work of choice.

Yet Lincoln could never entirely banish the demands of office. Counselors, members of his cabinet, and others came to discuss war plans. He himself put pen to paper while living at the cottage: more important than any correspondence or memorandums that he produced at his retreat was the draft of the Emancipation Proclamation, the document that made the abolition of slavery an official goal of the war. Even as the Proclamation took shape, the men around Lincoln knew, as his secretary John Hay noted on the day the president read a draft to the cabinet, that this was a "momentous document."

Though Lincoln had told his inner circle in July 1862 of his decision to free the slaves, there had been political factors to consider before it could be published. These were not merely matters of party, since public opinion as a whole did not favor total emancipation. Timing was an issue too, as the war was not going well. At the suggestion of Secretary of State William Henry Seward, "I put the draft of the proclamation aside," Lincoln confided in Francis B. Carpenter, the painter later commissioned to record the first reading of the Emancipation Proclamation. In August, the Union forces were routed at the Second Battle of Bull Run, and Lincoln observed, "Things looked darker than ever."

In September, better news arrived. "Finally came the week of the Battle of Antietam," Lincoln told Carpenter. "I determined to wait no longer . . . [since] the advantage was on our side. I was then staying at the Soldiers' Home. . . . Here I finished writing the second draft of the preliminary proclamation."

The executive order was made public the following Monday, on September 22, 1862. It was hardly the last word, as the Emancipation Proclamation freed just the slaves in the ten Confederate states; those in slaveholding border states on the Union side would be freed later. Only with the passage of the Thirteenth Amendment of 1865 (approved by Congress in January, ratified that December) would the total abolition of slavery be achieved.

⬦⬦⬦⬦⬦⬦⬦

At the Soldiers' Home, the reminders of war seemed forever at hand. A hundred and fifty disabled veterans lived on the property, as did Secretary of War Edwin Stanton in his own cottage. The first national cemetery was on the premises too. The interment of soldiers who had died carrying out his orders was a daily sight for President Lincoln, who was often seen in the night hours walking the grounds. He spoke almost daily with soldiers, seeking firsthand information and opinions about the war and its progress.

In July 1864 the war came within earshot, when Camp Stevens, located a mile distant at the city's perimeter, was attacked by the Confederate Second Corps of the Army of Northern Virginia. Seeking to distract the Union Army from the siege at Richmond, General Jubal A. Early had marched across Maryland. As Early's men neared, Lincoln rode to Fort Stevens, where he stood atop a parapet, watching the Confederates at a distance of perhaps two hundred yards. "He stood there with a long frock coat and plug hat on, making a very conspicuous figure," one officer recalled. Only when a man standing nearby took a bullet in the leg did Lincoln remove himself from the line of fire.

On April 9, 1865, General Robert E. Lee, CSA, surrendered to General Ulysses S. Grant at Appomattox; the Civil War was effectively over. Four days later, Lincoln sought the quiet of the Soldiers' Home for the last time, riding the grounds on April 13, 1865. A Treasury Department aide who conversed with him noted that the president appeared tired and in a melancholy mood. The following day, John Wilkes Booth placed a derringer to the back of Lincoln's

Above: The so-called cottage was anything but small, with habitable spaces on all four levels. The Lincolns, together with a handful of servants, left much of the house unused.

Opposite: In this engraving, printed several years after Lincoln's death, he is surrounded by his family, including his wife, Mary Todd Lincoln; Robert Todd Lincoln, then in military service; and preadolescent Thomas "Tad" Lincoln. Another son, William Wallace Lincoln, who died during Lincoln's presidency, is memorialized in the portrait on the wall.
Augustus Robin, Engraver

head in his box at Ford's Theatre and fired. Shortly after seven o'clock the following morning, Abraham Lincoln died.

LOOKING FOR LINCOLN

The post-Lincoln histories of these two properties have been very different. Though he did not occupy the home after inheriting it, Robert Todd Lincoln maintained ownership of the Lincoln house in Springfield for nearly a quarter century after his father's death. A series of renters resided there, and for a time it became a rooming

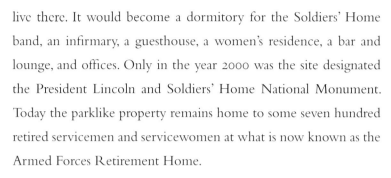

house. In 1883, an early collector of Lincolniana opened the house to the curious, charging two bits a head to view Lincoln-related items. A campaign was launched to persuade the state of Illinois to acquire the property and, in 1887, Robert Todd Lincoln freely conveyed ownership of the "homestead of the Late Abraham Lincoln." All that he asked in return was that Illinois maintain the property "in good repair and [provide] free access to the public." A 1971 Act of Congress established the Lincoln Home National Historic Site, to be administered thereafter by the National Park Service.

Today the house at Eighth and Jackson, restored to its circa 1860 appearance, is the centerpiece of a larger restoration project, which includes a dozen other structures in the immediate neighborhood. A further sense of Lincoln's Springfield in the downtown area is to be gained from visits to the Old State Capitol and Lincoln's law office, which have also been restored to their mid-nineteenth-century appearance.

In contrast, President Lincoln's Cottage at the Soldiers' Home would welcome a varied mix of residents in the years after the Civil War. Presidents Rutherford B. Hayes and Chester A. Arthur would

live there. It would become a dormitory for the Soldiers' Home band, an infirmary, a guesthouse, a women's residence, a bar and lounge, and offices. Only in the year 2000 was the site designated the President Lincoln and Soldiers' Home National Monument. Today the parklike property remains home to some seven hundred retired servicemen and servicewomen at what is now known as the Armed Forces Retirement Home.

The National Trust for Historic Preservation returned the Lincoln Cottage to its Lincoln-era appearance in a seven-year, $15-million restoration. Unlike the fully furnished Lincoln Home in Springfield, which contains some fifty Lincoln artifacts and many period pieces, the Lincoln Cottage has few furnishings, in part because the caretakers lack both original Lincoln objects and firm evidence of the house's early appearance. The focus instead is on Lincoln's ideas, in particular the Emancipation Proclamation. Visitors listen to "historical voices" (period readings of Lincoln's and others' words) and view video screens with images that portray the rituals of the household, its residents, and events and issues of the Lincoln era. The Home and the Cottage offer an intriguing counterpoint: the two quite distinct museum experiences convey a sense of the man and his connection to these private places at separate moments in his eventful life.

Left: The pine bead-board walls in the room Lincoln used as his library had twenty-three coats of paint, which the restorers laboriously removed. Note also the lozenge (diamond-shaped) windows, a detail characteristic of Gothic Revival homes.

Opposite: Abraham Lincoln and his youngest son, Tad (born 1853), often played checkers. The boy was a great favorite among the infantry guards, who dubbed him a "3rd Lieutenant."

ULYSSES S. GRANT COTTAGE

ULYSSES S. GRANT
(1869 – 1877)

WILTON, NEW YORK

"And so he wrote on and on.
General Grant, the savior of our Union,
General Grant, commander-in-chief of
1,000,000 men, General Grant,
eight years President of the United States,
was writing, writing of his own grand deeds,
recording them that he might leave
a home and independence to his family."

JULIA DENT GRANT, *MEMOIRS*, CIRCA 1889

INTIMATIONS OF MORTALITY

The most popular man in America moved to the mountaintop. "There is little heat there," explained physician John H. Douglas. "It is free from vapors, and above all, it is among the pines, and the pure air is especially grateful to patients suffering as General Grant is suffering." The man credited with saving the Union now had a place to rest and recover himself.

The preceding year had been hellish, all the more so because their lives—his and wife Julia's—had seemed so happily settled. Their new brownstone just off New York's fashionable Fifth Avenue on Sixty-sixth Street delighted Julia, while "Ulys," as she called him, was exhilarated by the world of Wall Street and the company of men such as Jay Gould and J. Pierpont Morgan. He had joined the investment firm his son Ulysses Jr. (known as "Buck") had founded with Ferdinand Ward. Ward's preternatural gift for making money on Wall Street had made the elder Grant's daily visits to the Grant and Ward office at 2 Wall Street a pleasure. Dividends poured in at such a rate that the old general remarked to his wife, "Julia, you need not trouble to save for our children. Ward is making us all rich."

Then, on Tuesday, May 6, 1884, the firm of Grant and Ward went bankrupt, crushing the financial fortunes of both generations of Grants. It became apparent that investors had been paid with other people's money; unbeknownst to Grant and his son, Ferdinand Ward and another partner had maintained a second set of books that, upon examination, revealed assets of just $60,000 against the stated public capitalization of $15,000,000. In a last-ditch effort to save the bank, Grant himself had personally borrowed $150,000 from William H. Vanderbilt, to whom, as a matter of honor following the bankruptcy, Grant signed over the title to his house, furniture, and military memorabilia. On the day of the debacle, Grant was left with $80 in his pocket.

That summer, another blow struck with terrible finality when General Grant experienced an intense pain in his throat. Eminent physicians, microscopists, and other medical men were consulted.

Previous page: The expansive porch wraps around three sides of the two-story cottage. Grant found the breezy quiet of the site a welcome antithesis to the steamy city and the clamor of its multitudes.

Left: President Grant, photographed by Mathew Brady in his studio. *Library of Congress / Prints and Photographs*

Opposite: Grant's last weeks were spent surrounded by family, including his wife, sons, and grandchildren. They enjoyed the mountaintop house, equipped as it was with a comfortable porch and this parlor.

Located eleven miles north of the well-known spa at Saratoga Springs, New York, the cottage at Mount McGregor, protected by tall pines, was just what the doctor ordered for Ulysses S. Grant.

Grant's omnipresent cigar disappeared, but over the winter of 1884–1885, the diagnosis of his malady went from "a complaint with a cancerous tendency" to an "epithelial cancer of the malignant type that was sure to end fatally." General Grant, despite the presence of generous friends and the affection of his family, was penniless *and* dying.

Yet the ever-resourceful general conceived a way of restoring the family fortune. He determined to put pen to paper, initially to write a series of articles about his war experiences for *Century* magazine. But by June 16, 1885, on his arrival at Mount McGregor, he was nearing completion of a more comprehensive work. He most fervently hoped that the publication of his two-volume *Personal Memoirs of U. S. Grant* would save his family from penury.

THE LITTLE GENERAL

Grant was a man many underestimated. When he enrolled at West Point at age seventeen, the five-foot-one Grant displaced all of 117 pounds. He would grow in every sense of the word in the years to come—President Grant measured almost five foot eight—but he would never become a man who could win advancement by virtue of his physical appearance.

A Westerner born Hiram Ulysses Grant, he fortuitously became U. S. Grant due to an error in his nomination papers to West Point. After graduating from the military academy in 1843, Second

Lieutenant Grant was jeered at in Cincinnati when attired in his dress uniform; thereafter he cultivated an apparently careless manner of dress. Even at the climactic moment of his life, one he surely understood would stand forth from the pages of the history books (the surrender on April 9, 1865, at Appomattox), when the grandee Lee arrived in a pristine uniform, Grant met him, according to an aide, "covered with mud and in an old faded uniform looking like a fly on the shoulder of beef."

As a young officer, he had fought in the Mexican-American War, rising to the rank of captain. In the peace that followed, he performed quartermaster duties stationed in the Pacific Northwest. Far from his wife and young son, he found solace in the whiskey bottle and, confronted with accusations of drunkenness, resigned from the Army in 1854. His reputation for drinking, probably exaggerated, would shadow him the rest of his life.

He tried his hand at farming, which proved to be the low point of his young life (these years are well remembered at the Ulysses S. Grant National Historic Site in Missouri; see *Visitor Information,* page 241). After his return to the military in June 1861 as colonel of the Twenty-first Illinois Regiment of Volunteers, his rapid success in battle led to a rise through the ranks. He was by nature a problem solver—his experience as a quartermaster demanded it—and his unpretentious, no-nonsense character won him the respect and affection of his fighting men. His understated leadership style led the rank and file to make remarks such as "Ulysses don't scare worth a damn" and "He look as if he meant it." But it was results on the battlefield, including victories at Shiloh (1862) and Vicksburg (1863), that led President Abraham Lincoln to give Grant command of all Union forces. Grant's Western origins and an independence surprising in a military man all contributed to the working bond between Grant and Commander in Chief Lincoln. For both men, their task was a dual one: to save the Union, which also meant "that slavery must be destroyed" in order to erase, as Grant himself put it, the "stain to the Union."

A series of battles—at the Wilderness, Petersburg, and Richmond—would bring the war to a close but at a terrible price.

Above: "During his last days, the General worked almost continually on his book," reported the stenographer hired to help him. The temporary office set up in a rear room at the cottage served as a desk and editing center. Here, surrounded by papers and reference documents, Grant's son Fred was charged with confirming facts, since his father brought the same determination, candor, and good sense to the pages of his *Memoirs* that he had to his soldiering.

Right: Grant's publisher and benefactor, Samuel Clemens.
Library of Congress / Prints and Photographs

"Unconditional Surrender Grant," as he was called by some, prosecuted the war despite horrendous casualties; at Shiloh alone, the 23,000 men killed, wounded, or missing outnumbered all the losses in all the American wars to that date. That was a diminutive down payment on the slaughter that followed (more than 600,000 would die during the four-year war). With victory, however, came the appreciation of a nation. The town of Galena, Illinois, where he had resided before the war, presented Grant with an impressive brick home (see *Visitor Information,* page 241).

When his turn to run for president came in 1868, Grant did not campaign. Instead, he and Julia traveled to New York, St. Louis, Chicago, and points west, where he refused all invitations to speak. The following March, at age forty-six, he became the youngest

SAMUEL L. CLEMENS, PUBLISHER

Mark Twain distrusted publishers—so he decided to become one himself. Together with his business manager, he founded Charles L. Webster and Company, and the first book bearing the Webster imprint was one of the greatest American novels of all time, *Adventures of Huckleberry Finn* (1885).

A friend of Ulysses Grant, Clemens was outraged when he heard the terms the Century Company had offered for the right to publish Grant's *Personal Memoirs.* When Clemens offered to double the royalty or to pay 70 percent of the net profits, Webster and Company acquired a second title for its list.

Clemens personally oversaw the marketing of the book and the editing of the proofs. He offered the inexperienced author encouragement, comparing Grant's writing to *Caesar's Commentaries* for its "simplicity, manifest truthfulness, fairness and justice toward friend and foe alike, . . . and soldierly avoidance of flowery speech." He understood that his investment depended upon the ailing general's ability to complete the book, and when summoned by Grant at the end of June 1885, Clemens went immediately to Mount McGregor. He and one of Grant's sons worked all night on June 28–29 to incorporate Grant's edits. Clemens described the fledgling author—and dying man—to a friend: "The old soldier battling with a deadly disease yet bravely completing his task, was a figure at once . . . pathetic and . . . noble."

The first volume of Grant's *Personal Memoirs* appeared five months after Grant's death. Two months later, on February 27, 1886, Clemens presented the Widow Grant with a check for the astonishing sum of $200,000. At the time, it was the largest royalty payment ever made by a U.S. publisher.

president yet inaugurated. In his inauguration speech, which he wrote himself, he reminded his listeners that he was accepting an office he had not sought.

He was reelected in 1872 by a generous margin, not only with a mandate from the North but also having carried several former Confederate states. During his administration, he worked to reintegrate the South while also maintaining the freedom of former slaves. For the era, he took a surprisingly enlightened view of the Indian, although his attempts to treat Native Americans with fairness came to a sudden halt after an ill-informed, fair-haired general named Custer marched into legend at Little Bighorn, thereby empowering others in Washington bent on extermination. Grant's years in the White House were also marred by his stubborn refusal to abandon ill-chosen friends, some of whom contributed to the scandals that unfolded, particularly during his second term.

But in his last weeks, U. S. Grant sought to explain his life, in particular his role in the war between the states. That he was perhaps the most gifted writer ever to become president made it possible—if only he could live long enough to complete the job.

GENERAL GRANT'S COTTAGE

With unseemly candor, W. J. Arkell, co-owner of the Mount McGregor property, with its adjacent Balmoral Hotel, later explained his ulterior motive for welcoming the ailing former president. "I thought if we could get [the general] to come here to Mt. McGregor, and if he should die there, it might make the place a national shrine—and incidentally a success." Whatever the auspices, an exhausted Grant found the two-story home comfortable.

Grant's unaffected manner remained unchanged, despite his enervated state. He was unable to walk more than a few steps unas-

sisted. A solution of water and cocaine offered some relief from the pain. He was wasting away, living on a diet of tea and soft fruit—his family dined at the Balmoral—but he was determined to finish the book he had begun. Limited to a pained whisper, the general resorted to "pencil talk," using scribbled notes to communicate with his family and with Harrison Tyrell, his devoted African American valet.

In a sense, the world was watching: in March, a *New York Times* headline had proclaimed, "Sinking into the Grave . . . Dying Slowly from Cancer." A full company of reporters had followed him to Mount McGregor; at the Balmoral, telegraph lines had been installed to deliver the latest word on Grant's condition.

Grant wrote a preface, dated July 1. He regularly coughed up blood from hemorrhages in his throat. Periodically his doctor administered morphine or injections of brandy. On July 4, he spent the day rewriting the closing of his book; for another week he revised his pages about the end of the Civil War. Then, on July 19, he put down his pencil. The book was done. On July 23, at 8:08 a.m., the general faded away.

He left a superior book, and not only because Grant insisted it be meticulously correct, all facts checked. Though Grant had not distinguished himself at West Point, finishing twenty-first in a class of thirty-nine, he was a natural writer. Even during wartime, according to one of his Civil War aides, "He wrote nearly all his documents with his own hand. . . . His thoughts flowed as freely from his mind as the ink from his pen." In writing his *Personal Memoirs,* he produced a 275,000-word book in a year, its prose style efficient, at times elegant. It isn't a work on his life; it is a book devoted almost entirely to his war. Yet the character of the man came through.

An immense audience would buy and read this book: it sold 318,000 copies and generated $450,000 for his heirs. But equally gratifying, perhaps, to the deceased Grant would have been his emergence as a unifying figure—in the long funeral procession that marched to his burial site in New York's Riverside Park, former CSA officers and men marched proudly alongside those of the Grand Army of the Republic.

Above: A few evenings after completing his book, Grant expressed his wish to lie down; as they helped him into a bed in the parlor pictured here, his family knew it was the end.

Right: The risk of choking had forced Grant to sleep upright in a chair for months; here, in the study at what is now called the Grant Cottage, he slept in an upholstered armchair, his feet elevated on a facing chair.

Opposite: The dying man, pen in hand, editing his memoir on the porch at the cottage at Mount McGregor, less than a month before his death.
Library of Congress / Prints and Photographs

BENJAMIN HARRISON PRESIDENTIAL SITE

BENJAMIN HARRISON
(1889 – 1893)

INDIANAPOLIS, INDIANA

"A home is life's essential to me

and it must be the old home."

BENJAMIN HARRISON TO HIS SON
RUSSELL HARRISON, DECEMBER 3, 1895

◇◇◇◇◇◇◇◇◇◇◇

THE WIDOWER'S RETURN

Even as president, Benjamin Harrison (1833–1901) was very much a family man. His White House was home to four generations, ranging from his father-in-law, age ninety, to a newborn granddaughter. The president himself was known to don a full Santa costume to greet his three grandchildren beneath the tree (it was the first decorated Christmas tree ever in the White House). The role was one to which he brought both a full beard and a jolly rotundity.

Yet on March 4, 1893, as he bade his cabinet farewell at trackside in Washington, he knew well that his return to his Indianapolis home would be a mournful one. The sixteen-room mansion on North Delaware Street had been built for him and his wife, Caroline Scott Harrison. Constructed in 1875, the house had been a collaboration, and together he and Carrie had chosen the Eastlake-style

furniture. Among the reminders of her contributions were the many pieces of fine porcelain she had decorated with her floral renderings.

But she herself would not be there to welcome him home.

The previous autumn, Caroline Harrison had succumbed in their White House bedroom after months of battling pulmonary tuberculosis. Then too Harrison had returned to Indianapolis to stand at graveside as the remains of his wife of four decades were interred. A week later, the nation had turned the incumbent Harrison out of office—Grover Cleveland, whom he had beaten four years before, was reelected—but that seemed a minor sadness to the man his wife had called the "General." As he told a political confidant in the hours after his defeat, "For me there is no sting in it. Indeed after the heavy blow the death of my wife dealt me, I do not think I could have stood the strain a re-election would have brought."

He would resume his life in Indianapolis, where, at age twenty, he and Carrie had arrived from their native Ohio in 1854. His law

practice had flourished, and he soon launched a political career with a successful run for Indianapolis city attorney in 1857. Three years later, he won the office of Supreme Court reporter, running on the antislavery platform and campaigning for Republican presidential candidate Abraham Lincoln. With the coming of the Civil War, he helped organize the Seventieth Indiana Regiment, then rose rapidly in its officer corps, first as Lieutenant Harrison, then as colonel. In 1864, after commanding a brigade in General William Tecumseh Sherman's march on Atlanta campaign, he was brevetted a brigadier general.

When the war ended, he had resumed his flourishing Indiana law practice. With the added stature of his distinguished war service,

he sought the governorship of his adopted state, pointing out to the voters that his Republican Party mission would be to right some of the growing wrongs of Reconstruction. As he told the state convention in 1872, he wished to see to it that "the cabin of the negro, which always afforded a refuge for our soldiers, . . . shall be rendered secure against the assaults of the old supporters of slavery." Though his fellow Indianans did not elect him governor, the state legislature sent him to the U.S. Senate in 1881. His one-term presidency followed.

On arrival in Indianapolis in March 1893, the former president was greeted by hundreds of cheering admirers; as he wrote to his son that week, "I made no mistake in coming at once—there are no friends like the old ones." He was accompanied by his daughter Mary Harrison McKee and her children, six-year-old Benjamin and Mary Lodge, age four. As the former president unpacked his books, his daughter chose wallpaper and picked paint colors to brighten up the ten-thousand-square-foot house, which had been rented to a tenant for the previous four years. But the McKees would depart in the months that followed, leaving Harrison with his memories.

A POLITICAL HERITAGE

Benjamin Harrison was the direct descendant of a Patriot. His great-grandfather Colonel Benjamin Harrison had signed the Declaration of Independence, but despite a family tree with deep Virginia roots, some Harrison men looked west, and the Signer's son, William Henry Harrison, had struck out for the frontier.

William Henry had served in the Northwest Indian War in 1792–1794, which opened much of what is today's Ohio for settlement by Europeans. Subsequently he became governor of the Indiana Territory, which encompassed the future states of Indiana, Illinois, Michigan, Wisconsin, and eastern Minnesota. As commander of the Army of the Northwest, General Harrison masterminded a major victory during the War of 1812. That had been the Battle of the Thames, at which the feared Indian chief Tecumseh was killed (the British termed him the "Wellington of the Indians"). When William Henry was elected president in 1840, Benjamin Harrison, age seven, watched his grandfather leave for Washington. His own father having been a congressman, the adult Benjamin Harrison could lay claim to a family history of national leadership.

Nicknamed "Little Ben" by some of his admiring soldiers in the Civil War, the five-foot, six-inch Harrison nearly always had a cigar in his hand, but it was his rhetorical abilities that won him many votes. The twenty-third president was self-confident, a litigator of great gifts, and he brought to his campaigning and his presidency talents for both insightful analysis and artful persuasion.

Though some historians have tended to dismiss his accomplishments as president, his four years in office saw significant changes.

"BABY McKEE"

The press corps loved it: a president who routinely dined next to a two-year-old in a high chair. Benjamin Harrison McKee had the run of the White House and rode about its lawn in a cart pulled by a pet billy goat named "His Whiskers." The grandfather doted—"a jolly boy," observed the president, "not a bit spoiled." As the longtime White House doorman put it, the president's namesake became "one of the principal personages of the White House."

For a man whom some of his staff called "the human iceberg," Harrison clearly melted in the presence of the boy the nation knew as "Baby McKee." When his second marriage led to the estrangement of his daughter Mary McKee, the former president lost the familiar presence—if not the affections—of his grandson. As the grandfather wrote on March 2, 1895, "Grandpa came home from Richmond yesterday afternoon, and there was no little boy to meet him in the hall—but there was your bicycle—the first thing I saw to remind me of you. But the bicycle . . . could not talk and I didn't want to."

Opposite: Harrison and grandson Benjamin Harrison McKee, pictured in the White House.
Benjamin Harrison Presidential Site

Above: The arch in the front hall offers a view of the central winding stair and the service areas to the rear.

Unlike his grandfather William Henry Harrison, during whose brief tenure no new states were admitted to the Union, Benjamin Harrison welcomed North and South Dakota, Washington, and Montana in 1889, followed by Idaho and Wyoming in 1890. In his final weeks in office, he tried to annex Hawaii; although a divided Senate failed to act before he left office (Hawaii would not become American soil until 1898), Harrison helped establish a new climate for an expansionist foreign policy.

Harrison was an early conservationist. At a time when there was just one national park (Yellowstone, established in 1872), he designated Rock Creek Park (Washington, D.C.), Sitka National Historical Park (Alaska), Casa Grande Ruin Reservation (Arizona), Sequoia and Yosemite (California), and Pikes Peak (Colorado); in all, Harrison set aside some thirteen million acres as national forest preserve. His single term also saw significant legislation signed into law, including the Pension Appropriation Bill, which he had championed to guarantee care would be provided for the "men who saved the country." At a time when trusts such as Standard Oil were being accused of monopolistic practices, Harrison signed the Sherman Antitrust Act; if the legislation proved inadequate to the task, it was still the first federal law that sought to guarantee, as Harrison put it in his inaugural address, that "great corporations . . . more scrupulously observe their legal obligations and duties." Harrison also appointed Frederick Douglass, the nation's most prominent African American leader, to be minister to Haiti. In the last full year of his administration, Ellis Island became the nation's gateway for European immigrants: more than twenty million people would pass through in the course of the next several decades.

A TALE OF TWO WIVES

The first letter Benjamin Harrison wrote upon his return to Delaware Street was addressed to his late wife's niece, Mary Lord Dimmick. A widow, Mary Dimmick had been an intimate member of the White House household and had helped nurse her aunt in her last weeks. Though she called Harrison "Uncle Ben," the two

In a bedroom interpreted as that of Harrison's late-in-life child, an original portrait of Elizabeth hangs over a tall Renaissance Revival–style Harrison bed. She would earn a law degree and entry into both the New York and Indiana bars by age twenty-two.

had long found each other's company bracing, playing billiards and enjoying many energetic walks together.

Having been a valued companion to both Benjamin and Carrie in Washington, Mary was soon invited to Indianapolis. A discreet interval would pass during which they lived independent lives, but after her summons to the former president's bedside in the winter of 1895 (he was recovering from a dangerous bout with the grippe, the ailment soon renamed influenza), it became apparent that she and Benjamin would marry.

Like other families, presidential ones can be subject to conflict when it comes to widowed parents remarrying, and the former president's two grown children, Russell and Mary McKee, both regarded Mary Dimmick as an interloper. In the weeks before his remarriage in April 1896, both arrived in Indianapolis to remove their possessions from Harrison's Delaware Street home. To the father's great sadness, no members of either of his children's families

When Harrison returned to Indianapolis after his presidency, he converted his gentleman's library upstairs to his office. The bookcase was a gift from a German-born cabinetmaker grateful for Harrison's legal services; the large desk at the center of the room returned with the former president from the White House; and the longhorn chair was a gift to President Harrison from a Texas rancher.

were in attendance at his wedding to Mary Dimmick, a woman twenty-five years his junior.

In his retirement years, Harrison resisted the several entreaties made to him to reenter politics. He gave a series of lectures at Stanford University but subsequently refused the offer of both a professor's chair at the University of Chicago and the presidency of a bank. He tried a case before the Supreme Court and wrote many essays about the presidency and federal government, some of which appeared in the *Ladies' Home Journal* and most of which were later collected in a book, *This Country of Ours.*

Perhaps the happiest event of his retirement occurred on February 21, 1897, when a child was born to Benjamin and Mary Harrison; the baby was named Elizabeth after Benjamin's mother. Her birth led Harrison to refuse many offers to play the public role

of elder statesman, though the twenty-third president would travel to Europe in 1899 with his second family to pursue a matter of international law. The aging former president made a memorable sight aboard the SS *St. Paul,* striding the deck in the company of his two-year-old daughter, who was dressed in a red coat and hood. Just two years later he would die, age sixty-seven, at his Indianapolis home, on March 13, 1901, and be buried four days later beside his first wife, Carrie.

Mary Dimmick Harrison and her young daughter remained in the home until 1913. At Mary's death at age eighty-nine, her remains were returned to Indianapolis and buried with her husband and Aunt Carrie at Crown Hill Cemetery.

SAGAMORE HILL

THEODORE ROOSEVELT
(1901 – 1909)

OYSTER BAY, NEW YORK

"The house is comfortable, filled with reminders of the stirring life its owner has led in camp and on the hunting-trail.... But it is homelike rather than imposing. It is the people themselves who put the stamp upon it,—the life they live there together."

JACOB RIIS, *THEODORE ROOSEVELT, THE CITIZEN* (1904)

✕✕✕✕✕✕✕✕✕✕

THE SUMMER WHITE HOUSE

T he man of the house wore a flannel shirt and rough trousers. A handkerchief was tied around his neck and a wide-brimmed straw hat shaded his eyes. Dressed much like the other farmworkers, he joined them as they wielded their pitchforks, racing to get the newly mown hay to the barn before the graying sky released its rain.

For the twenty-sixth president, it was all in a day's work.

While some chief executives are best encountered in Washington's corridors of power, Theodore Roosevelt (1858–1919) was never more himself than when at home at Sagamore Hill. In the summer of 1906, the president was youthful and energetic (five years earlier, at just forty-two, he had become the youngest president ever to assume the office when his predecessor, William McKinley,

succumbed to gangrene, the result of an assassin's bullets). During the summer doldrums of his presidency, Roosevelt regularly sought to escape the torpor of Washington, journeying to his home on Long Island Sound in June, usually remaining until mid-September.

Whether swinging a scythe, chopping wood, or building fences, Roosevelt found the active life suited him. Told after his graduation from Harvard in 1880 that he should restrict his activities due to a weak heart, he had assiduously built himself up; even during his presidency, he prided himself on his skills as a pugilist (though one sparring partner delivered a blow that left him blind in one eye). Roosevelt had his solitary pleasures too, and as a devoted birdwatcher he liked nothing more than to take guests on a whispered bird-spotting tour around the property he knew so well.

The New Yorker Roosevelt brought to office a manner that was typified by intellectual rigor as well as physical vigor. He read a book a day and had written several himself, including a well-regarded naval history of the War of 1812, published when he was just twenty-three. Possessed of a photographic memory, he could draw upon a deep well of knowledge. As his son Theodore remembered after his death, "It made little difference into what channels the conversation turned. Sooner or later Father was able to produce

---

Previous page: Roosevelt built his home atop a spit of land on the north shore of Long Island; a passionate outdoorsman, he led his family on many activities on and around the Sagamore Hill property grounds — hiking, canoeing, and working.

Left: Theodore Roosevelt a year after taking office as president.
Library of Congress / Prints and Photographs

Opposite: The Sagamore house has broad verandas, just as Roosevelt ordered.

information which often startled students of the theme under discussion. . . . It was never safe to contradict him on any statement, no matter how recent you might feel your information was." The elder Roosevelt rarely stopped talking or moving; his physical presence was hyperkinetic. He seemed to be interested in everything, issuing the expletive "Bully!" when something pleased him. Peering through his pince-nez spectacles in a manner both aristocratic and hearty, the man with broad shoulders and a booming voice was a presence to be reckoned with.

Roosevelt had made an uneasy peace with the press, and during the summer of 1906 he permitted Sherman M. Craiger of *Town & Country* to observe the family rituals. Craiger reported that the vacationing Roosevelt hosted no formal entertainments that summer, though the president did deliver the oration at the local Independence Day celebration in Oyster Bay. The business of the country went on too, as Roosevelt's secretary and staff occupied three rooms over the village store, Morris Grocery, where he visited daily. But he spent as much time as possible with his family.

One day, Craiger reported, the entire family loaded their gear into a pair of boats and set off for a distant shore, their destination Eaton's Neck. As he often did, the president pulled the oars in one boat, accompanied by his wife, Edith, and their two younger sons, Archibald, twelve, and the baby of the family, Quentin, eight. Eldest son Theodore Jr., age eighteen, occupied the other boat along with his sister Ethel and some Roosevelt cousins. Several hours of rowing were required to cover the twelve-mile distance, and further activity ensued on arrival, with swimming, fishing, and the eventual reward of broiled chicken, hard-boiled eggs, and sandwiches from picnic hampers.

The outing ended with a return trip to Sagamore Hill, the long row home lit by the light of an August moon.

THE HOUSE ON THE HILL

Theodore Roosevelt's house today overlooks fields and forest, where breezes waft in from Long Island Sound, cooling the generous piazza in summer. For Roosevelt—naturalist, hunter, and parent nonpareil—this meeting of the land and water was the perfect setting. Yet even as the plans had been drawn for the house, events almost conspired to prevent its construction.

Mr. and Mrs. Theodore Roosevelt were expecting their first child in the New Year when, in late 1883, Roosevelt, then a member of the New York State Legislature, commissioned two young New York architects, Hugh Lamb and Charles Alonzo Rich, to design a home, along with stables and entrance lodge, for the 155-acre property he had purchased adjacent to other Roosevelt estates. He anticipated a large family, and plans were prepared for a twenty-three-room home, but before he could approve them, Roosevelt was struck a terrible blow. Just two days after delivering a daughter, his wife died unexpectedly of kidney failure; as if one shocking loss

was not enough, Roosevelt was already reeling from the death of his mother, just hours earlier that very day, of typhoid fever. The grieving Roosevelt penned a large X atop the page in his diary for Thursday, February 14, 1884, adding only, "The light has gone out of my life." At twenty-six, he was the father of a newborn child, Alice Lee Roosevelt, and about to bury the two most important women in his life.

Recognizing that Alice would need a place to grow up, Roosevelt decided to proceed with construction and, the following month, approved the drawings for the home and an estimated construction cost of $16,975. The architects had followed his wishes, designing "a library with a shallow bay window looking south, the parlor . . . occupying all the west end of the lower floor [and] big fireplaces." But the grieving client chose not to stay and supervise the build, instead departing to work his ranch in North Dakota, riding his horse, carrying his rifle, herding cattle, hunting, and learning the ways of the West on the banks of the Little Missouri, where he would remain off and on during the nearly two years it took to complete the house. He left his infant daughter in the care of his older sister, Anna. Known as "Bamie," she appeared to be on her way to

spinsterhood, suffering as she did from Pott's disease, a tubercular arthritis that had left her stooped and in nearly constant pain.

The house was to have been called Leeholm, in honor of his wife, Alice Hathaway Lee, but later Roosevelt renamed the estate after a Native American chief, Sagamore Mohannis, whose tribe, Roosevelt believed, had signed away its right to the land in the seventeenth century. Roosevelt remarried, taking a childhood friend, Edith Kermit Carow, as his wife in London in December 1886, and his first wife was never to be spoken of in the household. In his autobiography, written three decades after her death, she went unmentioned.

The first story of the house was of brick, built atop two-foot-thick foundations; on the second and third floors, the cladding consisted of patterned shingles, in keeping with the local Long Island vernacular, with some surfaces resembling fish scales, others shingled in a diamond pattern. Though built as a summerhouse—the Roosevelts maintained homes at different times in Manhattan, Albany, and Washington—the well-built house was never solely a summer place, with its eight fireplaces and two up-to-date hot-air furnaces in the basement. Over time, the structure would remain largely unchanged, with only the addition of a formal reception room to the home's north side during Roosevelt's presidency. After he declined to run for another term in 1908, the family assumed year-round residence at Sagamore Hill.

As Roosevelt had hoped, his family grew rapidly after he remarried, and in the ensuing decade, Edith delivered four sons and a daughter. During that span Roosevelt's public prominence expanded too. He became President Benjamin Harrison's civil service commissioner after the 1888 election; despite Harrison's defeat in 1892, the incoming president, Grover Cleveland, chose to keep the popular Roosevelt in his post, where he had sought to substitute competence for patronage in appointing federal officials. Roosevelt went on to serve as president of New York City's police board but lobbied hard to be appointed assistant secretary of the Navy when McKinley was elected chief executive in 1896. In that post, he helped position the Navy for the war that broke out two years later in the Philippines and Cuba.

He resigned shortly after war was declared on Spain to volunteer as a lieutenant colonel in the First U.S. Volunteer Cavalry. In June and July of 1898, he and his troops, known as the "Rough Riders," engaged Spanish forces in Cuba as the Americans prevailed at the decisive Battle of San Juan. Back on the mainland, newspaper accounts of their bravery under fire as they charged up a ridge overlooking Santiago de Cuba added to Roosevelt's visibility and popularity. Later that year he was elected governor of New York.

In 1900 he joined incumbent McKinley on the Republican presidential ticket, and Roosevelt proved himself a very effective campaigner on the national stage. While McKinley ran a front-porch campaign, rarely leaving his home in Canton, Ohio, Roosevelt traveled some 21,000 miles; a gifted orator, he gave almost 700 speeches. The McKinley-Roosevelt ticket handily defeated Democrat William Jennings Bryan, with 292 electoral votes to Bryan's 155. Barely six months after Roosevelt was sworn in as vice president, bullets from anarchist Leon Czolgosz's gun raised him to the nation's highest office.

THE CONSERVATION PRESIDENT

When he took office in September 1901, Roosevelt chose to keep McKinley's cabinet intact. But in almost every other way, he made the presidency his own. He became, in Thomas Edison's words, "the most striking figure in American life," bringing his usual passionate engagement to the presidency.

During his seven and a half years in office, he took up the cause of the Panama Canal and saw that it was constructed. In the arena of foreign affairs, he promulgated the "Roosevelt Corollary" to the Monroe Doctrine, stating the right of the United States to use its "international policy power" to intervene in the affairs of smaller countries in the Americas in the interests of economic stability (more bluntly, he saw the role of the United States in terms of a West African proverb: "Speak softly and carry a big stick"). He was awarded the Nobel Peace Prize for his role in the negotiation of the Russo-Japanese peace treaty in 1906. When it came to domestic matters, he prided himself on his concern for middle-class Americans, promising a "square deal." In attempting to limit the sway of large corporations, he earned a reputation as a trustbuster. He helped advance consumer protections, signing into law the Meat Inspection Act and the Pure Food and Drug Act.

Yet perhaps his most enduring contribution was as a conservationist. When he took office, some 80 percent of the nation's woodlands remained, and extraction industries—oil and mining—were virtually unregulated. Roosevelt relied upon a chief counselor, Gifford Pinchot, whom he named chief forester of the U.S. Forest Service, and in keeping with Roosevelt's love for natural places, his administration declared 150 national forests forever wild and established 51 federal bird reservations, along with 5 national parks and 18 national monuments. In total, approximately 230 million acres—an assemblage of land greater than the areas of the original thirteen states—were permanently preserved.

Roosevelt left office in 1909, having chosen not to seek another term, despite wide popularity. But more than a century has since passed and, though scholars consistently rank him among the top

Above: A contrast to the more masculine spaces in the house, Edith's genteel drawing room (called the parlor until renovated in 1901) was the place in which Christmas presents were opened at Sagamore Hill.
Sagamore Hill National Historic Site / National Park Service

Right: Although Theodore had a larger-than-life presence, it was Edith who ran the house from her desk in the drawing room.
Sagamore Hill National Historic Site / National Park Service

MOUNT RUSHMORE

The standing of Theodore Roosevelt in the early twentieth century is suggested by the sixty-foot-tall likeness of his face that looks down from Mount Rushmore. He is in very good company indeed, shoulder-to-shoulder with George Washington, Thomas Jefferson, and Abraham Lincoln.

A South Dakota historian named Doane Robinson actually conceived the idea for the giant work in 1923, but sculptor Gutzon Borglum decided upon whom to represent. Located in the Black Hills region, the Mount Rushmore National Memorial was carved between 1929 and 1941, before insufficient funding brought the work to a halt (Borglum's original conception had been to portray the four presidents from head to waist).

Although the immense monument commemorates four great presidents, in the view of some Native Americans the faces also personify the unhappy history of the American Indian during the nineteenth century, not least because it was constructed on land that, as late as 1868, had been granted "in perpetuity" to the Lakota Sioux tribe. Yet in honoring Roosevelt, the site seems appropriate, with its rich array of native flora and fauna, as Mount Rushmore itself is home to a great variety of birds, its ecology largely unspoiled.

five presidents of all time, the charismatic Roosevelt seems to have a diminishing hold on the American imagination.

In part that is a consequence of time: no one alive today can know the truth of the description offered by an English visitor to Sagamore Hill in the waning weeks of his presidency. "You feel the activity, the impetuosity, the enormous virility of President Roosevelt," wrote Charles Dawbarn in the *Pall Mall Magazine* in January 1909. "He has the staccato kind of speech by which words are curiously, but not unpleasantly, underlined. As he talks, as he becomes animated in developing some congenial topic, his eyes almost close up behind the pince-nez, and he seems to smile through his teeth." Not so many Americans recognize that look today, and still photographs can only suggest his vitality. Fewer still, perhaps, would recognize the complex man that Dawbarn termed a "scholar and high-principled gentleman, happily combining these traits with a great, wholesome taste for the out-of-doors." As *Arsenic and Old Lace* (in which a character believes himself to be Theodore Roosevelt) has faded from the theatrical repertory, the man who lent his name to the stuffed toy known as the *teddy bear* has grown less distinct in the public memory.

Yet Roosevelt's home in Oyster Bay suggests much about the man and his complex legacy. He was the naturalist president but also an avid hunter who lined the walls of his home with game trophies. He was born to wealth, yet he won admiration from those less well-to-do by delivering on his promises of a "square deal" for all. He was a student of war, and a warrior who won the Nobel Peace Prize.

Sagamore Hill dates from another era; it wasn't a place for a telephone, for example, as Roosevelt hated the device and permitted the installation of one at his waterside home only during his presidential years. He had it removed when he left office. Back at his estate, he became once again *Colonel* Roosevelt (he forbade those around him to call him *President*). He was happy in his place; as he once wrote to Edith from a late-in-life return to electioneering, "I *never* want to leave Sagamore again!" He would die there in his sleep on January 6, 1919, at just sixty years of age.

Above: The Roosevelt children were famously required to ask each dinner guest at least one question; and when there were no guests, the conversation was always a series of teachable moments.
Sagamore Hill National Historic Site / National Park Service

Opposite: Sagamore Hill National Historic Site / National Park Service

Right: Roosevelt distrusted technology—for years, the only telephone he permitted at Sagamore Hill was in the bowels of the house, down in the kitchen. The home was not electrified until 1918.
Sagamore Hill National Historic Site / National Park Service

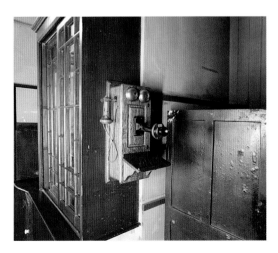

Above: This was a family place in more ways than one. Many members of the household spent time in this library, and in this relaxed room hangs a portrait of Theodore Roosevelt Sr., accompanied by other portraits, including those of the younger Roosevelt's heroes, Ulysses S. Grant and George Washington. The namesake son described his father as "the best man I ever knew."
Sagamore Hill National Historic Site / National Park Service

Right: Up on the third floor, built into the roofline, is the Gun Room. Though used as a study (Theodore Roosevelt wrote his book *The Rough Riders* there in 1898), this was also the place where the guns were stored and the life of a hunter was celebrated with a Kodiak bear rug and a cattle-horn chair.
Sagamore Hill National Historic Site / National Park Service

Above: Just inside the North Room, which was added in 1805, stand two immense tusks, as if to guard the entrance. Beyond them in the paneled entry hall the visitor gets an immediate sense that this is the home of a huntsman, given the many mounted heads of game.
Sagamore Hill National Historic Site / National Park Service

Right: When at Sagamore Hill, President Roosevelt carried out many of the duties of his office at this desk.
Sagamore Hill National Historic Site / National Park Service

WOODROW WILSON
HOUSE

WOODROW WILSON
1913 – 1921

WASHINGTON, D.C.

"The man who is swimming against the stream

knows the strength of it."

WOODROW WILSON

◇◇◇◇◇◇◇◇◇◇

ARMISTICE DAY, 1921

T

he central figure was supposed to be an anonymous casualty of the Great War. The United States planned to inter an unknown soldier on November 11, 1921, just as the French and British had done a year earlier. But the focus shifted when Woodrow Wilson unexpectedly stepped back into the public view.

A coffin on caissons departed the Capitol, pulled by six great black horses, their hooves muffled. The mourners followed, led by President Warren G. Harding, shoulder-to-shoulder with General John J. Pershing, who had commanded the American expeditionary force in Europe. The long, solemn parade included cabinet secretaries, governors, senators, congressmen, justices, military officers, and Medal of Honor winners.

An open carriage came next. Although everyone else was on foot, a special exception had been granted to former president Woodrow Wilson. His fragile health made it impossible for him to walk the length of Pennsylvania Avenue. He sat, bracing himself with his cane, his wife, Edith, at his side. His trusted African American valet, Isaac Scott, rode in front with the driver of the rented victoria.

Thousands of people crowded the sidewalks, watching in respectful silence as the Unknown Soldier rolled past. But whispers were heard moments later when the man in the pince-nez and the unmistakable silk top hat came into view. Over the murmur, first one call of greeting was heard, then another. As the procession continued along the route to the White House, a smattering of applause echoed. By the time the carriage stopped before the national mansion where Wilson had lived for eight years, the voices swelled into cheers for the man whose vision and idealism the nation still held in high esteem.

Near the West Gate to the White House precinct, President Harding looked on. His invitation to Wilson, though written in longhand, had been an afterthought, but now he bowed to the

Previous page: The drawing room, large enough for a Steinway grand piano, was decorated with a fine tapestry that had been a wedding gift to the Wilsons in 1915 from the people of France.

Left: Wilson negotiates the stairs, cane grasped in his right hand, with his man Isaac Scott supporting him on his paralyzed left side.
Woodrow Wilson House / National Trust for Historic Preservation

Opposite: Washington's newest neighborhood, Kalorama, was just beyond the bounds of L'Enfant's city grid. The Wilson House has a deep lot, and the rear of the home overlooked a generous garden.

unlikely man of the moment, the occupant who sat rigid in the halted carriage. With the attention of the crowd entirely upon him, Wilson, his face severe, acknowledged the ovation, raising his tall silk hat with his good hand while the other sat immobile in his lap. With that, the driver directed the carriage out of the cortege, heading home to S Street.

On reaching his quiet residential neighborhood a few minutes later, the former president found that another crowd awaited him. Though Wilson disappeared into his three-story brick residence, people continued to amass outside. According to reports in the *New York World* the following day, some twenty thousand people jammed

the street when, several hours later, the front door opened and Wilson reemerged. A flag hung overhead as he laboriously descended the steps. He greeted three disabled soldiers seated in a car at curbside.

He moved to address the crowd. He was a practiced orator, but the man who had given countless political speeches, pleaded for peace, and led his nation into war could no longer rise to his former rhetorical heights. With tears running down his cheeks, his voice quavering, he said his thanks simply. Then the son and grandson of Presbyterian ministers offered a benediction. "God bless you," he said to the crowd. His wife now at his side, he groped for her hand and, accompanied by Isaac Scott and Edith, returned to the house.

Above: With a doctor never far away, Wilson's medical kit was always at hand.

Opposite: The great portrait that looms over the table is of Edith Bolling Wilson. Though the Wilsons entertained, the former president himself rarely ate here, as his stroke had greatly impaired his ability to eat and he was reluctant to dine in company.

If it was a failed performance by his younger standards, he gave the crowd what they wanted. As one editorial writer had it, the former president—physically crippled and mentally debilitated by a series of strokes, his party voted out of office and the passion of his later life, the League of Nations, rejected—still represented for many people "a living link with their noblest phase."

Woodrow Wilson (1856–1924) had become, observed *Collier's* magazine, "The Man They Cannot Forget."

THE LAST HOUSE

Born Thomas Woodrow Wilson in Staunton, Virginia, the twenty-eighth president led a peripatetic life. As a young man, he resided in Georgia, North Carolina, New Jersey, Baltimore, and Virginia in pursuit of his studies. He practiced law in Georgia before deciding to teach politics, which he did at Bryn Mawr, Wesleyan, and the College of New Jersey (renamed Princeton University in 1896). A professorship gave way to the college presidency at Princeton, and eight years later his victory in the 1910 gubernatorial election meant relocating temporarily to an inn, then to a rented house (New Jersey in that era provided no year-round accommodations for its chief executive). But the governorship itself proved only a brief stopping place on his way to the White House in 1913.

Eight years later, relocation to his last house offered a new permanence. Moving day was occasioned by Harding's inauguration on March 4, 1921. A widower, Wilson had remarried in 1915, and his second wife, Edith, choreographed the move to 2340 S Street with her usual vigilance. Her concern was that "my dear one" be as little discombobulated as possible. The moving men from Smith's and Company were instructed to take careful note of the arrangement of Wilson's bedroom, and upon their arrival at their new home that afternoon, Mr. and Mrs. Wilson found everything in its place. Edith had ordered a bed that matched the Lincoln bedstead in which the president slept at the White House. Her husband's shaving stand occupied a place by the window. The desk in the corner, dating from his Princeton days, was the repository for private papers.

The Wilsons had assembled an eclectic array of objects. Many dated from his long association with Princeton, but there were gifts from foreign dignitaries, and even a Graphoscope movie projector, which had been a source of entertainment in the White House. The grand library space on S Street accommodated much of his eight-thousand-volume library.

The five-year-old house was new to the Wilsons, who had purchased it just three months earlier. They discussed retiring elsewhere, but other cities lost out to Washington because the capital had been Edith's home since her schoolgirl days. The former president also desired easy access to the Library of Congress, as he still dreamed of writing a long-contemplated book on government.

A number of renovations had speedily been made to the handsome brick Georgian Revival house. Men from the Otis Elevator

Company removed the trunk-lift mechanism and installed an electric elevator in the existing shaft. A new door had been cut in a side wall to ease Wilson's access to his Pierce-Arrow limousine. The changes had been essential to accommodate the semi-invalided Wilson.

The house on S Street today remains much as it did in Wilson's time, pristine and packed with Wilson's contents. It is a place where one can consider the fading figure of the man who lived the last three years of his life there.

"THE WAR TO END ALL WARS"

When President Woodrow Wilson ran for reelection in 1916, a campaign slogan—"He kept us out of war"—reminded Americans that, even as war raged in Europe, Wilson had spent much of his first presidential term working to maintain his nation's neutrality. Yet by April 2, 1917, he found German submarine activity unconscionable and asked for a declaration of war. As he told Congress, "The world must be made safe for democracy."

Wilson has been described as the first truly internationalist American president, and after the war was won, he set about trying to live up to his declaration promise. He traveled to Europe and presented his peace terms (known to history students as Wilson's "Fourteen Points"), which included a bold plan for the creation of the League of Nations, a world body empowered to settle future international conflicts.

Newsreels from the time reveal President Wilson, his erect carriage giving him the look of a man taller than his six-foot height, accepting unprecedented acclaim amid large European crowds. The peace document that emerged from the negotiations differed from Wilson's idealistic outline, but the chief executive had become a world presence. He was a guest at Buckingham Palace in 1918, the first American president to be so honored. He returned from an audience with the pope bearing a grand gift of a mosaic, which today is on display at his S Street house. The Norwegian Nobel Committee soon recognized his efforts at the peace negotiations, awarding him the 1919 Nobel Peace Prize.

At home, however, Wilson encountered strong opposition. The treaty he signed in France required the advice and consent of the Senate, with a two-thirds majority vote needed for ratification. Finding the votes weren't there, Wilson took his case directly to the people, giving thirty-two major addresses in twenty-two days in September 1919.

Wilson's health had always been fragile; on his cross-country journey, it rapidly deteriorated. When the presidential train departed Pueblo, Colorado, to race back to Washington, its principal passenger was a desperately ill man. The left side of Wilson's face sagged, his speech had grown indistinct, and saliva escaped the downturned corner of his mouth. In retrospect, it appeared that other episodic illnesses as far back as 1906 had probably been ministrokes, but on October 2, 1919, when he collapsed in his White House bathroom, a massive stroke paralyzed his left side and robbed him of vision in one eye.

At Edith Wilson's order, the seriousness of his medical condition would remain a closely held secret. Wilson's physician, Dr. Cary Grayson, did release regular bulletins; overwork and exhaustion were said to be the cause of the president's failure to appear in public—reportedly he was on the road to recovery. But cabinet meetings ceased, and pardons, proclamations, and even laws went unsigned.

Opposite: The house was fully staffed and the cook was in charge of an efficient, state-of-the-art range.

Left: This portrait of Wilson hangs in his S Street home. It was painted after Wilson's death by the Polish-born artist Stanislav Rembski.
Woodrow Wilson House / National Trust for Historic Preservation

Left: Wilson worked at his desk in the library, but this was also an entertainment space. A movie screen rolled down from the cornice of the bookshelves; using a Graphoscope projector given them by actor Douglas Fairbanks Sr., the Wilsons watched silent movies.

Opposite: Edith's bedroom—complete with her daybed, cheval mirror, and a portrait of her husband—remains much as it was during her time of residence. She would stay in the home until her death, living out a thirty-seven-year widowhood on S Street.

Behind closed doors, Wilson had become more patient than president. His wife and closest advisers protected him from the demands of running the country. As the renowned Philadelphia neurologist F. X. Dercum advised Mrs. Wilson, "Every time you take him a new anxiety or problem . . . , you are turning a knife in an open wound. His nerves are crying out for rest, and any excitement is torture to him."

The first lady discouraged talk of resignation, and Vice President Thomas Riley Marshall, a former governor of Indiana, was reluctant to assume the presidency in the absence of hard information concerning Wilson's condition. As for Wilson himself, he confided in Grayson in the months that followed that he would consider resigning "[if] I become convinced that the country is suffering any ill effects from my sickness." His once flexible and robust mind, however, had so narrowed that Wilson not only did not resign but held out vague hopes for a third term. Only after the Democratic convention selected a ticket headed by Ohio governor James M. Cox, with Franklin D. Roosevelt as his running mate, were Wilson's hopes ended. And in November, the Democrats were trounced by Warren G. Harding and Calvin Coolidge by an electoral college vote of 404 to 127.

The soon-to-be-former president had become, in his wife's pet phrase, "our beloved sufferer." He would never regain his physical and mental vigor. He could not rise from a chair unassisted. After months in bed, he had to relearn how to walk as he dragged his useless left leg; the tapping of his cane would be a constant for the rest of his life. His attention span was brief, the breadth of his once-encompassing mind narrowed. A man characteristically in strict control of himself found his emotions often welled up, and tears spilled.

Though few outside the inner circle understood how gravely ill he was, Wilson's stroke meant his vigorous leadership of the nation was effectively over. Perhaps most painful of all to Wilson, any hope of passage for the League of Nations faded with his incapacity to lead and persuade his countrymen.

"OUR BELOVED SUFFERER"

In keeping with Edith's wishes and those of Dr. Grayson, who would be an almost constant presence in the home, the patterns of life at the S Street house were carefully regimented. At first Wilson had few visitors; he took his meals in his bedroom. After a time, the

regimen was eased and the former president was permitted one visitor a day, and Georges Clemenceau, David Lloyd George, and Franklin Roosevelt came to visit. Edith was never far from hand, a nurse tended Wilson at night, and Isaac Scott was at his beck and call.

Patterns emerged. Each morning after breakfast Wilson would ride the elevator to the ground floor and the room called the "Dugout." John Randolph Bolling, Edith's brother, was quartered there, and Bolling, a hunchback crippled since his youth, functioned as Wilson's secretary, taking dictation and helping Wilson maintain a voluminous correspondence. Wilson exchanged letters with many former servicemen, in particular men incapacitated by war injuries. As Admiral Grayson explained, "Between him and them there was a mutual recognition of comradeship—they had been broken in the same cause."

Another denizen of 2340 S Street was Ray Stannard Baker. A former journalist, Baker had been Wilson's press secretary during the talks that resulted in the Treaty of Versailles. Wilson granted Baker first access to his papers in order to write a book on the peace conference; in time, the first volume would be followed by numerous other books on Wilson. Baker established quarters in a third-floor bedroom, next door to Margaret Wilson, the president's remaining unmarried daughter, who often practiced her singing there.

Wilson's days at S Street were those of a man in decline. He was by no means addled; nor did he live in a state of constant depression. Although he managed to regain some strength in his profoundly damaged left side, in January 1924 his health worsened and his organs began to fail. Wilson knew his end neared and told Dr. Grayson, "The machinery is worn out. I am ready." Wilson died in his S Street home on February 3, 1924.

Today the house offers glimpses of Wilson's life. He knew its spaces, he inhabited its halls, he died in his bedroom on the third floor. Its contents belonged to him, from his suits and presidential chair to the books and objects gifted to him as president. This was the house where, in a sense, he went to die. Yet, as the crowd who cheered him on Armistice Day and this remarkable house suggest, he proved to be a man whose memory would refuse to fade away.

CALVIN COOLIDGE STATE HISTORIC SITE

CALVIN COOLIDGE
(1923 – 1929)

PLYMOUTH NOTCH, VERMONT

"He is just what the country needs,

a quiet, simple, unobtrusive man,

with no isms and no desire for any reform."

OSWALD GARRISON VILLARD

BY THE LIGHT OF A KEROSENE LAMP

Having been a mayor, governor, and president of the Senate back in Massachusetts, Calvin Coolidge was accustomed to setting the agenda. But as the nation's vice president? The social dinners and his speeches amounted mostly to pointless talk; at cabinet meetings and as presiding officer of the Senate, he found his role to be little more than that of listener. After more than two years in Washington, Coolidge truly understood that his office was utterly without influence.

With the Senate in recess and President Warren G. Harding on a two-month national train tour, Coolidge, along with his wife, Grace, and their two sons, made his way to Vermont in early July 1923. His father, Colonel John Coolidge, aged seventy-eight, had admitted that he could use some help tending to repairs and other chores on the farm in Plymouth Notch, the tiny town (population: twenty-nine) where the vice president grew up. The Coolidge sons, John, a month shy of his seventeenth birthday, and Calvin Jr., age fifteen, would be put to work. For the vice president, the prospect of three weeks back in Vermont offered a welcome respite from the Washington routine.

Wednesday, August 2, was a typical day. Coolidge helped a neighbor with the haying, operating a horse-drawn hay rake. Grace took her daily constitutional. A press photographer recorded an image of the vice president, mallet and chisel in hand, performing tree surgery on an old sugar maple. Shortly after nine o'clock, the day ended when the Coolidges retired to their upstairs bedroom.

Thursday proved a different day indeed. A few minutes after midnight, the vice president awoke to the sound of a tread on the stair, accompanied by his father's trembling voice calling his name. He brought shocking news, just arrived from San Francisco: *President Harding was dead.*

As Coolidge later remembered, "I knelt down and . . . asked God to bless the American people and give me the power to serve them." He and Grace dressed and descended the narrow wooden stair in the simple farmhouse to the sitting room. He dictated a note of condolence to Mrs. Harding, then drafted a quick statement for the

Previous page: On the day after the swearing in, a reporter asked Coolidge's father, who was sitting on the porch of his farmhouse, whether he thought his son was up to the challenge of being president. "I think he'll do fairly well," John Coolidge replied.

Left: Calvin Coolidge, tree surgeon.
Vermont Historical Society

Opposite: The fourteen-by-seventeen-foot sitting room at John Coolidge's farmhouse gained fame—and a new name—on August 3, 1923, when in the early hours of the morning, it became the "Oath of Office Room."

press as the first newspaperman appeared at the door, accompanied by a local congressman. The word was out.

John Coolidge made his way to the hamlet's general store and the only telephone in Plymouth Notch. He reached Secretary of State Charles Evans Hughes, a former justice of the Supreme Court. Colonel Coolidge asked whether, as a notary public, he might conduct a presidential swearing in. "That's fine," Hughes said.

No photographers were on hand, but the scene that unfolded soon entered the public's imagination, evocative as it was of a rural America that was already sliding into history. In dramatic chiaroscuro, Calvin Coolidge was sworn in as his wife, Grace, and other figures watched. In the semidarkness, the father recited the oath; the son, his face illuminated by an oil lamp on the table before him, repeated it and added the closing words "So help me God." The son signed the document in triplicate, the father affixed his notary seal.

Having been duly sworn in at 2:47 a.m., the thirtieth president of the United States went back to bed. His time of vice presidential

irrelevance had come to a sudden end, and he would need all the energy he could muster in his new role.

"A TYPE ENTIRELY NEW TO WASHINGTON"

When asked several years later what his first thought had been upon being awakened to learn he had inherited the presidency, Coolidge paused briefly to consider the question. His expression unchanged, he replied with his usual mix of candor and caution, "I thought I could swing it."

There were plenty of politicians in Washington who were less certain. In the months before Harding's death, some forty members of Congress in Coolidge's own Republican Party went public with their desire to replace him on the 1924 ticket. He had been very much overshadowed by the likable Harding, whose perpetual smile contrasted with the vice president's characteristic schoolmaster seriousness. But the man who some laughingly dismissed as "Silent Cal" would prove attractive to the American people.

His life story had an everyman appeal, starting with his date of birth, which had been on July 4, 1872. John Calvin Coolidge Jr.

Above: The Coolidges were among the first settlers in the hamlet of Plymouth Notch; John Coolidge arrived in the 1780s when he bought land here with his mustering-out pay from the Continental Army.

began his education in a one-room schoolhouse. After years of illness (probably tuberculosis), his mother died when Calvin was twelve, in the same room where, four decades later, he took the presidential oath. The boy did chores on the dairy farm, kept the wood box full, boiled sap for the farm's primary cash crop, maple syrup, and fished and hunted in the streams and hills around the "Notch."

After graduating from Amherst College, he clerked in a law office in nearby Northampton, Massachusetts. Within a year of opening his own practice, he ran for city councilman, the first of a series of local offices he would hold. He met Grace Goodhue in 1904. She was watering the garden at the Clarke School for the Deaf, where she taught and he rented a room. He had been shaving, standing near a window, dressed in a union suit and a hat, and her laughter at the sight of him caught his attention. They married a year later, and her lighthearted temperament complemented his, her charm and social ease softening his stiffness.

He served a term in the Massachusetts House of Representatives, then won election to the mayoralty of Northampton in 1909. Back in Boston by 1912 as a state senator, he soon rose to president of the Senate but came to national attention only after his election to the governorship of the Bay State.

The newly chartered Boston Police Union went on strike in September 1919. Within days, rioting and violence on the city's streets prompted Governor Coolidge to intervene, summoning the National Guard to restore order. In a telegram to American Federation of Labor president Samuel Gompers, he asserted, "There is no right to strike against the public safety by anyone, anywhere, any time."

His words reverberated across the country. He had been decisive in the face of what some saw as dangerous radical elements, possibly a domestic manifestation of the unrest abroad, where Communists had led revolutionary outbursts not only in Russia in 1917 but in Germany and Hungary in 1919. When the Republican Party convened in Chicago the following June, ten ballots were required to select Harding as its presidential candidate. After Coolidge's name was brought forward as his running mate, a single roll call taken to echoes of "We want Coolidge!" put him on the ticket by a better than 4-to-1 margin.

Coolidge was at his hotel in Boston when he fielded the call from Chicago. He turned to Grace and told her he had been nominated.

"You are not going to accept it, are you?" she inquired.

"I suppose," he replied, his face expressionless, "I shall have to."

DEATH OF A SON

When Calvin and Grace Coolidge arrived in Plymouth Notch in the summer of 1924, they were struggling to put more than the heat of Washington behind them.

In June, Calvin Jr. had returned from playing tennis on the White House grounds with a blister on his toe. An infection set in, and his entire foot became inflamed. When the infection spread to his bloodstream, the boy became gravely ill, and despite emergency surgery at Walter Reed Hospital, he died on July 7 at age sixteen.

Back on the land that the Coolidges had tilled for five generations, the president mourned the loss of the son who, he remembered, "looked like my mother's people, particularly my mother." During their August visit, Grace took flowers to the boy's grave site each day. The president was observed sitting for long periods, shaded by sugar maples, gazing toward the surrounding hills.

In his memoir some years later, Coolidge offered a revealing aside concerning the death of his son Calvin. "When he went," wrote the still-grieving father, "the power and the glory of the Presidency went with him."

THE SUMMER WHITE HOUSE

In August 1924, Plymouth Notch became the summer White House, just as Roosevelt's Sagamore Hill had some years earlier. President Coolidge had accepted his party's nomination for president, and his hometown was temporarily transformed with his arrival. The second floor of the general store and post office became the nation's executive offices. A reception was held for Vermont neighbors. A few days later, a more famous party arrived to call upon the president. Henry Ford, Thomas Alva Edison, and Harvey Firestone offered their support and had their picture taken with the man who was coming to symbolize the prosperity Americans were enjoying. "The United States is lucky to have Calvin Coolidge," Edison observed. Henry Ford predicted Coolidge would win that November.

In the coming months, Coolidge campaigned little but was aided by the radio, a new medium well suited to his nasal voice, careful enunciation, and conversational style (his 1923 presidential address had been the first to be broadcast to the nation over the radio). But his popularity seemed based on his nature as a matter-of-fact man whose approach fit the tenor of the times.

His personal style would help him weather the scandals that had rocked Harding's final days. Two members of the cabinet, Navy Secretary Edwin Denby and Interior Secretary Albert B. Fall, were forced to resign, and the latter would eventually go to prison for bribery in connection with oil leases in the Teapot Dome scandal. But Coolidge somehow remained above it all, a man who seemed to embody such verities as faith, Yankee thrift, common sense, and public service. His bedrock dignity helped restore a sense of trust in the office of the president.

Above: Calvin, Grace, and John Coolidge, along with Calvin Jr. (*left*), the summer the boy died.
President Calvin Coolidge State Historic Site / Vermont Division for Historic Preservation

Left: The Coolidge farmhouse is a textbook example of a New England big house, little house, backhouse, and barn plan. The horse barn at right was added by John Coolidge for horses on the upper level, pigs below.

As Henry Ford predicted, Calvin Coolidge won reelection in 1924. His presidential style emerged as that of an old-school manager: "The way I transact the Cabinet business," he explained, "is to leave to the head of each Department the conduct of his own business." These men included several valuable holdovers from Harding's tenure, among them Secretary of the Treasury Andrew Mellon and Secretary of Commerce Herbert Hoover, who would succeed Coolidge as president.

At a time when Wilsonian progressivism and internationalism were falling out of favor and conservatism and isolationism were on the rise, Coolidge's Jeffersonian view of the federal government seemed a good fit. He thought a lesser national role preferable for Washington, along with a greater role for state and local government. He believed business was America's engine, as expressed in his oft-quoted (and misquoted) remark that "the chief business of the American people is business." As president, he reduced the deficit, cut taxes, and sought to make government more efficient. Yet in 1928, despite broad popularity, he announced he would not be a candidate for another term.

On the day Coolidge left office, Walter Lippmann observed, "Surely no one will write of those years since August 1923, that an aggressive president altered the destiny of the Republic. Yet it is an important fact that no one will write of those same years that the Republic wished its destiny to be altered."

Calvin Coolidge was a smooth-faced, mild-mannered man, with a gift for listening. Though chary with words in conversation, he drafted his own speeches and, after his retirement, wrote an autobiography that offered many clues to the man and his presidency. It wasn't that writing came easily to him; for Coolidge, it was a matter of good Yankee discipline. "I always knew that there was some water in my well," he observed, "but that I had to pump to get it."

Calvin Coolidge died of a heart attack at age sixty on January 5, 1933. His grave is marked by a simple stone that is of a piece with those of seven generations of Coolidges in the small cemetery at Plymouth Notch, Vermont.

Above: The newly minted president, recorded on canvas by Herman Hanatschek in 1924. *President Calvin Coolidge State Historic Site / Vermont Division for Historic Preservation*

Left: The Community Room over the Grange became the headquarters during the summer of 1924 for Coolidge's staff and the eighteen Secret Service men detailed to protect the chief executive.

SPRINGWOOD

FRANKLIN DELANO ROOSEVELT
(1933 – 1945)

HYDE PARK, NEW YORK

"He was one of the few statesmen
in the twentieth century, or any century,
who seemed to have no fear of the future."

ISAIAH BERLIN

A BEAUTIFUL FRAME

T he father was of a certain age. Nearly fifty-five, the recently remarried James Roosevelt doubled his wife's years, but on the evening of January 30, 1882, it was Sara Delano Roosevelt whose health was in crisis.

Sallie, as her husband called her, had finally felt the first contractions at seven thirty the previous evening, a fortnight after her pregnancy had reached full-term. Neither the nurse nor the doctor in attendance was able to speed the baby's progress, and Mrs. Roosevelt's screams of agony seemed to grow more intense. Finally, after twenty-four hours of labor, the doctor administered a dose of chloroform to the exhausted Mrs. Roosevelt. It didn't seem to be enough, but when he gave her another, Sallie began gasping for breath and, to Mr. James's horror, promptly lost consciousness.

As she lay on the mahogany double bed upstairs at the Roosevelt home in Hyde Park, her skin taking on the bluish tinge of hypoxia as her lungs processed too little oxygen, her husband could only wonder whether mother and child were dying before his eyes.

◇◇◇◇◇◇◇◇◇◇

Previous page: The 1915 renovation was a collaboration, as Franklin and his mother, Sara, directed the architects Francis Hoppin and Terence Koen to enlarge the Victorian home, built as it was to resemble an Italianate villa. The result is a pretty Georgian Revival façade with decorative details such as the columned portico, balusters at ground level, and a new attic story decorated with swags that capped the half-round and oculus windows.

Left: James Roosevelt's Springwood, in the late nineteenth century, before his wife and son remodeled the home in 1915.
Franklin D. Roosevelt Library

Opposite: The largest room in the house, the library dominates the stone south wing that was added in 1915. Roosevelt often worked here on his stamp collection and played games with his children, but this was also, upon occasion, the site of the much-anticipated evening cocktail hour, where the business of the day was quickly left behind as Roosevelt mixed drinks and regaled his guests with his favorite stories. When the Roosevelts welcomed King George VI and Queen Elizabeth in 1939 with a tray of cocktails in this room, Franklin confided to the king that his mother, who sat nearby, didn't approve of cocktails. "Neither does my mother" was the reply as the royal guest reached for a drink.

This was to be the first Roosevelt child born at the house on the tall bluff. The family had resided for three generations at Hyde Park on the Hudson, some ninety miles north of Manhattan, but only after an 1865 fire destroyed the previous Roosevelt house two miles away had Mr. James acquired this property. The run-down estate on 110 acres had consumed his attentions after 1867, as he set about making improvements. He built stables for the horses that

were his passion, which included trotters as well as riding and driving horses. He added to his holdings too, and soon his dairy herd of Guernseys, Jerseys, and Alderneys were pastured on a property that amounted to more than nine hundred contiguous acres. He renamed the place *Springwood*.

An informed observer approaching the seventeen-room mansion along the winding drive would have recognized the style as

Above: Franklin Delano Roosevelt was born in this room; after his mother's death in 1941, her furniture was returned to this space to restore the room to its appearance on the occasion of FDR's belated birth on January 30, 1882.

Opposite: Smiling as usual, Eleanor Roosevelt photographed on a New York City sidewalk in 1940.
Franklin D. Roosevelt Library

Italianate. Seen across a broad green, the low-pitched rooflines were supported by characteristic brackets, and the long façade was lined with a covered veranda. The three-story Tuscan tower at the south end of the wood-frame house took in an expansive view of the Hudson River. James's attentions meant the house had been refurbished too, with Brussels carpets on the inside, just the proper shade of green paint applied to the piazza, and newfangled indoor plumbing.

After the sudden death of his first wife in 1876, James had wooed the much younger Sara Delano. Like him, she came from well-established New York roots. Her family had made its money in whaling, the China trade, and even opium importation; descended from a seventeenth-century Dutch immigrant named *Rosenvelt,* the Roosevelts in six generations had made their gains in Manhattan real estate, West Indian sugar, and dry goods.

Despite the difference in their ages, James and Sara had seemed a suitable match to her father. (Her previous suitor had not: Warren Delano had dismissed Stanford White, then a young draftsman of no particular prospects, as the "red-headed trial.") In 1880, middle-aged James, his rounded face framed by bushy gray sideburns, married the young and statuesque Sara, who stood five feet, ten inches tall. The newlyweds went on an extended European tour before retiring to Springwood upon learning that Sara was with child.

⬦⬦⬦⬦⬦⬦⬦⬦

At 8:45 p.m., the baby emerged. But the newborn showed no signs of breathing, and his skin, like his mother's, had a bluish tinge. Even when slaps were delivered to his bottom, he did not respond. Only after the doctor put his mouth over the baby's and blew repeatedly into his lungs did the child cry out and begin to breathe on his own.

Sara recovered in the coming weeks, but there would be no more babies. The center of her life would be her son. She breast-fed her child; she delegated little of the care for the boy in the way that many women of her class and time usually did. James doted on the child—the boy called him "Popsy"—and at his side the lad learned to ride horses and to sail the large Roosevelt yacht. In the winter they would reside at the Roosevelt town house in New York, but together the child and his parents traveled often, touring Canada and many American states in their private railroad car, the *Manon,* which was fitted out as a suite of rooms with brass and mahogany trimmings. Master Franklin would see England repeatedly, and after his father developed heart problems, the Roosevelts remained for sustained periods in the German Rhineland so that James could take the waters. Summer months were spent off the Maine coast at Campobello (the Cottage at Roosevelt Campobello International Park is today a historic site; see *Visitor Information,* page 241). But wherever he was, the boy lived a highly disciplined life of lessons, carefully chosen games and sports, and reading, often from the well-stocked shelves at Springwood. In early adolescence, a tutor arrived to drill him in Latin, math, and other subjects in preparation for the Groton School.

When he finally began his formal schooling at fourteen, two years or more later than most of the boys at Groton, he had only rarely been separated from his parents. If he was ready to face the world—and he soon proved that he was—part of the explanation

ELEANOR ROOSEVELT'S HYDE PARK

Franklin's fifth cousin proved as indomitable as the man she married. She mothered their children, but after Franklin's disabling illness in 1921, Eleanor became his eyes and ears too, reporting back upon the state of the nation, what people were saying, and how well government monies were being spent. She did it all despite an inherent shyness and the earlier discovery of her husband's love letters to her social secretary, clear evidence of his infidelity. Eleanor and Franklin's physical intimacies may have ceased after 1919, but in the years that followed she emerged as a powerful and much-loved personality in her own right, as well as her husband's essential public partner.

Even after Franklin's death in 1945, the widely admired Eleanor remained an influential presence. She wrote a six-day-a-week syndicated newspaper column, "My Day," from 1935–1962, in which she addressed matters both familial and public. A woman passionate about social justice, equality, and human rights, she remained an activist presence not only in American politics but in the world (President Harry S. Truman appointed her a delegate to the nascent United Nations in 1945, and she later served on the UN Commission on Human Rights).

Springwood had never truly become Eleanor's home. Even after she and Franklin married, her mother-in-law, Sara, remained mistress of the estate. Following the deaths of both Sara and Franklin, Eleanor took up residence nearby at Val-Kill, a rambling former factory two miles from Springwood, the only home she would ever own. Upon her death in 1962, her remains were interred at Springwood with her husband's. Today, the Eleanor Roosevelt National Historic Site at Val-Kill, as well as Springwood, interprets the independent life of the woman Truman called "the first lady of the world."

Top: One rainy afternoon in his boyhood, Franklin was discovered by his mother reading *Webster's Unabridged Dictionary;* in 1933, a photographer found the newly elected president paging through one of the folio volumes in the Springwood library.
Franklin D. Roosevelt Library

Bottom: Eleanor was the most public woman in Roosevelt's life, but Franklin's mother was certainly her equal in influence. Sara Delano Roosevelt's room, called the "Snuggery," was at the center of the household. The business of running Springwood was conducted in this cramped space, which retained many pieces from the old parlor after the 1915 renovation.

lay in the circumstances of his upbringing. As his mother explained, she worked to keep "Franklin's mind on nice things, on a high level; yet . . . in such a way that Franklin never realized that he was following any bent but his own."

As Sara's sister Dora put it, "He was brought up in a beautiful frame." Those early years of nurture, privilege, and love readied him to embrace a much larger world with confidence and to succeed at Groton and then at Harvard, where he became president of the *Harvard Crimson* ("Perhaps the most useful preparation," he later said, "[that] I had in college for public service"), and to excel with his eventual law studies at Columbia. But his childhood also left him deeply connected to the family home at Hyde Park. In Franklin Delano Roosevelt's mind, Springwood would always be "the center of the world."

GREAT EXPECTATIONS

By 1915, Roosevelt's public career was following in the path of his idolized cousin Theodore. Both Roosevelts had been elected to serve in the New York State Senate and had received appointments to be assistant secretary of the Navy (in Franklin's case, he assumed the jobs, respectively, in 1910 and 1913). Franklin's private life was proving productive too. In 1905, against his mother's wishes, he had married Teddy's niece, Anna Eleanor, and she had birthed five children in ten years. Another was expected.

With his large ambitions and growing family, the need was obvious: the house at Hyde Park had to be expanded.

His father had died almost fifteen years earlier, but Sara remained in charge at Springwood. Over the years minor changes had been made to the house (the staircase had been moved in 1892, the home electrified in 1908), but a more radical rethinking was required. Together, mother and son commissioned a respected New York architectural firm, Hoppin and Koen, to prepare a plan. The revamped house that resulted was a mingling of the architects' Beaux Arts training and Franklin's fondness for elements of the Dutch Colonial design native to the Hudson Valley.

The roof was raised on the existing house, allowing for the construction of a large playroom. At either end of the original structure, new fieldstone wings were added. The north addition had a common room for the servants and a schoolroom on the first floor, along with five servant bedrooms and a bath above. The south wing contained a spacious library down; three bedrooms up. The configuration of the principal rooms in the earlier house was largely retained, though the house doubled in size.

Sara Delano Roosevelt paid the bills and managed the yearlong renovation, during which the old clapboard cladding was removed and replaced with gray stucco for a look more compatible with the coursed rubble stone of the new wings. Other decorative touches added formality to what became a more imposing house, as the entry gained a columned portico and a fanlight over the door. A vernacular Victorian dwelling was transformed into an orderly and symmetrical statement that spoke for the means and expectations of the man of the house.

In the years that followed, Roosevelt's rise seemed likely to continue. In 1920 he was the Democratic candidate for vice president (along with Ohio governor James M. Cox), though the Republican pairing of Warren G. Harding and Calvin Coolidge won by an overwhelming margin. Roosevelt returned to his law practice, but less than a year later, on vacation at Campobello, he took to his bed. The diagnosis was polio, and for much of the next seven years, Roosevelt worked at his rehabilitation. He would never regain full use of his legs and, wary that people would think him unfit for public office, attempted to appear more mobile than he was, delivering speeches while standing (he wore iron leg braces) and taking pains to avoid being photographed in his wheelchair.

Eventually, he reentered politics and, in 1928, was elected governor of New York. After two terms in Albany, the fifty-year-old Roosevelt pledged at the Democratic convention in 1932 that, if elected, he would deliver "a new deal for the American people." That November he won a national mandate, carrying forty-two of the forty-eight states. He would win a total of four presidential elections as he sought to lead the nation out of the Great Depression and, eventually, to victory in war after the Japanese attack on Pearl Harbor, which he described as "a date that will live in infamy."

Historians and biographers have wrestled with the popularity of the politician and the complex personality of the man. Franklin Roosevelt was raised an Eastern aristocrat but seemed genuinely to like everybody, regardless of class or region. When he addressed people as "my friends," whether among a small group, in a public speech, or over the radio waves in one of his periodic "Fireside Chats" (many of which were broadcast from Springwood), all kinds of people were drawn to the man with the welcoming manner and a passion for conversation and company. The American people not only accepted his friendship but admired his implacability and the seemingly bottomless optimism that had been in evidence since his childhood. Everyone felt they knew this man, and most people liked him.

Yet there was also something unknowable about him, a private self, a reserve that no one penetrated. "He had no real confidantes," Eleanor, his wife of four decades, once remarked. "I don't think I

Roosevelt could no longer climb stairs after his disabling illness, so a trunk elevator was converted for his use. It was operated manually (note the ropes); Roosevelt, though his legs were nearly useless, had a broad-shouldered, well-muscled upper body.

The initial impetus for the gift was President Roosevelt's concern about his compendious records and collections, and in 1938 he announced his intention to donate his books, memorabilia, and voluminous correspondence and other documents to the federal government. His plan called for the erection of a library and archive on his Hyde Park estate, one to be built at no cost to the nation. The notion of establishing a presidential library was a new one, as no previous living president had seen fit to create an institution charged with conserving his legacy.

The public response to the popular president's plan was immediate. Some 28,000 Americans contributed to the effort, and on July 4, 1940, the library became the property of the nation. The Hyde Park estate, including Springwood, was given to the nation "to be maintained for the benefit of the public." (Another Roosevelt home, the "Little White House" in Warm Springs, Georgia, has also been preserved for visitors; see *Visitor Information,* page 241.)

Unique among presidential sites, the property at Hyde Park was Roosevelt's principal home throughout his life; even as president he traveled there often, making almost two hundred trips to Springwood in the course of his thirteen-year presidency. President Roosevelt spent languid summer days in the house that overlooked the Hudson; he ritually returned home at Christmas for his hearthside reading of *A Christmas Carol* to the children and grandchildren; he planned war strategies with Churchill there. After his death on April 12, 1945, his remains made one last pilgrimage to Hyde Park, traveling through the night past thousands of Americans who gathered to watch and grieve. He was bound for the resting place he had chosen, in his mother's rose garden.

was ever his confidante, either." He was variously described by trusted colleagues as "the most complicated human being I have ever known" and as possessed of a "thickly forested interior." As one member of his Washington brain trust once said, "No one could tell what he was *thinking,* to say nothing of what he was *feeling.*" For all his apparent accessibility, FDR was, in short, a deeply enigmatic man.

"THAT'S WHERE I'M GOING TO BE BURIED"

Although Springwood offers a superb vantage from which to consider Roosevelt and his many facets, the home never actually belonged to its most famous occupant. At his death in 1900, James Roosevelt had left it not to his son (then newly enrolled at Harvard) but to his widow, Sara; prior to her death in 1941, Franklin had asked his mother to deed the estate to the federal government.

Above: Franklin's bedroom is on the second floor at Springwood. Although Eleanor stopped sleeping here (her bedroom is adjacent), Fala slept on the chaise longue at the foot of the bed. Acquired in 1940, the Scottish terrier became Roosevelt's traveling companion and America's most famous dog. Note as well the two phones at the bedside; one was a direct line to the White House.

Opposite: None of the wheelchairs Roosevelt used at Springwood were standard-issue; all were adapted from household chairs because the factory-made invalid chairs of the day were too wide and bulky.

EISENHOWER NATIONAL HISTORIC SITE

DWIGHT D. EISENHOWER
(1953 – 1961)

GETTYSBURG, PENNSYLVANIA

"In a place like Gettysburg, the visitor . . .
may easily forget that history was also
made here in quiet lives, on farm
and village street, through a century before
the battle, through a century after it."

DWIGHT D. EISENHOWER, *AT EASE* (1967)

THE MEMORY OF WAR

T he name Gettysburg conjures up visions of the bloodiest confrontation of the Civil War, a three-day battle at which the Union and Confederate armies sustained casualties of some fifty thousand men. But to Dwight David Eisenhower (1890–1969), the crossroads town in south central Pennsylvania would be replete with memories and hopes, martial and marital.

Eisenhower first visited with his West Point classmates in 1915 to study the crucial battle that had taken place in July 1863. But by the time the Army ordered him to return to Gettysburg in 1918, another war was being fought, this one in Europe. By then Eisenhower was a fast-rising graduate of the U.S. Military Academy, just given his first command. He was to establish Camp Colt for the new Army Tank Corps.

The tank—originally known as a "landship"—was a recent invention, and though no American tanks had yet been manufactured, Eisenhower was charged with training recruits in its battlefield use. Until the first French prototype arrived, the resourceful Eisenhower improvised, mounting naval cannon and machine guns on flatbed trucks. They were deployed on a training ground at the base of Big Round Top, a site on the Gettysburg Battlefield where many Civil War soldiers had died.

Though he would have preferred to be at the front in Europe, camp commander Eisenhower did have the consolation of returning home each evening to his wife, Mamie (he and Mary Geneva Doud had married in 1916), and their infant son, Doud Dwight (known as "Icky"). During their months at Camp Colt, the brevetted lieutenant colonel took his wife on long rides, regaling her with details of the deeds of the officers and men at the Battle of Gettysburg (she later recalled that "he knew every rock of that battlefield"). The

Previous page: A simple and deteriorated farmhouse was transformed by the Eisenhowers; it remained a rambling home after the renovation was completed in 1955, but one better suited to a president and first lady.

Left: President Eisenhower (*left*) with three budget advisers (Maurice Stans, Percival Brundage, and James R. Killian) on his Pennsylvania back porch in December 1957.
Eisenhower National Historic Site

Opposite: The property was a working farm before and during the Eisenhower years, with a need for fuel to power the tractors, trucks, and other equipment.

posting lasted less than a year, but the experience of Gettysburg would remain with the young officer.

As a boy, he had begun what would be a lifelong study of war. He memorized General George Washington's 1783 farewell address and devoured accounts of the campaigns of Napoleon and Frederick the Great. His youthful studies reached into the distant past too. "The battles of Marathon, Zama, Salamis, and Cannae," Eisenhower would later write, "became as familiar to me as the games (and battles) I enjoyed with my brothers and friends in the school yard." As a career officer, his time at Camp Colt was followed by a series of staff jobs; as a family man, he and Mamie mourned the death of Icky from scarlet fever in 1921 but the following year welcomed the birth of another son, John Sheldon Doud.

Eisenhower worked his way up through the ranks in Washington in the War Department, as an aide to General Pershing on the American Battle Monuments Commission, and as the personal assistant of Army Chief of Staff General Douglas MacArthur. His rise accelerated after the Japanese attack on Pearl Harbor, and he became the supreme commander of the Allied Expeditionary Forces and a five-star general. In charge of planning Operation Overlord, the invasion of Northern Europe that commenced with D-Day in 1944, he was tasked with nothing less than to "land in Europe and, proceeding to Germany, [to] destroy Hitler and all his forces."

Given his accomplishments in war and his appreciation of military history, perhaps it is not surprising that, after almost four decades of living a peripatetic military life, General Eisenhower's search for a more permanent place took him and Mamie back to Gettysburg. There they found a 189-acre farm located, as Eisenhower himself would put it, "next to the fields where Pickett's men had assembled for the assault on Cemetery Ridge."

A RETIREMENT DREAM

Mamie and Ike (his nickname dated from childhood) were visiting George and Mary Allen at the old stone house the Allens had bought near Gettysburg. The Eisenhowers' friends encouraged them

"Gettysburg," wrote Eisenhower in his memoir *At Ease* (1967), "was a demonstration of what a tiny portion of a nation's number can accomplish in the shaping and the making of history."

to buy a country house nearby; Mary and Mamie knew each other from the years when Colonel Eisenhower was a staff officer in Washington, D.C., and Ike and George had become fast friends in London during the war, when George was chairman of the Prisoner of War Committee of the American Red Cross.

All at once, several pieces fell into place. Having retired from active military service in 1948, Ike was in his third year as president of Columbia University. He was anticipating his eventual retire-

ment and, in the meantime, desired "an escape from concrete into the countryside." He was not a Pennsylvanian by birth, as he was born in Denison, Texas, and grew up in Abilene, Kansas (the Eisenhower Birthplace State Historic Site in Denison is open to the public; see *Visitor Information,* page 241). But his family had both a past and a present in Pennsylvania, as Eisenhower ancestors had immigrated there a century earlier, and two of Ike's brothers resided in the state. As for Mamie, after living in thirty-three different homes during

her husband's military career, she wanted "a place that conformed to her notions of what a home should be."

Driving down a dirt road in October 1950, they found what they wanted. At the end of a half-mile private drive, they saw a house and an immense barn. The home was more than a hundred years old and, the general noted, would require a good deal of work. But immediately to the east was the Gettysburg Battlefield, and the Blue Ridge Mountains rose toward the western sky. Inside the house Mamie was greeted by the smell of frying potatoes, while Ike found a range of farm outbuildings to tour outside.

A deal was soon struck. The purchase price was $40,000, which included not only the farm but one of the largest barns in the county, two Allis-Chalmers tractors, twenty-four Holstein cows, a dozen heifers, and five hundred leghorn hens. The present owner would work the farm for another year, easing Ike's transition into retirement and a return to the rural life he had known growing up, when his chores had included milking a cow and collecting eggs.

And for his wife? "Mamie," observed her husband, "had found the place she wanted."

But life happens to generals as well as to everyone else. A month after the purchase was finalized, President Harry S. Truman telephoned, and before they could even take possession of their farm, the Eisenhowers sailed for Europe on Washington's birthday in 1951. In a few short weeks, he had to take a leave of absence as Columbia's president, acceding to Truman's request that he serve as supreme commander of the new North Atlantic Treaty Organization (NATO). Later that year, yet another summons to public service reached him. Massachusetts senator Henry Cabot Lodge arrived in Paris with word the general had a passionate following within the Republican Party that wished to enter his name as a nominee for president. Eisenhower was dubious; only after he saw a film of a Madison Square Garden rally the following February did he agree to be a presidential candidate. It was the sight and sounds of 33,000 people chanting, "We want Ike!" that persuaded him of "the longing in America today for change."

After the results were tallied that November (with 55 percent of the popular vote, Eisenhower and running mate Richard M. Nixon won thirty-nine of forty-eight states), Mamie understood that, as eager as she might be to occupy the redbrick farmhouse in Gettysburg, the White House would be their next stop. As she remarked to Ike after moving back to Washington, "I still have no home of my own."

THE EISENHOWER FARM

Although they could not yet take up residence at their Gettysburg property, the Eisenhowers did begin to remodel the home to their tastes. They hired architect Milton Osborne to prepare plans, and Mamie's charge to him was to change as little as possible. But the pre–Civil War house, once its skeleton was revealed by the builders, required more radical surgery.

The brick proved to be merely a veneer, behind which were the decaying remains of a much earlier pioneer log cabin. Though some oak beams and a summer kitchen fireplace with its bake oven were salvaged, much of the rest of the house had to be dismantled. An essentially new house soon rose on the site and, by the time the reconstruction was completed in March 1955, the home had become what architect Osborne termed a "modified Georgian farmhouse." In short, the dilapidated early structure had been reinvented as a postwar dream house, one that bore a certain resemblance to the countless postwar houses built for the men who had served under General Eisenhower.

Certainly it was larger than most—this was an officer's house—with five bedrooms and five bathrooms, as well as a kitchen, a laundry, and an office for Eisenhower. In furnishing the formal dining and living rooms, Mamie consulted New York interior designer Elizabeth Draper, who had helped decorate the White House and the president's house at Columbia University, but the casual sunporch facing east would prove to be the Eisenhowers' favorite place to relax. At the far end of the house was a small apartment, quarters for Sergeant John Moaney and his wife, Delores. He had been Ike's orderly and valet since 1942 (Ike called him "my old companion"); Delores was the household's cook.

The president began using the home as an occasional weekend retreat from his presidential duties, but the house entered the public consciousness when, late in 1955, it became the temporary White House as Eisenhower convalesced from a heart attack (myocardial infarction) that autumn.

During his second term in office, Eisenhower regularly brought visitors, often notable international figures, to Gettysburg. The presidential country retreat at Camp David was only twenty miles away, just minutes by helicopter, and Eisenhower invited Indian prime minister Jawaharlal Nehru, West German chancellor Konrad Adenauer, and British prime minister Harold Macmillan to inspect his farm. Although it was in the midst of the Cold War, he brought Soviet premier Nikita Khrushchev to the farm too, introducing him to his grandchildren and showing him his horses and award-winning Black Angus cattle. Behind the wheel of his Crosley runabout, Eisenhower found that such farm visits provided opportunities to talk about something other than diplomatic matters. It was, as Eisenhower put it, a way "to get the other man's equation."

For the general, it seemed perfectly logical to take old military colleagues on a tour of the Gettysburg Battlefield, to show British field marshal Montgomery and Charles de Gaulle of France the scene of the great American battle. The veterans of World War II walked the rolling Pennsylvania hills, their aides trailing behind, as they reviewed cannon sites and terrain, considering the strategies and lessons of a long-ago war. As de Gaulle remarked to Eisenhower on his visit, "Victory often goes to the army that makes the least mistakes, not the most brilliant plans."

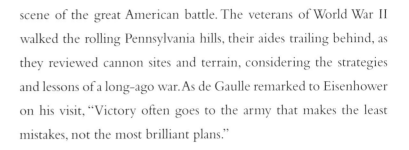

Left: The dining room features a suite of furniture that was almost as well traveled as the Eisenhowers. Mamie purchased the dining room table and chairs in 1927, and they went with them to many subsequent posts.

Right: The living room was often used for greeting first-time visitors, though Ike thought the space too stiffly formal, with its mix of presidential gifts, Mamie's collections, and some Victorian heirloom furniture from her family. The marble mantel was a gift from the White House staff. Found beneath a porch, the mantel had originally been installed in the White House during a remodeling in the nineteenth century.

MAMIE EISENHOWER

When Ike met Mamie, she was petite (five foot one), eighteen, and a child of privilege who lived both in San Antonio, where Ike was a young officer at Fort Sam Houston, and in Denver. Four months later, on Valentine's Day 1916, their engagement was made official. During a marriage that endured fifty-three years, she proved an adaptable military wife—but it was her spirited style as first lady that endeared her to the American public.

She was famous for her fondness for flowers (especially gladioli), the color pink (one paint company in the 1950s offered "First Lady Pink" as a color choice), and the "Mamie bangs" hairdo she adopted after the death of her first son. A skilled hostess, she welcomed world figures to the White House with the same aplomb that she brought to her many public appearances before an adoring public (after her husband's political slogan became "I Like Ike," a variant version soon appeared: "We Like Mamie").

Her military marriage meant periods of long separation (nearly three years during World War II), and she resented such intrusions on their lives as "dirty tricks." But in a volume of collected letters (*Letters to Mamie*, 1978), her husband's love and affection are apparent. "You should not forget that I do miss you and do love you, and that the load of responsibility I carry would be intolerable unless I could have the belief that there is someone who wants me to come home—for good."

She weathered rumors of her husband's affair with his driver, Kay Summersby, and gossip that Mrs. Eisenhower drank a little (the likely explanation was an inner-ear disorder called Ménière's disease that affected her balance). Popular for her bright, unaffected manner (she often referred to herself as a homemaker), she disliked giving speeches but as first lady maintained a grueling schedule of appearances and prided herself on writing to those who wrote to her. After her husband's death, she made annual pilgrimages to his grave in Kansas.

On the evening of January 20, 1961, snow fell as the chauffeured limousine turned up the lane toward the farmhouse. As the big car continued toward the farm complex, its two escort cars turned and headed back to Washington. The Secret Service had seen the former president safely home (protection for former presidents did not become the norm until after the Kennedy assassination). The Eisenhowers—Mamie and now *former* president Dwight D. Eisenhower—were home at last, after forty-five years of public service.

Above, left: On the day of their thirtieth wedding anniversary, Mamie and Ike pose in front of his Crosley golf cart.
Eisenhower National Historic Site

Above, right: In the former milk house, the U.S. Secret Service established its command and communications offices.

Opposite: The sunporch was Ike's favorite room. He worked on his oil paintings here, having taken up painting at age fifty-nine. He and Mamie played cards, read, entertained friends, and watched television in this casual space. Their favorite show? *I Love Lucy.* Despite Lucy's alleged association with possible Communists, Ike invited the cast to the White House.

On Eisenhower's watch, the interstate highway system had come into being, as had the Department of Health, Education, and Welfare. The year 1959 saw the first American satellite launched into orbit and Alaska and Hawaii granted statehood. Though remembered by some as a simple and happy time after two decades of war and depression, the 1950s also saw the coming and going of McCarthyism, the emergence of what Eisenhower himself had dubbed the "military industrial complex," and the 1954 Supreme Court ruling in *Brown v. Board of Education,* which helped cue the first phase of the Civil Rights movement.

With the new decade and his new life in Gettysburg, Eisenhower would derive great pleasure from his successful cattle business. He played golf, maintained an office at nearby Gettysburg College, and wrote his memoirs. Though they retained life tenancy, the Eisen-

howers donated their home to the National Park Service in 1967. Mamie would remain in residence for another ten years after Ike's death in 1969, and following her passing, the house was opened to the public in 1980.

Today the farmland and rolling hills around the Eisenhowers' chosen place have changed little. Acreage is leased to local farmers who are required to raise Black Angus and cultivate the same crops that the general did. And the house too remains very much as Ike and Mamie knew it. The visitor to Gettysburg may tour the Eisenhower farm to consider the last years of the thirty-fourth president, as well as visit, just as Ike liked to do, the scenes of war memorialized on the great battlefield nearby.

JOHN FITZGERALD KENNEDY BIRTHPLACE

JOHN F. KENNEDY
(1961 – 1963)

BROOKLINE, MASSACHUSETTS

"Children are the world's most valuable

resource and its best hope for the future."

JOHN F. KENNEDY, JULY 25, 1963

NOVEMBER 25, 1963

O n that bright but brisk November day, a funeral procession drew the attention of the nation and of the world. Perhaps a million people lined the route of the cortege from the U.S. Capitol to St. Matthew's Cathedral, then on to Arlington National Cemetery. Countless millions around the world watched the nonstop coverage of the funeral on television. The images are unforgettable: the riderless black horse; the folding of the flag; the wee boy in short pants, John F. Kennedy Jr., saluting his father in farewell.

Yet for a few thousand grieving Americans, those hours were spent on a streetscape in the comfortable Boston suburb of Brookline. Former neighbors and other mourners had their own memorial service at a quiet strip of middle-class houses just a few blocks from the main thoroughfare of Beacon Street.

They chose to gather there because of a routine domestic event that had occurred forty-six years earlier, on May 29, 1917. Tended by

Dr. Frederick Good, anesthetized with chloroform, Rose Fitzgerald Kennedy had given birth to her second son in the master bedroom at 83 Beals Street. Within a few years, the house had lost its Kennedy connection, as young Jack hadn't yet turned four when his father, Joseph P. Kennedy, sold the home and moved his growing family a few blocks away to a bigger, grander Queen Anne–style house with turreted corners and a wraparound porch. But the Kennedy connection wasn't entirely forgotten, as in 1961 the town of Brookline placed a bronze plaque at street side, marking the home as the new president's birthplace.

Barely two years later, as echoes of the three shots fired at Dealey Plaza in Dallas reverberated, the death of a president inspired talk of making the tall wood-frame house, then privately owned and the residence of an aging widow and her son, a place to com-

---

Previous page: The family nursery at John F. Kennedy's birthplace—thus the Kennedy cradle, which Jack and all his siblings slept in. There's a teddy bear too, a recently marketed child's toy that took its name from Theodore Roosevelt.

Left: On a gray day in November 1963, perhaps ten thousand mourners stood together, shoulder-to-shoulder, on Brookline's Beals Street.
Temple Kehillath Israel

Opposite: Colonial Revival in style, the house at 83 Beals Street boasts a spacious porch. Rose Kennedy remembers using it as a children's play area. "With a folding gate to block the entrance, the children would play there in fresh air and in full safety and, moreover, with the full panorama of neighboring life to entertain them."

memorate John F. Kennedy. After the funeral, citizens of Brookline started the conversation concerning the establishment of a house museum, but plans stalled. In 1966, the Kennedy family took charge, and one of Rose Kennedy's nephews purchased the house on behalf of the family. She then set about restoring the place as she remembered it. Work progressed, but before completion another Kennedy tragedy intervened when an assassin's bullets ended Robert F. Kennedy's life on June 6, 1968. Finally, on the late

president's birthday in 1969, the site was dedicated and gifted to the National Park Service by the Kennedy family.

A spontaneous outpouring of grief and loss on a Brookline street had transformed a modest house into a national monument, where the visitor then—as now—encountered the home, guided by the warm and affectionate tones of Rose Kennedy in an eighteen-minute taped tour, as she recollected the life of the house in Jack's early boyhood.

BOSTON POLITICS

The groom purchased the house before the wedding in the fall of 1914. Already showing signs of early success—that year, at just twenty-five, Joseph Patrick Kennedy had become one of the youngest bank presidents in the nation when he took over the Columbia Trust Company—Joe Kennedy paid $6,500 for the house on Beals Street. The five-year-old home was no mansion, but it suited his young bride. "It was a nice old wooden-frame house," Rose recalled decades later, "with clapboard siding; seven rooms, plus two small ones in the converted attic, all on a small lot with a few bushes and trees."

After years of courting, Joe and Rose's marriage was one of mutual affection, but it was also a merging of political power, as both husband and wife were third-generation Irish Americans whose fathers had done well. Rose's father, John Francis Fitzgerald, had won a series of elective offices, including three terms in Congress. Known as "Honey Fitz" for his singing voice (he liked to close his campaign speeches with a song, his signature being "Sweet Adeline"), his rise had culminated in two terms as mayor of Boston. During his years at city hall, Rose, by then a handsome young woman, had been her father's most visible companion (a retiring woman, her mother remained at home with Rose's two younger brothers). For his part, Joe's father too had been the beneficiary of the rising tide of Irish influence in Boston, which was shouldering aside the long-dominant upper-class Boston Brahmins. The senior Kennedy had held numerous appointive offices and met with success at the polls, serving multiple terms in both the Massachusetts House of Representatives and the Senate.

As Joe and Rose settled into married life, they would make only one minor change to the structure of their home, adding a bay window to the dining room. But their family changed almost from year to year, with the arrival of Joe Jr. in 1915, John in 1917, Rosemary in 1918, and Kathleen in 1920. Despite her exposure to political life, Rose's education at convent schools in Boston, Holland, and New York had set her on a domestic course, as she herself said, to devote her life to "*Kinder, Kirche, und Küche* (children, church, and cooking)."

The Kennedys were well-to-do, their fortunes rising. Living in a streetcar suburb, they were among the first in their neighborhood to have a car—Joe surprised Rose one evening when he arrived with a brand-new Model T Ford. Their automobiles were apt symbols of Joe's success, with the Tin Lizzie followed by a Pierce-Arrow in 1917 and, after they left Beals Street, a chauffeur-driven Rolls-Royce. Located on nearby Abbotsford Road, their next home was larger (twelve rooms), cost more ($16,000), and came with a garage in which to store the Kennedys' more prestigious automobile.

Joe, Rose, and their children would remain in Brookline only until 1927, when Joe, having moved on to the brokerage business, took his ventures to New York. Their wealth (by the end of the decade, he was a multimillionaire) and their status continued to rise. In addition to their New York home, other holdings in the Kennedy real estate portfolio soon included seasonal homes, with the purchase of estates in Palm Beach, Florida, and on Cape Cod, where Kennedy descendants still gather at the so-called Kennedy Compound in Hyannisport, Massachusetts.

Despite fragile health (a life-threatening bout with scarlet fever at age two had been the first of many serious ailments), their second son would prosper in the privileged world his parents came to inhabit. His father was a fixture in the administration of his friend Franklin Roosevelt, serving as the first chairman of both the Securities and Exchange Commission and the Maritime Commission. Joe's next assignment, as the United States ambassador to the United Kingdom, took the family abroad. There Jack's travels in England and on the Continent during the lead-up to World War II led to his senior honors thesis at Harvard College; when published a year after his graduation as *Why England Slept,* it became a bestseller.

Above: According to Rose Kennedy, the family often ate dinner in this room: "My husband and I sat at the main table, of course, and the children, when very small, sat at a small table and joined us at the big table as they grew older." The room was also a place to display the wedding gifts the couple had received, which included Limoges porcelain, silver flatware, and cut glass. The dining room table, sideboard, and buffet are original to the home.

Opposite: President Kennedy at a 1962 news conference.
Abbie Rowe, NPS/John F. Kennedy Presidential Library and Museum

Right: Located over the front door with a view of the street, Rose Kennedy's boudoir was the control center. From her desk in this, the smallest room in the home, she ran the household as wife, mother, and manager of the servants. She prided herself on what the British press called her "American efficiency," keeping index cards for each child, recording inoculations, illnesses, and other information. This was her office, her escape, her place.

During the war, Lieutenant (Junior Grade) Kennedy was decorated for his bravery after his boat, *PT-109,* was sunk in the Pacific, adding to the young man's luster. In 1946 he won election to Congress; after three terms as a congressman, he defeated incumbent senator Henry Cabot Lodge Jr. He was elected president in 1960, beating Richard Nixon in a race remembered for the narrowness of his victory (the margin was just 0.1 percent of the popular vote) and for the famous Kennedy-Nixon debates in which the confident young man with the strong Boston accent won over the television audience.

A YOUNG BOYHOOD ON BEALS STREET

Rose Kennedy remembered that books fascinated her son Jack. "He gobbled books," she wrote in her memoir, *Times to Remember* (1974), and his early favorites included such animal tales as *Billy Whiskers: The Autobiography of a Goat* and *The Adventures of Reddy Fox,* the latter by New England writer Thornton Burgess. He would move on to romantic adventures, including Sir Walter Scott's fictional tales of chivalry. The man who would later adopt Camelot as a personal metaphor for his presidency demonstrated a taste much earlier for the legend of the British king. His mother remembered him "reading and rereading his copy of *King Arthur and the Round Table.*" Today in the restored house, a children's edition of Malory's *Le Morte d'Arthur* is on display in the nursery.

Rose Kennedy looked to her recollections in restoring the home, but she also consulted an interior decorator. An employee of the Boston department store Jordan Marsh & Company, Robert Luddington, helped her replace items that were no longer in the family ("good, solid, serviceable, conservative furniture in the taste of the times," Rose explained). He found a soapstone sink and the coal and gas stove, and attempted to find matches for remembered wallpaper. He also suggested the taped tour and, when Mrs. Kennedy's memory failed her, supplemented the decoration and design with memories from his own childhood (fewer than a quarter of the objects on view at Beals Street were owned by the Kennedys).

Above: A studio portrait of the Kennedys, taken in 1921, the year after the move from Beals Street. Pictured are (*left to right*) Joe Jr., Jack, Rosemary, Eunice, and Kathleen, along with parents Joe Sr. and Rose.
John F. Kennedy Presidential Library and Museum

Opposite: The formal parlor and the more casual sitting room were common in the nineteenth-century American house, but the two spaces would gradually meld in the new century into what became generally known by the 1930s as the living room. At the Kennedy house, this living room was part of daily family life as well as a place to entertain guests. The advance of technology was also apparent: in addition to a Boston-made piano (a wedding gift from Rose's uncles), the Kennedys had a Victrola.

When the house was completed, Rose Kennedy made television appearances, including one on *The Merv Griffin Show,* to publicize the opening of the home.

The house as re-created offers a personal view of life circa 1917, but Rose Kennedy's approach was less than all-inclusive. Catholicism was at the core of her personal identity, and she took her children on almost daily visits to St. Aidan's, a nearby Roman Catholic church ("I wanted them to form a habit of making God and religion a part of their lives, not something to be reserved only for Sundays"). Yet religion is largely unrepresented in the home (for example, no crucifix is on view). In the same way, her taped tour omits all mention of the servants, despite the fact that, from the

earliest days in residence, the Kennedys shared the home with staff, including a maid of all work and a nursemaid who lived in two attic rooms. Such omissions remind us that the 1960s were a time when Catholicism was a political liability and the Kennedy scions were sometimes accused of being rich and spoiled.

For all its eccentricities, the place offers an opportunity to wonder about the boy who would grow up to become a president and who, after his assassination ended his presidency with terrible abruptness, left a legacy that still engages historians a half century later. By November 1963, President Kennedy had already sent many young Americans abroad under the auspices of the peace corps and laid plans for man to land on the moon, but his major legislative initiatives (among them bills that anticipated the Civil Rights Act of 1964, Medicare, and federal aid to education) were still pending in Congress when the rifle shots took his life. His successor, Lyndon Johnson, would win passage of these reforms, many of them after his election as president in his own right in 1964, together with two-thirds Democratic majorities in Congress.

Kennedy surely launched a great wave of change, but Johnson applied the rubric by which it came to be known—the Great Society—and signed the bills into law. We cannot know how a longer-lived John Kennedy might have fared in his further dealings with Russia, Cuba, and Vietnam, or how different his reputation would be today had he lived to run for reelection and even to retire from the presidency, still a relatively young man. But at 83 Beals Street, a shy and introspective boy is remembered, as is his mother, the woman of whom Jack Kennedy once said, "She was the glue. She's not as forceful as my father, but she was the glue."

Opposite: Note the earthenware pot on the cookstove. In Rose Kennedy's 1969 taped tour, she remembered, "We always ate Boston baked beans on Saturday night. . . . Everyone had their special recipe for Boston baked beans and piccalilli, which was usually served with them."

Above: Note the twin beds in the master bedroom (Rose recalled them as "fashionable" at the time). Jack was born in this room in the nearer bed.

LOOKING BACKWARD

In the late 1960s, Rose Kennedy sought at the John Fitzgerald Kennedy Birthplace to reproduce the look and character of the home she had known fifty years earlier. The result was a demonstration that the past is not a fixed destination.

Everyone's memories of a given moment or event are subjective and selective, colored by remembered emotions. Even perspectives on earlier times assembled by scholars from documents, period images, and other evidence are necessarily incomplete. The knowledge and attitude of the seeker, the time elapsed, and a hundred other factors color our view of the past. In the case of Rose Kennedy's re-creation of life in Brookline during the World War I era, a warmth and nostalgic simplicity are evident, but there's also a lack of some sociological details she chose to suppress; the result is worthy of the America rendered by her contemporary Norman Rockwell for the *Saturday Evening Post*.

Yet the Kennedy home on Beals Street remains a unique and important historic site both as a place of pilgrimage and, ironically, *because* of Rose Kennedy's angle of approach and what it reveals. The re-created house is accurate in most of its particulars, to some extent because her soft focus is now supplemented by interpreters with a more encompassing view. In the decades since the JFK site was conveyed to the National Park Service, the discipline of historic preservation has been transformed; today's professionals are not interior decorators but students of the past who ask harder questions and conduct thorough research. To the historiographer, how people have chosen to look at the past is itself revealing and important; to a casual historian such as the visitor who steps across the threshold at Beals Street—or, for that matter, at any presidential site—what is on display is but part of the story and is to be regarded as an invitation to learn more about the president and his times. See *For Further Reading*, page 248.

LYNDON B. JOHNSON NATIONAL HISTORICAL PARK

LYNDON JOHNSON
(1963 – 1969)

JOHNSON CITY, TEXAS

"This country has always been a place
where I could come and fill my cup . . . and
recharge myself for the more difficult days ahead."

LYNDON JOHNSON, SPEAKING OF HIS
NATIVE TEXAS HILL COUNTRY IN 1957

THE BOYHOOD HOME

Almost from the moment of his birth, expectations were high for Sam and Rebekah Johnson's firstborn child. The boy was four hours old when his grandfather, showing the baby to a neighbor, predicted he would "be governor of Texas some day." The child's name would come from a lawyer friend (surname: Linden), adding another level of expectation. Though neither his father nor his grandfather lived to see it, Lyndon Baines Johnson (1908–1973) would exceed even their lofty dreams.

One reason would be the boy's mother, Rebekah Baines, who had graduated college (Baylor Female College in Belton, Texas). She had grown up the daughter of a prominent attorney in prosperous Fredericksburg, a sophisticated place for early-century Texas, with both electricity and paved streets. While her move to dusty Johnson City and a house without running water was a shock, she channeled her considerable energies to good effect.

Her instruction was such that Lyndon knew his letters before turning two, recited Tennyson and Longfellow at three, and could read at four. After the family moved to a three-bedroom house in Johnson City when Lyndon was five, Rebekah tutored children in the neighborhood too, teaching dancing, etiquette, manners, and even English as a second language. She trained her precocious eldest child to know he was of a better class and to believe he could do anything. Much later, her son would remember her as "a constant, dogged, determined influence on my life."

The father held sway over his boy too. Initial success in real estate investments meant Sam Johnson's was one of the area's more prosperous families (their Model T was the second car in town). Though Sam spent twelve years in the Texas legislature, his influence on his tall son—Lyndon was already six feet tall at age thirteen—wasn't always what Rebekah had in mind. Sam spent many evenings seated in a brown rocker on the porch, regaling his friends with stories, swapping jokes, and talking local county politics. "Mother found

Previous page: The little stone house that was the original home was subsumed by later wood-frame additions at the LBJ ranch. The result is a pleasing assemblage of boxes with shadowed porches.

Left: Johnson, photographed in 1965, in a characteristic pose. As one newsman said of him, Johnson "made the phone an instrument of national policy." *Yoichi Okamoto/LBJ Library*

Opposite: The sleeping porch was the best place to escape the Texas heat that lingered through the night.

Above: Johnson's boyhood home, restored to look as it did circa 1924, the year that Lyndon graduated from high school. At each of the four corners of the house's footprint are porches with deep overhangs that screen the interior from the heat of the sun.

Opposite, left: In addition to the big wood-fired cookstove, the Johnson kitchen had a smaller kerosene stove for use in the summer to avoid turning the entire house into an oven.

Opposite, right: In the dining room Rebekah Baines Johnson drilled her son every morning. It was a place of pedagogy, the son remembered, where spelling and arithmetic lessons were taught.

little of interest in those nightly sessions," Johnson remembered many years later. "To her, such politics were low and dull, and so were Daddy's friends. . . . Mother was interested in national politics, not local. I think she was hoping that someday my father would run for national office."

Another formative influence on the young Johnson was his place. Geographers call the rolling terrain west of the state capital at Austin the Edwards Plateau, but colloquially it's Texas Hill Country. It's a raw, rugged landscape, higher and drier than East Texas, a semiarid land of tall grasses, scrub brush, and hearty trees. Most of the year, the creek beds are dry, and only the perennial rivers run with water. The first Johnsons settled hard by the Pedernales River before the Civil War, and the clan remained, in the town and along the river.

Unlike in many other parts of Texas, the railroad had yet to arrive here in the early-twentieth century; the poor quality of the land and falling agricultural prices meant ever more limited pros-

pects. In Johnson's boyhood, almost no one he knew got rich; in fact, he saw his father's fortunes declining. Near the end of his life, the former president recalled those years. "My daddy always told me that if I brushed up against the grindstone of life, I'd come away with far more polish than I could get at Harvard or Yale. I wanted to believe it, but somehow I never could."

THE YEARS AWAY

After graduating from high school, Johnson wanted to see another part of the world. Rejecting his mother's demand that he go to college, he lit out for California. At sixteen, he found an independent life, washing dishes and clerking in a law office. Almost three years would elapse before he would seek higher education, and it wasn't at an Ivy League university.

He arrived at Southwest Texas State Teachers College as the self-confident boy (some said spoiled) that his mother had nurtured, but one possessed of a boundless curiosity about politics. A fellow student remembered lanky Lyndon as "seeking information from any and all professors and he talked to them at length [about] . . . anything political." He ingratiated himself with the president of the college, who encouraged him to pursue politics rather than teaching. But before he could, his need to earn tuition money exposed him to another segment of society.

He spent a year teaching at a Mexican American elementary school in South Texas cattle country. Despite feeling exiled in Cotulla, a town later described by Lady Bird Johnson as "one of the crummiest little towns in Texas," he became a passionate teacher. The memory of these lonely days would inform his thinking decades later when, as president, he shaped the umbrella policy known as the Great Society. "My students were poor," he told Congress in a major 1965 address concerning the Voting Rights Act, "and they often came to class without breakfast, hungry. They knew even in their youth the pain of injustice."

Back at college, he proved an adept political organizer, winning friends among local Democrats. He earned his degree and found

work as a teacher, but it was only a matter of time before he took a political job as secretary to newly elected Texas congressman Richard Kleberg. The wealthy heir to a ranching fortune, Kleberg was more interested in golf than government, and left his young aide effectively in charge of his Washington office. "This skinny boy was as green as anybody could be," remembered a senatorial aide who watched Johnson's transformation. "[W]ithin a few months he knew how to operate in Washington better than some who had been here for twenty years."

New Deal Washington had become his home, but it was back in Texas on political business in Austin in 1934 that he met Claudia Alta Taylor. A few months before, she had graduated from the University of Texas; within twenty-four hours of their first meeting,

Lyndon asked the woman called Lady Bird to marry him ("purdy as a lady bird," an African American nursemaid had said of her as a little girl). Three months later they were husband and wife.

The following year he was tapped to run the Texas branch of one of Franklin Delano Roosevelt's programs, the National Youth Administration, a job he performed with characteristic energy, earning the admiration of Eleanor Roosevelt, among others. With the death of a local congressman in February 1937, Johnson ran for the empty seat. He threw himself into the campaign and, despite surgery to remove his appendix two days before the election, returned to Washington a congressman. One of his first initiatives was to help establish an electrical cooperative that transformed life in his native Texas Hill Country.

BUYING BACK THE RANCH

By 1948, Congressman and Mrs. Lyndon Johnson had wealth as well as position. With an inheritance from Lady Bird's father, they had purchased KTBC in 1942; the Austin radio station had been the beginning of a burgeoning communications empire. Their family now included two preschool daughters, Lynda Bird and Luci Baines. Johnson decided that his decade in Congress, though interrupted by service in the U.S. Navy during World War II, had readied him for a seat in the upper house. A previous try for the Senate had ended in defeat, but the outcome this time around would be different.

The 1948 race for the open seat was close, with Johnson winning by a mere 87 votes (and thereby gaining him the sobriquet "Landslide Lyndon"). As was often true of rural Texas politics of the era, some of the ballots in his column were more than likely fraudulent, delivered by South Texas political operatives. But once he

Even when taking a cooling dip in the pool, Johnson wanted a telephone at hand, so he had a special raft fabricated for a floating phone.

joined its ranks, Johnson, as one of his aides remembered, "took to the Senate as if he'd been born there. From the first day on, it was obvious that it was *his* place." After the election of 1950, he became second in command of the Democratic majority as Senate whip, then ascended to majority leader in 1955. By 1956 he coveted the Democratic presidential nomination. Back in Texas, he had also acquired a country estate, as befitted his status as a member of the nation's most exclusive club.

⬦⬦⬦⬦⬦⬦

For Lyndon Johnson, his was a victorious return to the Hill Country. He had left to do good but had done so well he was able to acquire in 1951 the most impressive of the several family properties along the Pedernales River in Stonewall, Texas, some fifteen miles from Johnson City.

The original stone house that stood on the property had been constructed in 1895. Enlarged twice (a wood-frame addition was attached to the north elevation around 1900 and a two-story ell constructed in 1912), the house had been home during Johnson's childhood to his father's sister and her husband. Uncle Clarence Martin was a local lawyer and judge, and Lyndon had warm memories of family gatherings at what he called "the *big* house on the river." By the time he acquired the 243-acre property, however, the house had come to resemble what Lady Bird called "a Charles Addams cartoon of a haunted house."

Johnson was undaunted: his ownership of the ranch would be a mark of status, among both Texans and his brethren in the Senate. It would be a Texas spread where he could entertain at lavish barbecues and unwind from the pressures of public life. But it was also a homecoming. As he wrote to his mother a few years later from Washington, "I want to be roaming up and down the river with my beagle dog as I did when I was a boy."

Lady Bird took charge. She began with the landscape, planting a lawn and trimming trees to open up the view of the riverbank. She hired an Austin architect, J. Roy White, who, for the next thirty years, would be Lady Bird's collaborator. At first, White engineered a renovation in 1952, adding closets and bathrooms, restoring ram-

shackle porches. After a heart attack that nearly took Lyndon Johnson's life in 1955, a pool and cabana were added. In 1957, J. Roy White designed an office addition.

As Johnson's national prominence rose, so did that of his ranch. A 3,570-foot asphalt landing strip was constructed to save travel time. As majority leader, Johnson welcomed powerful friends and foreign dignitaries such as Mexican president Adolfo López Mateos. As vice president—Johnson's presence on the 1960 ticket helped Kennedy carry Texas and much of the South—he welcomed Chancellor Konrad Adenauer of West Germany and Field Marshal Muhammad Ayub Khan of Pakistan. The ranch was a place apart from the urban America of skyscrapers. At the LBJ ranch, where cattle grazed and grasses grew tall, the Johnsons' guests were reminded that America's roots were in working the land and in its wide-open spaces.

Above: Showing off his land was one of Johnson's pleasures. He would climb behind the wheel of his car, typically a convertible, and drive across his pastures, often at high speed, taking along guests, reporters, and friends. During his presidency, he would escape the watchful eyes of Secret Service agents, showing off his cattle as he crisscrossed the more than two thousand acres of the ranch.

Left: Lyndon Johnson greets members of the German press, along with columnist Drew Pearson, beneath the spreading oak at the ranch in 1967.
Mike Geissinger / LBJ Library

THE TEXAS WHITE HOUSE

The schedule for November 22, 1963, called for a day of politicking in Dallas, followed by a short flight to the Hill Country, where Jack and Jackie Kennedy were to be the guests of the Johnsons. But the gunfire heard at Dealey Plaza changed everything. That afternoon, Air Force One headed to Washington; once in the air, Lyndon Johnson was sworn in as the first Texan president.

Johnson's sudden ascent to the nation's highest office after John F. Kennedy's assassination would also mean a transformation for the ranch. Major improvements in infrastructure—transportation access, security, communications, and administration—were well under way by the time the new president arrived to celebrate Christmas 1963, as he would several times during his presidency. The changes at the ranch were all the more important because Johnson, more than any of his predecessors, regularly ran the business of the country from his home, which was soon termed the "Texas White House." As many as one hundred people—cabinet officials, staff,

support personnel, family, and guests—would make the trip from the nation's capital to the Hill Country, often accompanied by an even larger press contingent. The Johnsons would stay for much of July and August, and visit again for a long stay in November and December, with periodic shorter visits the rest of the year.

Johnson would spend a quarter of his presidency at his Texas residence, and the ranch looks much as it did during his presidential years. For many present-day visitors, that continuity makes it a suitable place to look back at the 1960s, when American society, seemingly so steady and stable in the previous decade, experienced seismic changes.

Some pundits called him the "accidental president," but once he took office, Lyndon Johnson's parliamentary skills, honed in Congress, and his personal predilections—many of them dating from a childhood informed by the difficulties of life in the Hill Country—enabled him to shape the programs that he described as the War on Poverty and the Great Society. There were education measures that funded schools and offered college grants for low-income students, but Medicare and Medicaid were also Johnson-era creations. He signed into law the Clean Air Act (1963), the National Historic Preservation Act (1966), and the first Endangered Species Act (1966). For African Americans, the Civil Rights Act (1964) and the Voting Rights Act (1965) fundamentally altered their roles in society.

Yet Johnson's place in history will also be defined by a fixed notion that shaped his foreign policy: as he once told his ambassador to South Vietnam, Henry Cabot Lodge, "I'm not going to go down in history as the first American president who lost a war." The decision to stay the course in Vietnam was, to Johnson, a matter of national honor; for an ever-more-vocal portion of the electorate opposed to the war, it made him the enemy. Even today, that tension affects perceptions of the man and his place in history.

Johnson decided in March 1968 not to seek reelection; in January of the following year he retired to his ranch. He would live out his days there, dying four years later, on January 22, 1973, just hours after his successor in the Oval Office, Richard M. Nixon, called to tell him that a cease-fire had been reached in Vietnam.

Above: Johnson's insistence on personally monitoring the media meant he was almost never disconnected from either a television or a radio. When it came time for the evening news, he watched all three major networks simultaneously. In an era long before today's ubiquitous remote, he had a device engineered that enabled him to raise or lower the volume so he could be sure to hear what was being said about him.

Opposite: The chair at the head of the table looks a bit out of place—it's recognizably an executive office chair—and Lady Bird did not look with favor upon it. But Johnson held court in upholstered comfort, periodically interrupting the proceedings to talk on a telephone that was mounted just out of sight on the table's undercarriage. No doubt Mrs. Johnson liked that even less.

Right: During LBJ's recuperation from his 1955 heart attack, the living room at the ranch was temporarily transformed into the majority leader's office, complete with secretaries and ringing phones. A dedicated office space was clearly needed, and the result was a twenty-eight-foot-square structure, which accommodated desks for Johnson and two secretaries, as well as a portrait of a beloved dog.

RICHARD NIXON
BIRTHPLACE

RICHARD M. NIXON
(1969 – 1974)

YORBA LINDA, CALIFORNIA

"The one sure thing about politics is that

what goes up comes down,

and what goes down often comes up."

RICHARD NIXON

"THE SETTING WAS IDYLLIC"

I was born in a house my father built." So remembered Richard Nixon (1913–1994) in the opening line of his bestselling autobiography, *RN: The Memoirs of Richard Nixon* (1978). The year of his birth was 1913, during the coldest January anyone could remember in an unincorporated settlement some thirty-five miles south of Los Angeles (today's city of Yorba Linda). For most of the year, it was more Edenic, as inhabitants of the farming community of some two hundred people could enjoy the sight of the Pacific to the southwest, a view of the San Bernardino Mountains to the north, and air perfumed with the aroma of lemon and orange trees.

Named after an English king (Richard the Lionhearted), the boy was the second in a brood of five brothers. Dick, as he was known in the household, spent his first nine years living in the little house on the small hill, amid the eight acres of his father's grove of lemon trees. An irrigation canal a few feet from the house brought water to nourish the trees, from which his father, Frank Nixon, worked hard to extract a living.

After losing his mother at eight, Francis Anthony Nixon had dropped out of school at eleven and left home at fourteen. He worked as a motorman on a streetcar in his native Ohio before drifting west. He became a ranch hand in Whittier, where he began to attend Quaker meetings (the town was named for Quaker poet John Greenleaf Whittier). There he met Hannah Milhous, daughter of a Quaker elder. After a four-month courtship, they were married. For a time they remained in Whittier, but Frank eventually decided to seek his fortune as a farmer.

As a parent, he was a disciplinarian and a believer in corporal punishment, though Dick managed to master his father's rules well enough that, as he later remembered, his brothers more often than he "felt the touch of the ruler or the strap." His father was a shouter, partly due to growing deafness but mostly because he liked nothing better than an argument. As one neighbor remembered, "You would make him happy if you argued on either side." Though a quiet, self-contained lad, his second son certainly absorbed something from his father's fondness for disputation: Dick distinguished himself early as a sophomore member of his high school debate team and, later, as a successful college debater.

Nixon's mother, Hannah Milhous Nixon, was of another breed. Hannah was devout, and the Nixons raised their boys in the Quaker faith, worshipping in Dick's early years at the Yorba Linda Friends Church, which the Nixons had helped organize. As the only female in the house, Hannah was patient—the word *saintly* was used to describe her by several who knew her—but, as Nixon himself remembered, she was also "intensely private in her feelings and emotions." She would be physically as well as emotionally distant during Richard's childhood; when he was a baby she wet-nursed another child, and later she spent two years in Arizona with his ailing brother Arthur, who would die at age seven of tuberculosis.

Previous spread: The plain small house where Richard Nixon was born, framed by an immense California peppertree that Frank Nixon planted in 1914; the Richard Nixon Presidential Library and Museum complex is visible to the rear. The one-story house had five rooms on the main floor, with the boys' bedroom built into the pitched roof at the rear.

Above: The original Crown piano once again has pride of place in the sitting room. Nixon took up the piano at age seven and played throughout his life. He favored show tunes and the music of Duke Ellington.

In the cramped bedroom at the top of the narrow (twenty-two-inch-wide) stairs, the boys—Dick, Harold, Don, and Arthur Nixon—all slept. "It was crowded. We sometimes had arguments. But except for occasional pillow fights, we all got along famously."

Richard spent extended periods during his early years away from his immediate family with aunts. The poles of his childhood would be his mother's peaceful and kind but remote demeanor and, in the son's words, the "scrappy, belligerent fighter" that was his father.

Richard Nixon exhibited his intellectual capacity early on. As a kindergartner he recited long poems from memory; at age six, the precocious boy took to reading the newspaper. Like many bright children, however, he kept to himself. "Dick was always reserved," recalled his younger brother Donald, ". . . the studious one of the bunch, always doing more reading while the rest of us were out having more fun."

Life in Yorba Linda wasn't easy. At first, the house had neither electricity nor indoor toilets. Over the years, the clay soil proved ill-adapted to growing citrus, and the Nixon farm failed. At age nine, young Dick Nixon moved with his family to nearby Whittier, where, for much of his adolescence, he would help out in the family store his father ran, with the gas pumps out front and his father doing the butchering out back.

BEYOND WHITTIER

Richard remained at home even after he matriculated at Whittier College, helping to run the store. Yet he managed to play football (his career was distinguished more by his discipline and desire than by his on-field talent). He acted in plays, earned academic honors, and was elected student body president. Though not much of a dancer himself, his key campaign pledge was to end the Quaker college's prohibition of dancing.

Academic success at Whittier College helped him win a scholarship of $250 to Duke University Law School, a sum large enough to cover his fees for the year. In 1937 he was awarded his law degree, having earned the respect of his classmates at Duke (remarking upon the long hours the Californian spent at the library, one classmate observed that Nixon had "what it takes to learn the law—an iron butt"). He returned to Whittier and joined a law practice, which eventually led to an involvement with local Republican politics.

Top: In Frank and Hannah's bedroom, a still life of dresser, mirror, and family photos.

Bottom: In a houseful of males, Mrs. Nixon had a small space to call her own, which Nixon remembered as very much his mother's realm.

Above: In the bedroom—and in this bedstead, which she shared with her husband—Hannah Milhous Nixon gave birth to son Richard on January 9, 1913. "Our family doctor," Nixon later wrote, "wrapped me in a blanket after delivering me and put me in a laundry basket to keep warm." The friendship quilt on the bed was a wedding gift to Frank and Hannah.

Opposite: As Richard Nixon himself remembered, "The back rooms were my mother's domain. . . . But the most special room was the kitchen. My mother was an excellent baker. Her specialty was angel food cake."

A continued interest in amateur theatricals introduced him to Thelma Catherine Ryan. After meeting at the first rehearsal for a George S. Kaufman and Alexander Woollcott melodrama, *The Dark Tower,* Dick told the slim, hazel-eyed "Pat" Ryan that one day they would marry; two years later, in 1940, they did. After the United States entered the war, he and Pat moved to Washington, where he served in the Office of Price Administration before shipping out to the Pacific. As a line officer, he rose to the rank of lieutenant commander in the U.S. Navy.

After the war, Richard Nixon's passion—and instinct—for politics emerged full-blown. Invited by a Whittier banker to run for Congress, he won a seat in the U.S. House of Representatives in 1946, defeating an incumbent Democrat whom Nixon managed to associate in the public mind with Communists. Once in Washington he became a national figure, in large part for his role in the Alger Hiss affair. Hiss, who was accused of being a member of the Communist Party during government service, denied it before the House Un-American Activities Committee, of which Nixon was an active member. Hiss subsequently served time in federal prison for perjury. During his second term in Congress, Nixon ran for the Senate, and it was during the 1950 Senate race that he gained a new moniker. After his campaign referred to his opponent, Helen Gahagan Douglas, as the "Pink Lady," the opposition returned the favor, dubbing the Republican candidate "Tricky Dick."

In 1952, the thirty-nine-year-old Nixon was elected as vice president, helping bring first convention delegates and then voters to his running mate, Dwight David Eisenhower. Nixon served two terms as the nation's vice president, but his string of electoral victories came to an end when John F. Kennedy defeated him by a narrow margin in the presidential contest of 1960. A second defeat in the California gubernatorial race of 1962 found Nixon, exhausted and hungover the day after his defeat, snarling at reporters, "You won't have Nixon to kick around anymore because, gentlemen, this is my last press conference."

The promise proved premature. After six years out of office—the "wilderness years," he called them—Nixon defeated an old Senate colleague, Hubert Horatio Humphrey, for the presidency in 1968.

THE NIXON PRESIDENTIAL LIBRARY AND BIRTHPLACE

For many people, the memory of Richard M. Nixon involves a helicopter. On August 9, 1974, a small army of photographers

Richard M. Nixon, in a familiar pose, bidding farewell to the presidency.
Richard Nixon Presidential Library and Museum

recorded the ascent of Marine One from the South Lawn of the White House. The Sikorsky VH3A aircraft carried the former president—that day he had become the first (and, thus far, the only) man to resign the office—to an uncertain future. A month later Nixon would learn his fate, when President Gerald Ford granted "a full, free, and absolute pardon." Thirty years on, that helicopter, long retired from presidential use, was restored and installed on the grounds of the Nixon Presidential Library in Yorba Linda, where visitors are invited to step aboard.

Nearby is Nixon's birthplace, still in its original location. It was a kit house, which was common in the early years of the twentieth century. Sears, Roebuck and Company and Montgomery Ward, among other purveyors, sold such houses by mail order. The customer purchased a design pictured in a catalog, and the precut pieces arrived by rail packed in a boxcar. Following the specifica-

tions and instructions provided, the purchaser could assemble a sturdy, inexpensive domicile; the construction of the Nixon home may well have been a community affair, with neighbors and Friends arriving to raise the roof. The cost to Frank Nixon was in the range of $1,000 and the result was a bungalow-style home.

After the Nixons departed in 1922, a variety of private owners resided in the home for a quarter century. In 1948, the Yorba Linda School District assumed ownership, and the modest home became the custodian's residence for what later was named the Richard Nixon Elementary School. In 1978, the home was acquired by the Richard Nixon Birthplace Foundation; since 2006, the site, including the Richard Nixon Presidential Library, which contains some eighty thousand square feet of exhibition, library, storage, event, and other spaces, has been administered by the National Archives and Records Administration.

A COMPLEX LEGACY

The Richard Nixon Presidential Library and Museum seeks to aid scholars and the general public alike in understanding a man whose name, nearly two decades after his 1994 death, still provokes controversy.

His was an eventful—and often paradoxical—presidency. He inherited a war in Southeast Asia and, during his years in office, expanded the bombing campaign in North Vietnam and ordered an invasion of Cambodia. The latter provoked antiwar demonstrations across the nation; at one of them, on the campus of Kent State University in Ohio, four students were killed when National Guardsmen fired upon rock-throwing protestors. Yet it was also Nixon who ended the war, when the Paris Peace Accords were signed in January 1973 and American troops, who had numbered more than half a million, came home.

Though a longtime antagonist of Communism, Nixon established new and productive relations with the USSR, signing treaties that limited strategic armaments. In 1972 he made an unprecedented trip to the People's Republic of China; the rapprochement opened political and trade relations, the ramifications of which have only become truly apparent in the years since President Nixon's death.

In a life replete with ironies, none was greater than the 1972 Nixon campaign. Despite the candidate's status as a popular incumbent facing a deeply divided Democratic Party, the Committee for the Re-Election of the President (known as CRP and, later, CREEP) dispatched a five-man team to break into the headquarters of the Democratic National Committee; the men were arrested in the act of installing listening devices at the DNC. That autumn, Nixon would win a remarkable forty-nine of fifty states (his opponent, George McGovern, carried just Massachusetts), only to be forced to resign in 1974 in the face of almost certain impeachment.

Nixon was one of the most memorable and polarizing men of his generation, a man whose jowls, trademark five o'clock shadow, and moody demeanor made him an appealing target for caricature. He was a public man famous for his secretiveness but one who possessed a remarkable knack for the memorable public moment. The American political vocabulary of the second half of the twentieth century is spiced with Nixonian terminology. There's his Checkers speech of 1952 (where he defended his use of campaign donations, disarming many with his refusal, since his daughters had grown fond of the animal, to return the cocker spaniel the family had been given). The 1959 "Kitchen Debate" gave the Cold War a human aspect (it was a spontaneous exchange between Vice President Nixon and Soviet premier Khrushchev, in which the two debated the virtues of Communism and capitalism while standing in an exhibition hall featuring an American kitchen). There were the Kennedy-Nixon debates of 1960; the White House tapes; the foreign affairs concept of détente; and, perhaps most of all, the Watergate scandal, as the presidency-ending break-in and its aftermath came to be known, having occurred at a then-obscure office complex in Washington, D.C., of the same name.

In his later years, Nixon sought to embody the notion of the elder statesman; the image of the former president seated at a piano in the U.S. embassy in Moscow playing "God Bless America" for Mikhail Gorbachev is striking. Jimmy Carter was the first, but many of those who succeeded him in office, including Reagan, Bush, and Clinton, all consulted the exiled Nixon. His rehabilitation advanced another magnitude when his library was dedicated at a ceremony attended by Gerald Ford, Ronald Reagan, and sitting president George H. W. Bush. But it was Nixon himself who told the crowd of fifty thousand, standing within sight of the home his father built, where he had been born seventy-seven years before, "Nothing we have ever seen matches this moment—to be welcomed home again."

The graves of Richard Milhous Nixon and Thelma Catherine Ryan Nixon at the Nixon Presidential Library and Museum.

JIMMY CARTER
NATIONAL
HISTORIC SITE

JAMES EARL CARTER
(1977 – 1981)

PLAINS, GEORGIA

"Plains has been a haven for us, drawing us
back when I left the navy, the governor's office,
and the White House. . . . Whenever we are away,
there is always a quiet yearning
to come back home."

JIMMY CARTER, *WHITE HOUSE DIARY*, 2010

AN ENDURING CONNECTION

I n Sumter County, nothing has changed — and everything has. To visit the rural Georgia town where both Jimmy and Rosalynn Carter were born is to journey into a sleepy, rural past; but the Carters are still here, a vibrant presence among the six hundred or so other residents, living in a modest ranch house built for them fifty years ago.

For the former president, Plains is a place where he relaxes and recharges after his many travels. He teaches Sunday school when he's in town, usually to a full house at the Maranatha Baptist Church. His old campaign headquarters in the train depot contains an exhibition devoted to his long-shot run and victory in the presidential election of 1976. With a number of Carter-related properties now administered by the National Park Service, there is a

museum and visitor center at the old Plains High School from which both Jimmy and Rosalynn, his wife of more than six and a half decades, graduated.

Yet it is the two Carter homes that offer the clearest view of the boy who grew up to serve as the thirty-ninth president of the United States. One is a simple house that has been restored to the Depression-era appearance of his boyhood. The other is his present home, to which he returned after his four years in the White House, only to embark on more than three decades of international statesmanship as perhaps the most active ex-president in United States history.

THE BOYHOOD HOME

In his memoir, *An Hour Before Daylight,* Jimmy Carter (1924–) describes the wood-frame house of his childhood. "Set back about fifty feet from the dirt road, it was square, painted tan to match the dust. . . . The rooms were laid out in 'shotgun' style, with a hall that went down the middle of the house dividing the living room, dining room, and kitchen on the left from three bedrooms on the right." The house was as plain and unadorned as Carter's prose.

Previous page: Carter's father ran a commissary on his farm, one where farmworkers could purchase basic foodstuffs, kerosene, household supplies, tobacco, and gas from the pump out front.

Left: Two Plains natives, Jimmy Carter and Rosalynn Smith Carter, in a contemporary photo taken at Jimmy's boyhood home.
Jimmy Carter National Historic Site / National Park Service

Opposite: During Carter's boyhood, the deep porch across the front of the house was the place the family spent much of its time in warm weather—which was, Carter remembers, "about nine months of the year." The pecan trees that shade the home were planted by the James Earl Carters, Jr. and Sr.

The source of water was a hand pump on the back porch. There was a privy in the backyard (and each bedroom had a chamber pot). As a boy, Jimmy was required to tote bucketfuls of water to the kitchen and to carry wood, sawed and chopped at the backyard woodpile, to feed the kitchen stove and the fireplaces. It wasn't until James Earl Carter Sr. ordered a windmill from a Sears, Roebuck and Company catalog that the family had a bathroom with a flushable toilet and a makeshift shower that used a bucket with holes in the bottom as a showerhead.

Jimmy was the oldest of four children in the Carter family, with two younger sisters, Gloria and Ruth, and a still younger brother, Billy, born in 1937. James and Lillian Gordy Carter grew most of their own food in a large fenced-in garden and nearby fields. They kept a small dairy herd of Jerseys and Guernseys, and raised hogs, sheep, and goats. Horses and mules were essential for the work of the farm. When chicken was on the menu, it was often Jimmy's job to catch and kill one of the hens or fryers kept for just that purpose. Corn—served as grits, hominy, or corn bread—was the staple grain of the household. With the barn, the sheds, a blacksmith and carpenter shop, and a network of fences, pens, and gardens, it was a busy and cluttered farm.

The Carter home stood in Archery, a tiny hamlet on the outskirts of Plains. Most of the Carters' neighbors were African American; at the time, segregation was the law, and the Carter farm relied upon black workers who lived in small clapboard houses on the property. The future president came to look upon one of those

men, Jack Clark, as a friend, having spent a great deal of time learning from him and visiting the home Jack shared with his wife, Rachel, who was also a child-care provider for the Carters. But, in the way of the times, the legal doctrine of "separate but equal" meant that, even in relations between a boy and a man he admired, there would always be a calibrated distance. Carter's mother, Lillian, was among the few whites who refused to see the color line. As her daughter-in-law Rosalynn recalled, "She was a registered nurse, and no matter who was sick, black or white, she was there. Always."

The complexity of race relations in the South was demonstrated on the night of the much-anticipated 1938 bout between Joe Louis, an African American, and German Max Schmeling. Several black neighbors asked Jimmy's daddy if they could listen on the Carters' battery-powered radio (electrification had yet to reach Archery). The radio was duly placed on a windowsill, but the fight didn't last long, as Louis quite literally came out swinging. His barrage of punches sent Schmeling to the canvas three times before the American was declared the winner, barely two minutes into the fight.

At Yankee Stadium, where the fight was held, all was in tumult; in Plains, Carter remembers, "We heard a quiet, 'Thank you, Mr. Earl,'" as the men left the yard, bound for a tenant house across the street. There, a loud and raucous celebration ensued that lasted all night. Carter, who would become the first Southern president in generations, wrote of the Louis-Schmeling fight decades later. "The mores of our segregated society," Carter explained, "had been honored."

THE NAVY AND AFTER

Plains was a little town with no movie theater or library. Though its churches had provided a core social experience for the Carter family (Jimmy Carter's Christian faith has played an important role throughout his life), the lure of the larger world proved irresistible to the young man. Appointed to the United States Naval Academy, Carter earned his degree in Annapolis, Maryland, then promptly married Rosalynn Smith, who was three years his junior. The couple embarked on the itinerant life of a military family, living in Norfolk, Hawaii, San Diego, New London, and Schenectady. Carter became a submariner, pursued graduate studies in nuclear physics,

---

Above: Jimmy Carter is still an essential man in his hometown, as this image of the main streetscape in Plains suggests.

Below: The bedrooms, like the rest of the house, are simple, functional rooms, with few decorations.

and was appointed to serve as a senior officer on the *Seawolf,* which was to be the nation's second nuclear submarine.

The expected course of the son's life changed when, in 1953, James Earl Carter Sr. was diagnosed with pancreatic cancer. Jimmy returned home on a week's leave to spend time with his dying father. Sitting at his father's bedside, he was struck by the sheer number of visitors, black and white, who came to express their gratitude to his father. Many confided in the young Navy lieutenant how important a role Mr. Earl had played in their lives. He had loaned money to needy neighbors, bought graduation clothes for children of families who hadn't the means, and even supported a widow for many years after her husband's death. Those deeds had been done quietly, with no public acknowledgment.

Inspired by his father's example, he resigned his commission and returned to Plains with Rosalynn and their three young sons. He assumed management of Carter's Warehouse, his father's farm-supply and seed company in Plains, as well as the family's agricultural holdings. His father had been a Georgia legislator, and Jimmy soon followed him into public service, first on county boards—school, hospital, library—before winning a seat in the Georgia Senate in 1962. He ran for governor in 1966 but, when no candidate won a majority of the vote, the legislature decided the election in favor of Lester Maddox. Four years later, however, Carter did win election to the state's highest office, and the Carters' home away from home became the Governor's Mansion in Atlanta. In December 1974, he announced his candidacy for president; his two-year quest resulted in a hard-fought electoral victory over Gerald Ford.

His four years in Washington are often remembered as a difficult time for the nation, with high inflation and interest rates, soaring oil prices, and the economy in recession. A revolution in Iran produced the most visible foreign-policy crisis of the Carter administration when sixty-six Americans were seized at the U.S. embassy in Tehran and held hostage for more than a year, leaving the president looking powerless as his country was called the "Great Satan." Carter did create the Department of Education, shape a coherent energy policy, and, together with Egyptian president Anwar Sādāt and Israeli prime

As a boy, Carter learned tool sense from his father, a blacksmith and woodworker; as a former president, he makes furniture in his wood shop.

minister Menachem Begin, advance the cause of peace in the Middle East with the Camp David Accords in 1978. But he didn't succeed in negotiating the release of the hostages in Iran until January 20, 1981, the day of Ronald Reagan's inauguration and the beginning of what Carter himself has called his "involuntary retirement."

COMING HOME

"When Jimmy lost the election in 1980," Rosalynn Carter wrote in her memoir, *First Lady from Plains,* "there was no question about where we would go: We would go home."

Home was the house that Jimmy, Rosalynn, and their sons had moved into in 1962 and where their fourth child, Amy, was born in

1967. The same comfortable but modest ranch-style house remains their residence today.

The garage has been converted into a woodworking shop — the president's staff, on his departure from Washington, gave him an array of tools and machinery to pursue his hobby. There's a guest house on the upper level.

The house itself is like millions of others across the country: two bedrooms, a parlor, a dining room, a kitchen, and a family room. A mixed-used library, office, and exercise room has been added at one end of the home. The place is a contrast to the grand homes where they spent time during Jimmy Carter's years in office. Both the Georgia Governor's Mansion and the White House are museums as much as they are domiciles, full of antique furniture, fine art, and other treasures. But at the home in Plains, much of the art came from Jimmy Carter's own easel, including landscapes and character studies. Many pieces of furniture too are his handiwork, fabricated and finished in his converted garage.

Plains has always been a place where Carter can put on his jeans, go fishing, visit with old friends on Main Street, or walk his fields and forest (he still owns acreage in Plains that produces cotton, wheat, peanuts, and timber). But when he left office, he was determined that his postpresidential days would be more than a mere retirement from public life.

He has become a prolific writer, with more than a dozen books to his credit, some of them on his political life but others that address his faith, aging, and international affairs. He's written a novel and a book for children too.

He has been a professor at Emory University in Atlanta for three decades, and the university is also home to the Carter Center, which, along with the Jimmy Carter Library and Museum, occupies a thirty-five-acre park on the outskirts of Atlanta. The Carter Center has established programs in more than seventy nations, many of them among the world's poorest, seeking to address issues such as conflict mediation, election monitoring, and disease prevention. Carter himself has traveled widely, visiting such trouble spots as North Korea, Haiti, Ethiopia, the Sudan, Palestine, and Bosnia. Habitat for Humanity and the Rosalynn Carter Institute for Caregiving are other organizations to which the Carters have committed their time and energy. Carter's good works in his post-presidential years have won him admiration and accolades, including the 2002 Nobel Peace Price for what the Nobel Committee called "decades of untiring effort to find peaceful solutions to international conflicts, to advance democracy and human rights, and to promote economic and social development."

Back in Plains, fifteen acres of the original Carter holdings in Archery have become the Jimmy Carter Boyhood Farm, a historic site that tells something of the story of Carter's boyhood but represents in a larger way how rural families lived in the South during the Great Depression. The farmhouse and other structures, including the Carter store and the home of Jack and Rachel Clark, have been restored to their circa 1937 appearance.

The private residence today remains just that—private and not open to the public—though the current Carter home and compound have been deeded to the nation and one day will be open for tours as part of the Jimmy Carter National Historic Site. The Carters these days typically divide their time between the residence in Plains and an apartment at the Carter Center in Atlanta, though their many commitments often take them overseas.

If Jimmy Carter is a man of the world—and surely he is—Plains has always provided him a sense of continuity. He returned after his naval service and after his presidency, and continues to do so following journeys to distant destinations. Plains has always been the place where Jimmy Carter comes home to renew his connection to the red soil of Sumter County.

Opposite: The home office, with walls of books to read and a computer on which to write them.

Right: The family room (*above*) is a tall-ceilinged and casual room, the parlor (*below*) more formal, with two of the former president's canvases hung over the sofa.

RANCHO DEL CIELO

RONALD REAGAN
(1981 – 1989)

SANTA BARBARA, CALIFORNIA

"We relax at the ranch, which, if not heaven itself,

probably has the same zip code."

RONALD REAGAN

◇◇◇◇◇◇◇◇◇◇

"IT SURE LOOKS LIKE GOAT COUNTRY TO ME"

With the arrival of the New Year, Ronald Reagan prepared to ride off into the sunset. In January 1975, after decades of public life as an athlete, broadcaster, star of B movies, trade union executive, corporate spokesman, and two-term chief executive of a state with an economy greater than that of most countries, he was about to vacate his corner office. He would journey southward, but before reaching Santa Barbara, he and Nancy would turn left off U.S. Route 101 onto a dusty, winding road that rose into the Santa Ynez Mountains.

Reagan had owned country properties before, including a horse ranch in Northridge and the 350-acre Yearling Row in Malibu, but Tip Top Ranch, as it was known to the locals, loomed as his own personal Eden. After eight years as governor, he was ready to leave

behind the demands he memorialized in a poem composed on his last day in office. "Budgets / Battles / Phone calls / Hassles," wrote Reagan. "Letters / Meetings / Luncheons / Speeches. / Politics and / Press Releases. / News confences / Delegations / Plaques and / Presentations. / Travels / Briefings / Confrontations. / Crises / Routines / Mediation." No

longer in harness to the people of California, he would be free to build fences out of old telephone poles, clear brush, and take daily rides on his favorite horse, the large black gelding known as Little Man. Though born in Illinois, Reagan had long since adopted the ethos of the Western cowboy as his own. "People who haven't tried it might be surprised," Reagan explained with characteristic folksiness, "how easy your thoughts can come together when you're on the back of a horse riding with nothing else to do but think about the decision ahead of you."

Nancy and Ronald Reagan had first seen the site north of Santa Barbara a year earlier. The steep, narrow country road zigzagged for seven miles up a rugged hillside to an altitude of some 2,400 feet, where granite peaks offered a towering view of the craggy Pacific coast. But the journey continued beyond the summit, since the unfancy ranch home was situated in an upland canyon. As Reagan recalled that first visit, "I thought, well, maybe somebody's got a house up here they call a ranch, but it sure looks like goat country to me. Where would you ride a horse?"

Previous page: The tack room in the barn contains a range of bridles and saddles; it was clearly a place of pride for Reagan the horseman.

Left: The nation's fortieth president, astride a horse, at his beloved ranch. *Young America's Foundation*

Opposite: An early-morning fog burns off at Rancho del Cielo.

As they eased down the dirt drive on the 688-acre property, the visitors passed through a stand of coastal live oaks. A nondescript house was set into a gentle slope, its porch opening to the north and east, but their eyes were drawn to the generous rolling meadow that seemed to meld with the sky at the horizon.

The Reagans purchased that ranch with its five-room adobe house in November 1974, and the soon-to-be-former governor had plans for the place. The rickety porch with a corrugated tin roof

Reagan converted a seasonal pool into a year-round pond by lining it to prevent leakage and filling it with well water. He dubbed it "Lake Lucky" in honor of Mrs. Reagan's mother, Edith Luckett, and stocked it with ornamental koi. He also gave Nancy a canoe; the two-person craft was called *Truluv*.

had to come off. The tiny bedroom would be enlarged, along with many of the too-small windows.

While more than eligible for Social Security—exactly a month after leaving office, Reagan would enter his sixty-fifth year on February 6, 1975—he remained a remarkable physical specimen: tall, upright, and muscular, possessed of a hankering for hard, physical work. With the help of former California Highway patrolmen Barney Barnett and Dennis LeBlanc, he would remake the ranch as he wanted it. He would give it a new name too, one suggested by the site itself. "You feel you are on a cloud looking down at the world," Reagan wrote of the place he chose to call *Rancho del Cielo*. In the Spanish of California's first European settlers, it means "Ranch in the Heavens."

THE REAGAN RANCH

Reagan's life plan in those early months of retirement appeared ambiguous. On the one hand, as Nancy wrote of their departure from Sacramento that January, "I honestly believed we were leaving politics forever." On the other, the man she called Ronnie refused to offer a definitive yes or no when asked whether he wished to be president. In the fullness of time, his ultimate destination would emerge, but what was abundantly clear in early 1975 was his desire to go to work on their new property.

The house in the mountains would be seasonal, but from late February to November it would be Reagan's backcountry escape. Coming and going on day trips that spring from the Reagan home in Pacific Palisades ninety miles away, Reagan and coworkers Barney and Dennis demolished a wall, cutting through the adobe bricks that had been made on site of native sand, clay, and water. They found that the original house, probably built around 1898, was sound, but they added a surface of metal tiles fabricated to resemble the clay tiles of mission-style architecture.

Inside the home, they opened larger windows to welcome more light into what had been a cramped and dark dwelling. Nancy helped lay a new tile floor. The old porch became a bright and spa-

cious family room, with a dining table, comfortable chairs, and a tall bookcase. In remodeling the kitchen, Reagan maintained his allegiance to an old employer from his days as a corporate spokesman, installing General Electric appliances.

A domestication of the acreage was undertaken too: clearing trails, building fences of recycled telephone poles (Reagan enjoyed wielding a chain saw, cutting the timbers into posts), and transforming a vernal pool into a permanent pond. The ranch remained far from a suburban tract: the human inhabitants of the Santa Ynez would always share the wild terrain with mountain lions, bears, and snakes, and Reagan and his ranch hands managed to capture more than a hundred of the latter, which they took beyond the borders of his property to deposit in a pond soon known as "snake lake."

Despite the pungent fragrance of wild sagebrush, everyone sensed the allure for Ronald Reagan of another life, one in national politics. His regular radio commentaries were popular. CBS correspondent Mike Wallace came to the ranch, and in October 1975 *60 Minutes* ran a profile titled "Mister Right." Reagan took Wallace for a ride in his jeep and told him that New Deal Democrat Franklin Delano Roosevelt was his inspiration ("He took his case to the people," said Reagan).

Once he declared himself a candidate for president on November 15, 1975, Reagan rose quickly in the polls. He would lose the Republican nomination a year later to incumbent Gerald Ford, but his speech at the 1976 Republican National Convention raised his national visibility. Summoned to the stage by chants of "We want Ron" from the floor, he addressed the packed auditorium in Kansas City and, perhaps more important, a national television audience. The speech he gave demonstrated the truth in the words of former governor Pat Brown of California, whom Reagan had beaten in 1966: "There's no more persuasive man in the United States on television than Ronald Reagan." Four years after the convention, Reagan defeated Jimmy Carter to become the nation's fortieth president.

THE WESTERN WHITE HOUSE

While the ranch had been an important private place in the time leading up to the 1980 election, Rancho del Cielo became Reagan's essential refuge for the next eight years. The presidential entourage would arrive on Air Force One at nearby Point Mugu Naval Air Station, where Reagan would board a helicopter for the last leg of the journey to the ranch. He kept the press corps at a discreet distance; along with White House staff members, the reporters and photographers took up residence in Santa Barbara, some thirty miles away, many at the Biltmore Hotel. Even the president's staff lived off the premises, and at night the Reagans had the ranch to themselves aside from the White House physician, a military aide, and a few

---

Opposite: The ranch was originally part of a larger Spanish land grant, but its first individual owner was José Jesús Pico. He paid $32 for the property and, during the last quarter of the nineteenth century, built the adobe home, grew vegetables and grapes, and raised livestock.

Below: Set beneath the overhang of the entryway is the now-famous "Tax-Cut Table," on which the fortieth president signed the Economic Recovery Tax Act in 1981.

United States Secret Service agents housed in a newly constructed compound nestled into a forested hillside behind the home.

The rituals at the ranch were well established. Reagan liked to rise before the sun, and his official day began with the arrival of mail and security documents brought by an aide. Once he had made his phone calls and written his letters, tending to what he called his "homework," he would saddle Little Man or a white Arabian stallion named El Alamein, a 1981 gift from the president of Mexico. The ranch and surrounding properties were crisscrossed with tree-lined riding trails and, often accompanied by Nancy, the president would while away the rest of the morning on horseback. Summoned by a big bell rung promptly at the noon hour, they'd eat lunch; in the afternoon, Reagan would work around the property, building fences, pruning madrone trees, delighting in the out-of-doors. In one two-week visit in 1984, Reagan, Barney, and Dennis built a patio and cleared a stretch of woods. After a day's work, as Reagan himself described a typical evening in his diary, it was "dinner by the fireside & early to bed."

Only rarely was the press corps welcomed at Rancho del Cielo, such as on the momentous occasion when, on August 13, 1981, he affixed his signature to the Economic Recovery Tax Act. That bill, which amended the tax code by cutting personal and corporate taxes substantially, was to be the centerpiece of Reagan's policy for stimulating economic growth. Barbara Walters was granted an interview at the ranch; she extolled the connection between the man and his place.

When Reagan was in residence at the ranch, the taping of his weekly radio cast was a regular event. The peace of the Reagan property was also penetrated occasionally by news of events in the wider world. One morning on his horseback ride, Reagan learned from an aide that the Soviets had shot down a Korean commercial airliner; on another day, Secretary of State George Shultz visited to brief the president on a trip to Moscow. Once, word arrived of a kidnapping in Lebanon. Vice President George H. W. Bush visited periodically, as did friends and family for celebrations. But trimming trees with Barney and Dennis was a more common occupa-

Nancy made no pretense of being a cook (there were quarters for a cook in the main house). The pass-through (*opposite*) linked the kitchen to the dining area.

tion at Rancho del Cielo than entertaining. Ronald Reagan would spend a full year of his presidency at the ranch, and he liked it best when he could confide in his diary, "Things seem quiet on the Presidential side—so far I'm just a rancher."

Rancho del Cielo offers a provocative comparison to the ranch of another prominent Californian, that of William Randolph Hearst. There are some shared characteristics, as both homes sit atop the spine of the Coastal Range. Both men were powerful and world famous; they saw their places as expressions of themselves, where they were able to commune with the California landscape they loved. But there the commonalities end.

Hearst inherited an immensely larger piece of property, some 250,000 acres, where the newspaperman and sometime politician chose to construct a castle; over a period of twenty-five years, he built himself a treasure-house of art and antiquities, a great sprawling complex of towers, pools, gardens, and 165 rooms. Hearst invited the rich, famous, and up-and-coming to his home, entertaining his guests lavishly from his kingly overlook.

In contrast, the Reagans' two-bedroom house was originally constructed by a Mexican laborer and homesteader who transported

building materials to the site on the back of a donkey. Reagan's collections amounted to a small library, a few cowboy images hung on the walls, and family memorabilia. While guests at Hearst's castle dressed for dinner, Reagan preferred jeans and denim shirts. He cut much of the cordwood that burned in his fireplace.

Even when he took the oath of office as president, Reagan recognized that his piece of California had a permanence that neither he nor the presidency had. When a heliport was constructed to ease his comings and goings at what had become the Western White House, Reagan decreed that it must be a temporary installation; when he returned to private life, he wanted the pristine hilltop to look as it did when he and Nancy first visited in 1974. Today wildflowers bloom in an alpine meadow where once was heard the whir of helicopter rotors.

Reagan left office in January 1989; five years later, he and Nancy went public with the diagnosis of his Alzheimer's disease. By 1997, the ranch was of no practical use to the couple, and Nancy put Rancho del Cielo up for sale. The Young America's Foundation, a student outreach organization devoted to conservative principles, acquired the property in 1998. Long associated with Reagan—the

Opposite, left: In the master bedroom the large bed is actually a pair of twin beds pushed together to become one. The house is an unpretentious place, little changed since the Reagans remodeled and decorated it in the mid-1970s.

Opposite, right: The tall credenza obscured the television during daylight hours, but Reagan, after a day of physical work and riding, liked to relax by watching TV in the evening before retiring early.

Above: A new interior space was created out of what had been a porch. Tall windows light the multipurpose room, with its casual wicker furniture, decorative throw pillows, and Mexican wall hangings.

foundation underwrote some of his early radio commentaries—the Young America's Foundation maintains the Reagan Ranch Center in downtown Santa Barbara, with a permanent exhibit devoted to the Reagans and Rancho del Cielo.

Largely unchanged, the ranch today, which is open only by appointment, offers a glimpse of Nancy and Ronald Reagan's chosen destination when they wished to be by themselves. The isolated mountain site wasn't Nancy's natural milieu—she thrived on the energy of society and city life—but she understood that, for Ronnie, Rancho del Cielo was a place where he could be himself. There are those who will see the isolation of the place as symbolic of the famously amiable man whom his own children regarded as distant; others will see the ranch as a reflection of the independent man who emerged to captain the conservative movement as no one else could. But with a smell of wood smoke in the air, the horses in the paddock, and a ground fog rising from the pond, it is possible to understand what Ronald Reagan meant when he said, "Rancho del Cielo can make you feel as if you are on a cloud looking down on the world."

Opposite: Fireplaces were the only sources of heat in the converted adobe dwelling. Though few signs are in evidence at Rancho del Cielo that the man of the house was a U.S. president, there is a presidential seal hanging over the fieldstone fireplace. In keeping with the workmanlike tone of the place, the medium is nails.

Above, left: Reagan occasionally played a game of bumper pool, but more often the table was piled high with newspapers.

Above, right: A mix of titles on a range of subjects lines the shelves. Reagan enjoyed novels: Western writer Louis L'Amour is amply represented, along with Larry McMurtry and Horatio Alger, whose male characters attained success through honest determination. In addition to the political novels of Allen Drury, one finds Whittaker Chambers's *Witness;* books on cowboy life; and multiple volumes by Reagan's friend, admirer, and political confidant William F. Buckley Jr., founder and longtime editor of the *National Review.*

BILL CLINTON BIRTHPLACE

WILLIAM JEFFERSON CLINTON

(1993 – 2001)

HOPE, ARKANSAS

"My grandparents and my mother always
made me feel I was the most important person
in the world to them."

BILL CLINTON, *MY LIFE* **(2004)**

◇◇◇◇◇◇◇◇◇◇◇

BILLY BLYTHE'S HOPE

On August 19, 1946, one of the three movie houses in town screened a recent Hollywood release titled *Young Widow*. On that very day, at 8:51 a.m., a more memorable drama involving another widow began to unfold at Julia Chester Hospital, with the birth of a six-pound, eight-ounce baby named William Jefferson Blythe III.

The new mother, Virginia Blythe, had lost her husband three months earlier when a blowout on a Missouri highway sent his speeding Buick careening across Route 60. The dark blue sedan rolled twice before coming to a halt, upside down, its radio still playing, the headlights illuminating the surrounding cornfields. The driver, Bill Blythe, was found drowned in a nearby drainage ditch.

When Virginia and her newborn left the hospital ten days after

the cesarean birth, she returned home—but not to the house she and Bill Blythe planned to share in Forest Park, Illinois. Instead, the former Virginia Cassidy, age twenty-three, with little money and a mother for the first time, arrived on her parents' doorstep.

The paint was peeling on the rented house on Hervey Street. Judging by their nightly arguments, the new mother's parents, Edith and James Eldridge Cassidy, could have used a marriage counselor. The town of Hope itself, a half-forgotten railroad terminus of fewer than ten thousand inhabitants, needed an economic rebirth. But little Billy Blythe, by whatever means, would emerge from such unlikely circumstances as a bright, engaging, happy, and much-loved boy, one with the talents and desire to become the only Arkansan ever elected president of the United States.

THE TWO MOTHERS

At Hope High School, Virginia Cassidy had been a bright and sociable young woman, a member of the student council and the National Honor Society. She worked on the school paper and acted in plays. A flirtatious girl remembered for her laugh and affection for almost

Previous page: This house in Hope, Arkansas, a squat box with a pyramidal roof, was the first home of Billy Blythe Clinton.

Left: Billy Blythe Clinton, cowboy.
Clinton Family Photographs

Opposite: Next to the sitting room downstairs, the largest room in the house is Virginia's room. Her parents gave her the master bedroom, and this is the space of both a mother (there's a child's crib) and a woman who cared about how she looked. Virginia liked makeup—mascara, eye shadow, eyeliner, and false eyebrows—and there is a dressing table like the one she owned, where she might have "put on her face."

WILLIAM JEFFERSON CLINTON   208

everyone, she graduated in the spring of 1941, just months before the attack on Pearl Harbor changed everything. Despite the times, she chose as her senior yearbook quote, "I'd like to be serious but everything is so funny."

Her parents had come to Hope when she was five months old to improve their prospects. Eldridge had married the girl next door back in Bodcaw, Arkansas (population: one hundred), and Hope seemed to them a great metropolis. Virginia, however, set her sights on a larger place and, after high school, enrolled in nursing school in Shreveport, Louisiana. It was there, on a midsummer night in 1943, that she met Bill Blythe, who walked into the Tri-State Hospital emergency room where Virginia was working the three-to-eleven shift. Though he arrived holding another woman's hand, less than two months later, on September 3, Virginia Cassidy became

Mrs. William Jefferson Blythe Jr. Five weeks after that, Bill Blythe shipped out with his unit for the duration of World War II.

Virginia completed her nursing degree, then returned to Hope and worked as a private duty nurse. When her husband came home after the war, the couple plotted their move to Chicago, where Bill Blythe had been offered a job selling heavy equipment. His unexpected death and the subsequent birth of Billy altered that plan, but the resourceful young woman soon devised a new strategy.

In the Cassidy house, the mother found that caring for her child was a collaborative affair. As Virginia described the experience, "Mother . . . was totally involved in showing me how mothering was done. She meant well, but I felt like a lowly student nurse again." "Mammaw" Cassidy was stout, standing barely five feet tall and weighing about 180 pounds. She proved an indomitable maternal presence, establishing a highly regulated schedule of eating, sleeping, and playing for Billy. Ironically, it was Edith's assertion of control over her grandson that enabled Virginia to seek a means of regaining her independence. When Billy Blythe was barely a year old, Virginia left for New Orleans, where she began nursing training at Charity Hospital to become a nurse anesthetist (it would prove a self-sustaining business, providing her with an income for some three decades). Billy remained in Hope, in Mammaw's care, for the next two years with only periodic visits with his mother.

117 SOUTH HERVEY STREET

Built in 1917 for the son of a local physician, Edith and Eldridge's home is, in architectural terms, a *Foursquare,* a trickle-down, middle-class variation of Frank Lloyd Wright's Prairie style. The two-story structure contains three bedrooms and a bath upstairs, and a living room, kitchen, pantry, and dining room downstairs. If the house isn't a memorable architectural monument, the efficient design, wide roof overhangs, and generous porch do convey a sense of Southern comfort.

After many years as a rental property, the home had assumed a certain shabbiness when, in 1938, the Cassidys moved in (they lost

their previous home to foreclosure in the depths of the Depression). As their prospects improved in the postwar era, they purchased the home and, by 1947, the house was freshly painted and the porch added to the street façade. There were also indications of the child in residence at number 117, as a sandbox, swings, and slide appeared in the side yard.

Today the house has been restored to look as it did circa 1950, a time of party lines (the Cassidys had one) and black-and-white television. But if its furnishings bring to mind the era of Ozzie and Harriet, it was another character of that era that Billy Blythe came to idolize. The fictional Hopalong Cassidy was a cowboy hero, and young Billy's boyhood worship of "Hoppy" resulted in a broken leg when he tried to jump over a rope wearing his heeled cowboy boots. At the head of the stairs, in Billy's small bedroom, a black cowboy hat rests on a boy's spool bed.

The furniture in the living room is a bit of a hodgepodge—the Cassidys were plain people, only a few years removed from a hardscrabble farm—and there is a smattering of children's objects (toy trucks, books, a child's rocker with a rush seat). Before her death of breast cancer in 1994, Virginia toured the house and offered the caretakers her recollections, providing many useful clues for the restoration.

The other denizens of the house are in evidence too, Mammaw in particular. She taught the boy his numbers and letters—consistent with family lore, there are playing cards attached to a sash window in the kitchen like those she used to drill him at the breakfast table. Billy Blythe proved a capable pupil, one who learned to read at three and began studying the daily newspaper at six.

Eldridge Cassidy was another important influence on Billy (the boy's first word, according to his baby book, was "Pawpaw"). A wiry man of five foot eight, Grandfather Cassidy had a fifth-grade education. He worked as an iceman and a clerk in a Hope liquor store, but in 1944 he opened a neighborhood grocery on North Hazel

---

Opposite: A working 1940s kitchen with water heater and stove crowded into a corner of the cramped space. Virginia Kelley, Bill Clinton's mother, remembered the stove had been a Blackstone.

Street, a short walk from home. He was a gentle and hospitable man, a storyteller suited to greeting the custom that came through the door of his store (see *A Store Across the Color Line,* right).

A new father figure would appear in Billy's life a few weeks before the boy turned four, when his mother married Roger Clinton. Something of a rogue (he supplied Eldridge Cassidy with bootleg whiskey for his store), Clinton was a charmer who wore well-pressed suits and cologne and whose legitimate business was the local Buick dealership. After the marriage, Roger, Virginia, and her son moved to their own home, a bungalow across town on Thirteenth Street in Hope, and eventually to Hot Springs. Billy's relationship with his

---

Opposite: The Clinton Birthplace feels very much of its time, with its large console radio and a Maxfield Parrish print for decoration.

Below: Just inside the front door is the living room, with seating for two generations of adults and a wee chair for the much-loved first child.

Above: Candidate Clinton, pictured in 1992, back home in Hope, Arkansas. *Clinton Family Photographs*

A STORE ACROSS THE COLOR LINE

In the era before supermarkets and convenience stores, Eldridge Cassidy sold stockings, basic foodstuffs, and snacks to kids who stopped by after school for Maid-Rite ice cream or sodas from the icebox. In dry Hempstead County, even some of the most reputable people in town would come to buy the bootleg whiskey that Eldridge kept in a cabinet beneath the register. Yet the store's location in a segregated town tells more about its importance than a list of its inventory.

Located just across the street from the sprawling cemetery where Bill Blythe Jr. was buried, the store sat on a fault line between Hope's white and African American communities.

Eldridge's store was among the few places in Hope where the races mixed freely. A frequent visitor to Hazel Street, young Billy Blythe played with black children in the neighborhood; from his early childhood, the color line made no sense to the boy, as he wondered why these playmates were forbidden to attend the schools he did. As a presidential nominee, Bill Clinton told America in his acceptance speech at the 1992 Democratic convention that his grandfather's way of doing business inculcated in him a sense of dignity and equality irrespective of race.

"When his customers, whether they were White or Black . . . came in with no money, well, he gave them food anyway. He just made a note of it. So did I." In the dedication of his autobiography, *My Life,* the former president cited his kindly grandfather as the man "who taught me to look up to people others looked down on, because we're not so different after all."

stepfather would prove difficult, as Roger Clinton (his nickname was "Dude") had a taste for gambling, alcohol, nightlife, and daredevil pals. But by first grade, the boy was calling himself "Billy Clinton."

RECOLLECTING AN ARKANSAN BOYHOOD

Located just off Interstate 30, not so far from the Texas border, Hope hasn't changed all that much since Billy Blythe's birth. The tallest structures remain the church steeples. Vestiges of the town's railroad past survive too, as the old train station has been restored as a visitor center. Hope's other chief claim to fame—after favorite son Clinton—is the annual Watermelon Festival, where whopping great watermelons grown each season by Hope's farmers are celebrated every August.

Even after the Clintons moved to Hot Springs, Billy returned to Hope to summer with his grandparents on Hervey Street, until the house was sold after Eldridge's death in 1956. But Clinton's other Arkansas connections have been many. During college he interned for Arkansas senator J. William Fulbright; after completing studies at Georgetown University, Yale, and Oxford, he returned to teach law at the University of Arkansas, before running for several state offices (when elected governor in 1978 at age thirty-two, he was the youngest in the nation). He, along with first lady Hillary Rodham Clinton, occupied the Governor's Mansion for a total of six terms prior to seeking the presidency in 1992. Dedicated in 2004, the William J. Clinton Presidential Center and Park, the repository of the papers of the forty-second president, is located on the banks of the Arkansas River in downtown Little Rock.

A much less imposing structure, the house on Hervey Street, now administered by the National Park Service, offers a glimpse of what life was like for young Billy Blythe. Less is known about his childhood than about the man he became, thanks to endless reportage and inquiries into his later public life. But even from the early years there are shadowy rumors and innuendos about Billy Blythe's paternity (he was born just eight months after his father's discharge) and Virginia's

five marriages, several of them to men with mixed marital histories (Bill Blythe had been married at least three times before, Roger Clinton twice). Roger Clinton's alcoholism and abusive behaviors were indisputable, and the free-spirited Virginia often seemed to be on the wrong side of Hope's strict moral code. As Bill Clinton himself once remarked, "Mom lived a large, messy, sprawling life."

In his early days in Hope, Billy formed important friendships. A kindergarten classmate, Mack McLarty, whose father owned the Ford dealership in town, would later become President Clinton's first chief of staff. Another of Billy Blythe's first playmates was Vince Foster—he lived next door to the Cassidys, and the boys played mumblety-peg together on their adjoining lawns; Foster would be Hillary Clinton's law partner in their Little Rock firm and then deputy White House counsel after the 1992 election.

Certainly there were aspects of Clinton's early childhood that were less than idyllic (he had no father, his mother was absent for much of his preschool life, and his grandparents were often in conflict), but young Billy seems never to have lacked affection. He may have been a needy, somewhat isolated, overweight, and precocious child, but, as the adult Bill Clinton would remember half a century later in his autobiography, *My Life,* "For all their own demons, my grandparents and my mother always made me feel I was the most important person in the world to them. Most children will make it if they have just one person who makes them feel that way. I had three."

Opposite: Bill Clinton's bedroom, complete with spool bed, Hopalong Cassidy bedspread, and cowboy hat.

THE GEORGE W. BUSH CHILDHOOD HOME

GEORGE H. W. BUSH
(1989 – 1993)

AND

GEORGE W. BUSH
(2001 – 2009)

MIDLAND, TEXAS

"It seems improbable in that little house on Ohio Street that there would be two presidents and a governor of Florida."

GEORGE W. BUSH, SPEAKING IN MIDLAND IN **JANUARY 2001**

◇◇◇◇◇◇◇◇◇◇

"WHERE THE SKY'S THE LIMIT"

George H. W. Bush made his way west at the wheel of a red Studebaker. A gift from his father, the car was new, as was the young man's degree from Yale University, class of 1948. Bush was traveling solo, having temporarily left his wife, Barbara, back in New England with their infant son, George Walker Bush, known as "Georgie." At twenty-four years of age, the much-honored aviator (he had been awarded the Distinguished Flying Cross) was bound for the oil fields of West Texas.

To "Poppy" Bush, as he long had been known to family and friends, the place didn't look so promising. Many years later, the forty-first president would write of his first glimpse, "It was all dry topsoil, tumbleweeds, and a few trees. . . . It was hard to imagine how the barren area around me could support cattle, or that under-

neath this arid soil might be a fortune, even several fortunes in minerals." Though there was little water for cultivation, billions of barrels of crude oil awaited in the Permian Basin, which in an earlier geologic time had been an inland sea. Oil from these deposits would account for about one-fifth of America's oil production in the 1950s.

Since its discovery in the 1920s, black gold had been making people in West Texas rich. A family friend had offered the young man a trainee job, having convinced him that the oil business was the best way to make money for someone who was willing to take risks. In the next several years, Bush would sweep floors, paint oil derricks, work as a clerk, and hit the road as a salesman for his employer, the International Derrick and Equipment Company, in Texas and California. But all the while he was learning the oil business, readying to launch himself as an independent oilman.

By 1951, he felt the time had come, and he partnered with a neighbor, John Overbey, in the Bush-Overbey Oil Development Company, Inc., based in Midland. The two men complemented each other. Overbey brought experience with the business model—they wouldn't drill for wells but buy and sell the rights to drill—and Bush possessed both the driving ambition to succeed and an ability to reach into the deep pockets of his extended family (whence came $400,000 to capitalize the venture).

Previous page: Its restoration required the removal of aluminum siding, asbestos, and lead paint, but the Bush house on Ohio Avenue was opened to the public as a museum in 2006.

Left: Father and son, photographed outside the Bushes' Midland, Texas, home, about 1955.
George W. Bush Childhood Home, Inc.

Opposite: Barbara Bush made curtains for the windows in the living room.

That same year, George and Barbara, along with their toddler daughter, Pauline (known as "Robin"), and five-year-old George, moved into a home on Ohio Avenue in Midland, Texas. It was a town with a motto that would prove prophetic: "Where the Sky's the Limit."

"LIFE SEEMED ALMOST TOO GOOD TO BE TRUE"

Built in 1939, the house that George and Barbara moved into was a comfortable one-story ranch. Sited on a quiet street amid other middle-class dwellings—a house painter, a surgeon, and a concrete contractor lived nearby—the fifteen-hundred-square-foot house had three bedrooms, with a fenced-in yard out back for the children to play in. The original structure had been renovated by a previous owner, who converted a garage into living space and inserted a bay window on the street façade.

The Bushes laughingly reported to relatives back east that, since there wasn't a lot else to do in Midland, they made friends. Though

Midland was a place with a strong sense both of community and of competition—fortunes were being made and lost in oil fields every day—it wasn't just another Texas town. The oil boom had drawn so many seekers that the little city could boast an enclave of educated Easterners, enough that—despite its size, with a population of roughly 25,000—Midland had Harvard and Princeton Clubs, as well as a Yale Club.

For the most part, these years were happy ones for the Bushes' oldest son. "Life in Midland was simple," George W. recalled in his recent memoir, *Decision Points* (2010). "I rode bikes with pals ... went on Cub Scout trips, and I sold Life Savers door-to-door for charity."

Although as a preschooler he practically lived in his cowboy clothes, his baseball uniform soon became more important. "My friends and I would play baseball for hours, hitting each other grounders and fly balls until Mother called over the fence in our yard for me to come for dinner." Baseball was important both to the boy and to his father. Poppy had been captain of the Yale baseball team, a slick-fielding first baseman who had led his team to the College World Series. Though Yale lost to USC in 1948, that year

Bush had been given the singular honor of accepting the original manuscript for Babe Ruth's autobiography from the Bambino himself, a donation to the university's rare book collection. As a father, Poppy coached his son's Little League team, and much later, as the occupant of the Oval Office, he kept a favorite baseball glove in his desk drawer.

But life in Midland, as Barbara Bush mused many years later, proved "too good to be true." The year 1953 began with the welcome arrival of John Ellis ("Jeb") Bush in February, but just weeks afterward, his three-year-old sister was diagnosed with leukemia. For seven months, the parents sought a cure, going back and forth to New York. After experimental treatments, Robin finally died on an operating table in October, just short of her fourth birthday, when last-resort surgery failed. The parents returned from New York and picked up seven-year-old Georgie at Sam Houston Elementary School and delivered the news. Though he had known she was ill, her death was a complete surprise. But what shocked him the most was his parents' grief. "On the short ride home, I saw my parents cry for the first time in my life." The need he felt to console his parents, many friends believe, was a factor in the shaping of his personality.

By the time the Bush family moved from Midland to Houston in 1959, George H. W. had accomplished his mission of achieving financial security for his family. His various oil ventures had morphed into an offshore drilling concern, Zapata Off-Shore Company, which made him one of the first independents with a

net worth in excess of a million dollars. That also meant he could pursue his next career: politics.

A REPUBLICAN FAR FROM HOME

Another Bush name had been on the ballot in 1952, as Prescott Bush, George H. W. Bush's father, had won a Senate seat in Connecticut. His son had supported his efforts from afar, but in Texas, the "Lone Star Yankee," as one biographer dubbed George H. W. Bush, was an anomaly. He met Lyndon Johnson in Midland in 1953, and his son Georgie would meet the Senate majority leader too, in Washington, D.C., in 1956 when Senator Prescott Bush introduced him ("I've got one of your constituents here," Prescott Bush said of his ten-year-old grandson, who remembered how Johnson's huge hand swallowed his). But neither George, then or later, would be swayed from the family's long Republican allegiance.

George H. W. would serve a new apprenticeship, this time to learn the game of politics, Texas-style. He ran for the Senate in 1964 but was one of many Republicans defeated by a ticket that elected Lyndon Johnson and Democratic majorities in both the House and Senate. Two years later, he won a seat in Congress. Though another run for the Senate in 1970 ended in defeat, he would subsequently serve as the United States ambassador to the United Nations during Richard Nixon's administration; as U.S. envoy to China; and as director of Central Intelligence for Gerald Ford.

On May 1, 1979, he announced his candidacy for president, and he and Barbara were soon traveling around the country to campaign. For a time, he gave Ronald Reagan a race, winning in Iowa. Eventually, however, he lost to the Californian, only to find himself sharing the ticket as Reagan's running mate. Eight years later, George Bush would win the office of the presidency in his own right.

A RETURN TO MIDLAND

George W. Bush's childhood years in Midland were followed by an adolescence in private schools; college at Yale, class of 1968; and

Left: The lifelong baseball fan George W. Bush, ready to play ball.
George W. Bush Childhood Home, Inc.

Opposite: There's Wedgwood identical to the china the Bushes had, along with mixing bowls and other objects common to the time period.

Above: A sunroom would be adapted by the Bush family as a nursery after the arrival of their third child and second son, called Jeb, in 1953.

Opposite: After removing as many as eight layers of paint from the knotty-pine walls, restorers found the ghosts of the now reconstructed bookcase in the bedroom of George Bush the younger.

Below: The telephone had its own niche in the hall, but the Bushes shared a party line in fast-growing Midland.

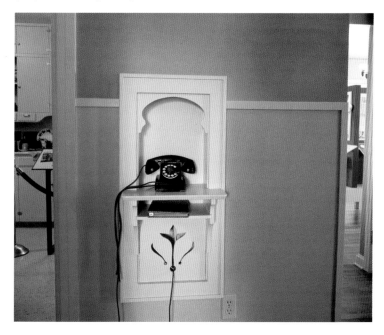

eventually an MBA degree from Harvard Business School in 1975. As he sought to establish himself in business, he followed in his father's footsteps, returning to Midland, by then a wildly prosperous city (according to the 1980 census, Midland had the highest per capita income in the nation). At this stage in his life, Bush later acknowledged, he was "young and irresponsible," a man who liked good company, good times, and to make his friends laugh.

His ventures in oil exploration weren't as successful as his father's had been, but during these Midland years, he married a native of the city named Laura Welch, whose father had built many of Midland's postwar homes (Laura Bush's mother still resides there). George W. ran for Congress in 1978 and, like his father, lost in his first election. ("It wasn't that people didn't like me," he quipped to a *Texas Monthly* reporter. "I finished a popular second.") By 1986, he was out of the oil business and working in his father's nascent presidential campaign. It was only after he had quit drinking alcohol, become the father of twin daughters, and embraced the Christian faith that he found his chance to make good, working in the sport that he had loved as a boy.

During his tenure as part-owner of the Texas Rangers, the team thrived, drawing fans to its new stadium in Arlington, Texas; Bush's initial investment of $600,000 eventually ballooned to $15 million. Flushed with success, George W. ran against incumbent governor Ann Richards and won the first of his two terms as Texas's chief executive. In 2000, the popular governor ran for president, and after a historically close election, a full month would pass before the Supreme Court would intervene in the process of recounting votes in Florida, finally declaring George W. Bush the winner over former vice president Albert Gore.

The Bushes thereby joined the Adamses—John and John Quincy —as the only fathers and sons to win election to the American presidency. Ironically, both Bush presidencies would be inseparably linked to the politics of oil, as well as to wars in the Middle East. After assembling an international coalition to invade Iraqi-held Kuwait, which won a signal victory in 1991, the elder Bush was defeated after one term by Bill Clinton in a campaign that centered

upon the faltering American economy. His son, who led the country into wars in Afghanistan and Iraq in the aftermath of the September 11, 2001, attacks, had better reelection luck, winning a second term, defeating Senator John Kerry in 2004.

The son took great pride in accomplishing promised tax cuts and a greater federal presence in education, exemplified by his No Child Left Behind Act (2001); the father played a key role in navigating a course for his nation through the uncharted terrain of a post–Cold War world.

As for Midland, Texas, the city today maintains its ties to energy: natural gas fields, oil derricks, and even towering wind turbines have risen from the vast arid range. For the man who became the nation's forty-first president, Midland was a stop on his way someplace else: he made friends and accumulated a fortune before moving on. For his son, however, a child born in the busiest year of the baby boom, Midland played a more formative role. As the *New York Times* reported in 2000 during the presidential campaign, "Midland . . . was a world of clear rights and wrongs, long on absolutes and devoid of ethical gray shades. It may be the source of some of Mr. Bush's greatest political strengths, the unpretentiousness and mellow bonhomies that warm up the voters." To see the house on Ohio Avenue is to visit the remembered simplicity of America in the 1950s.

OTHER PRESIDENTIAL HOMES

ASH LAWN-HIGHLAND
JAMES MONROE
225

GROUSELAND
WILLIAM HENRY HARRISON
226

SHERWOOD FOREST
JOHN TYLER
227

JAMES K. POLK STATE
HISTORIC SITE
JAMES K. POLK
228

MILLARD FILLMORE
HOUSE MUSEUM
MILLARD FILLMORE
229

FRANKLIN PIERCE HOMESTEAD
AND THE PIERCE MANSE
FRANKLIN PIERCE
230

ANDREW JOHNSON
NATIONAL HISTORIC SITE
ANDREW JOHNSON
231

SPIEGEL GROVE
RUTHERFORD B. HAYES
232

JAMES A. GARFIELD
NATIONAL HISTORIC SITE
JAMES A. GARFIELD
233

GROVER CLEVELAND BIRTHPLACE
GROVER CLEVELAND
234

SAXTON McKINLEY HOUSE
WILLIAM McKINLEY
235

WILLIAM HOWARD TAFT
NATIONAL HISTORIC SITE
WILLIAM HOWARD TAFT
236

HARDING HOME
WARREN G. HARDING
237

HERBERT HOOVER
NATIONAL HISTORIC SITE
HERBERT HOOVER
238

HARRY S TRUMAN
NATIONAL HISTORIC SITE
HARRY S. TRUMAN
239

ASH LAWN-HIGHLAND
JAMES MONROE
(1817 – 1825)
CHARLOTTESVILLE, VIRGINIA

James Monroe (1758 – 1831) was the third member of what some of their contemporaries called the *Virginia dynasty,* following his friends Thomas Jefferson and James Madison to the presidency. Like Jefferson, he had trained as a lawyer, then served as governor of Virginia and minister to France; during Madison's administration he also held the posts of both secretary of state and secretary of war.

His home in Charlottesville was built in part because of Jefferson, since Monroe, his wife, Elizabeth, and their daughter, Eliza, came to Albemarle County in 1789 at Jefferson's invitation (a second daughter, Maria, was born fourteen years later, at Highland). Jefferson's notion was to create an intellectual and social community —"a society to our taste," he said—and Monroe purchased 1,000 acres adjoining Monticello for $1,000.

The property eventually grew to 3,500 acres, with slaves operating the farm, which included timber, fruit orchards, vineyards (using Bordeaux grapes he imported from France), and cash crops of tobacco, corn, wheat, and grains. Monroe had threshing machines and a gristmill, and he imported merino sheep for their wool.

The house at Highland was built upon Monroe's return from his posting to France as minister. Construction began in 1797, and the Monroes moved in 1799. (The name Ash Lawn came later, after the family had sold the property.) It remained Monroe's primary residence for some twenty-five years. Several other owners made changes (notably a Baptist preacher named Massey, who added a Victorian front to the house). In the 1930s, an industrialist from Pittsburgh purchased the house for preservation; in 1974 it was given to the College of William and Mary, its present owner. Both Monroe and Thomas Jefferson were alumni of the college.

Highland wasn't a fancy house—Monroe himself termed it his "cabin castle." The son of a small planter, he was not a wealthy man. He also accumulated debts during his many years of public service and often expressed a strong belief in the simple life of a country farmer. He planned for many years to move to grander quarters and, when they sold Highland in 1825, their new home, Oak Hill, was more elaborate but still a farmhouse.

As president, Monroe acquired Florida from the Spanish in 1819. In 1823 he promulgated what came to be known as the Monroe Doctrine, a cornerstone of American diplomacy, in collaboration with Secretary of State John Quincy Adams. He had crossed the Delaware with Washington on Christmas night 1776, the first public appearance of many for a man who would prove an important actor on the American stage for the next half century.

James Monroe in a Goodman and Piggot engraving printed in the year of his inauguration, based on a C. B. King portrait. The Capitol is on view in the background.
Library of Congress / Prints and Photographs

Monroe's home, Highland, constructed at the turn of the nineteenth century, would become an ell to the rear of the larger Ash Lawn (the yellow structure, left) later in the century.
Ash Lawn-Highland

GROUSELAND
WILLIAM HENRY HARRISON
(1841)
VINCENNES, INDIANA

William Henry Harrison (1773–1841) spent fewer days in office than any other president, dying on April 4, 1841, a month after taking the oath. Yet Harrison remains an essential figure in the new nation's western development at the turn of the nineteenth century.

The youngest son of Benjamin Harrison V, a Signer of the Declaration of Independence, Harrison spent his early years at Berkeley Plantation, a fine mansion overlooking the James River in Virginia (Berkeley Plantation is also a historic site; see *Visitor Information,* page 241). At eighteen, he joined the military and was posted to the Northwest Territory. After his marriage to Anna Symmes, daughter of a prominent Ohio judge, and his service as a territorial delegate to Congress, he was appointed in 1800 to the governorship of the newly established Indiana Territory, which then consisted of what would become the states of Indiana, Illinois, Michigan, Wisconsin, and eastern Minnesota. In the territorial capital of Vincennes he constructed his mansion, Grouseland, named for the many game birds found nearby.

Grouseland was the first brick home built in Indiana, and it resembled the tall, brick, Georgian-style architecture that Harrison knew from Tidewater Virginia. Given its location, however, the solidly built house could also serve as something of a fortress: its basement contained a powder magazine; the freshwater well was within its walls; and the dormers on the third story could serve as battlements in the event of Indian attack.

Harrison's interactions with the Native Americans in his region proved central to his career, both as a military man and as a political appointee and politician. He negotiated numerous land treaties as governor but gained particular fame when, in 1811, his army defeated a confederation of Native Americans led by Tecumseh at a battle fought on the banks of the Tippecanoe River.

Harrison would subsequently serve as a congressman and senator from Ohio prior to running for president in 1836 (he lost to Martin Van Buren) and again in 1840. Harrison and his running mate, John Tyler of Virginia, campaigned under the winning rubric "Tippecanoe and Tyler Too."

Grouseland has been restored to appear much as it did during Harrison's residence; his son, John Scott Harrison, was born in the home, and, in turn, John Scott's son, Benjamin, would become the nation's twenty-third president. The collections at Grouseland also feature many items from the 1840 presidential campaign.

William Henry Harrison, president, as recorded by painter James Henry Beard and lithographer Thomas Campbell, probably in 1841, the year of the newly elected president's death.
Library of Congress / Prints and Photographs

An imposing house for frontier America in the early nineteenth century, Grouseland featured, among other details, a double portico and a bowed end wall overlooking the Wabash River.
Grouseland Foundation, Inc.

SHERWOOD FOREST

JOHN TYLER

(1841 – 1845)

CHARLES CITY, VIRGINIA

John Tyler was a tall, thin man with a long and narrow house to match. During his years in office, he became a president without a party — the Whigs expelled him for his independent ways — and Tyler defiantly embraced an intended insult from Henry Clay, naming his house Sherwood Forest after the Kentuckian compared him to the outlaw Robin Hood.

Anticipating retirement, John Tyler (1790 – 1862) had purchased the plantation of more than a thousand acres in 1842. He renovated an existing structure, constructing a long colonnade to link the free-standing kitchen to the east. To the west, he tied the house's three-story main block to his law office with a sixty-eight-foot ballroom, a space well adapted to the then-popular Virginia reel. The widower Tyler remarried in 1844, and Julia Gardiner Tyler helped remake their three-hundred-foot-long home in the Greek Revival taste of designer Minard Lafever.

Though his was among the most divisive presidencies in history, Tyler's arrival in office is of special significance. After learning of President Harrison's death, Vice President Tyler made haste to the capital, where he took the oath of office and issued a presidential inaugural address. Ignoring those who questioned his right to office (mail addressed to "Acting President Tyler" was returned unopened), he set an important precedent for the orderly transfer of power.

Another momentous event occurred in the waning days of Tyler's nearly four years in office when, just six days before James Polk was to be inaugurated, Tyler engineered passage in Congress of a joint resolution annexing the Republic of Texas, opening the way for Texas to become the twenty-eighth state.

After leaving office, Tyler devoted himself to working his plantation. A lifelong slaveholder, he emerged from retirement to chair the Virginia Peace Convention in 1861, a last attempt to avoid what would be the Civil War. Even as he addressed the convention in Washington, however, the government of the Confederacy was being formed in Montgomery, Alabama. Tyler was soon named a delegate to the Confederate Congress, but, a man of sickly constitution all his life, he died en route. In 1864, Sherwood Forest was sacked by United States Colored Troops, assisted by some of those who had been enslaved at the property.

The passing of the patrician John Tyler was not officially recognized in the nation's capital because of his allegiance to the Confederate States of America. He was the only former president not to be so honored.
Library of Congress / Prints and Photographs

Sherwood Forest remains the property of Tyler descendants, and some twenty-five acres of terraced gardens surround the house, along with a dozen original outbuildings, including the 1829 slave quarters and overseer's house.
Library of Congress / Historic American Buildings Survey

JAMES K. POLK STATE HISTORIC SITE

JAMES K. POLK

(1845 – 1849)

COLUMBIA, TENNESSEE

When Samuel Polk brought his eldest child home from college, the scholarly young man arrived at a tall house unknown to him. While the twenty-three-year-old James had been earning his degree at the University of North Carolina, Samuel had moved the family to a new home constructed in Columbia, Tennessee, on the banks of the Duck River. For the next six years, the Federal-style house on what is now the corner of West Seventh and South High Streets in the seat of Maury County would be James's on-again, off-again home as he read law (in Nashville), worked as a Senate clerk (in Murfreesboro), and built relationships with important Jeffersonian Republicans in Middle Tennessee. An enthusiastic supporter of Andrew Jackson, James K. Polk (1795–1849) would come to be known as "Young Hickory," a variation on his mentor's nickname.

Built in 1816, the house has a side-hall plan. The main entrance is flanked by sidelights with an elliptical fan sash above. The first floor consists of a stair hall that runs the depth of the house, open-ing onto a parlor and dining room, with bedrooms above. Built of handmade brick, it was a handsome and practical home for Samuel Polk and his large family; during James's residence prior to his marriage in 1824, it was home to James's parents, Samuel and Jane, and eight of their children, ranging from the future president to an infant brother.

Although Polk began his law practice in Columbia in 1820, he would serve in the state legislature in Nashville and, for seven terms, in the U.S. Congress, where he rose to Speaker. He served as governor of Tennessee for one term before he narrowly defeated Henry Clay in 1844 to become the nation's eleventh president, the only former Speaker to become chief executive.

A firm believer in the nation's "Manifest Destiny," President Polk acquired for the United States much of the Pacific Northwest as the Oregon Territory and, in the treaty that ended "Polk's War" (the 1846–1848 Mexican-American War), gained much of what would become the states of New Mexico, Utah, Nevada, and California. His four years in the White House also saw the establishment of both the U.S. Naval Academy at Annapolis and the Smithsonian Institution. Polk died of cholera three months after leaving office.

George Peter Alexander Healy painted this portrait of James Polk, who posed while in the White House in 1846.
James K. Polk Memorial Association

The only surviving Polk residence, Polk Place in Columbia, today is a repository for Polk objects, furniture, portraits, and memorabilia.
James K. Polk Memorial Association

MILLARD FILLMORE HOUSE MUSEUM
MILLARD FILLMORE
(1850 – 1853)
EAST AURORA, NEW YORK

Born with the century, Millard Fillmore (1800–1874) made good. This home in East Aurora, New York, stands at the fulcrum of a life that began in frontier poverty (his birthplace in western New York was a one-room log cabin with a dirt floor) and that culminated in Fillmore's service as the nation's thirteenth president.

He built this home for his wife-to-be, Abigail Powers. They resided here for the first five years of their marriage (1826–1830), prior to their departure to the growing city of Buffalo, twenty miles away. They met when she was twenty-one and a schoolteacher; the nineteen-year-old Fillmore had spent little of his boyhood in a classroom and, hungry for knowledge, he embraced the four-year course of study she laid out for him. He was elected to the state assembly in 1829; his three terms there would be followed by four terms in the U.S. Congress.

If his partnership with Abigail was a fulfilling one, Fillmore was less than a full partner after he was elected to the vice presidency in the 1848 election. Chosen for political and geographic balance, the two men

Fillmore was a tall and dignified Northerner; Zachary Taylor, who had won fame in the recent Mexican war, was a squat slave owner from Louisiana known as "Old Rough and Ready." The two men met only after the election and found little in common, and Fillmore had no role in Taylor's administration.

When Taylor died suddenly in 1850, Fillmore inherited both the office of chief magistrate and the intractable problem of slavery. Reversing his predecessor's position, he supported a series of five bills known as the Compromise of 1850. Their passage, historians believe, delayed the Civil War, but in Fillmore's time, the legislation satisfied no one with its further partitioning of the country into slave and nonslave states. The Fugitive Slave Law deeply angered many in the North, as it compelled the return of runaway slaves without due process. The electorate's general dissatisfaction with the state of the nation doomed Fillmore's hopes of being elected president in his own right.

The house on Shearer Avenue didn't start there. With the help of friends, Fillmore himself built the wood-frame home on Main Street in a country Federal style, with a small kitchen ell to the rear. After his departure, the house was moved twice. In 1975, the Aurora Historical Society acquired the home and restored it to its circa 1826 appearance.

An oil portrait of President Fillmore.
Aurora Historical Society

The restored Millard Fillmore House honors the memory of the young lawyer and his wife, Abigail; the birth of their first child; and the launching of the future president's political career.
Aurora Historical Society

FRANKLIN PIERCE HOMESTEAD AND THE PIERCE MANSE
FRANKLIN PIERCE
(1853 – 1857)
HILLSBOROUGH, NEW HAMPSHIRE AND
CONCORD, NEW HAMPSHIRE

Two homes that commemorate the life of Franklin Pierce offer a convenient means of looking at the nation's fourteenth president. The son of a celebrated Revolutionary War veteran, Franklin Pierce (1804–1869) spent his childhood at the Hillsborough homestead, arriving there as a babe in arms. His father's farm also served as a tavern, a stopping place for the likes of Daniel Webster. Pierce went off to Bowdoin College, where he met his lifelong friend Nathaniel Hawthorne. Trained as a lawyer, Frank Pierce soon took up politics. The amiable, handsome, and precocious young man seemed on his way to great things; he was Speaker of the New Hampshire legislature at age twenty-six and a U.S. congressman at twenty-eight, and became a U.S. senator four years later.

Pierce and his wife, Jane Appleton Pierce, had already lost one son in infancy when, in 1842, he resigned his seat in the Senate and the Pierces moved to what is today the Pierce Manse in Concord to raise their surviving sons, Frank and Benjamin. Pierce's law prac-

tice thrived, and he refused offers to rejoin the political fray. When the Mexican war began in 1846, he volunteered and rose to the rank of brigadier general. His war service and his record as a consistent party man in Congress made him an appealing choice for the ticket when, at the deadlocked 1852 Democratic National Convention, his name was put forward on the thirty-fifth ballot. He was elected by a large margin, despite having been out of politics for ten years.

Like most of the national politicians of the pre–Civil War era—including the men who occupied the White House before and after him, Millard Fillmore and James Buchanan—his attempts to address the unsolvable conundrum that was slavery made him more enemies than friends. His presidency was an undistinguished one and undoubtedly colored by the death of his third son just weeks before his inauguration (the second son had also died, in 1843, of typhus). Jane Pierce would spend her husband's entire presidency in mourning.

The Franklin Pierce Homestead is a handsome house, one suitable for a governor (Frank's father, Benjamin, was twice elected New Hampshire's chief executive), with imported French wallpapers and a second-floor ballroom. Built later, the Pierce Manse is a side-hall Colonial in design, with bold pilasters and a doorway in the Greek Revival style.

New Hampshire's only president as photographed by Mathew Brady.
Library of Congress / Prints and Photographs

The hip-roofed, Federal-style Franklin Pierce Homestead.
Sue Hofstetter

ANDREW JOHNSON
NATIONAL HISTORIC SITE
ANDREW JOHNSON
(1865 – 1869)
GREENEVILLE, TENNESSEE

Andrew Johnson (1808–1875) arrived in Greeneville at age seventeen with no formal education. Having apprenticed as a tailor, he opened a shop in this East Tennessee town. Eliza McCardle, the sixteen-year-old daughter of a local shoemaker, became his wife and tutored him in reading, writing, and arithmetic. His workmanship as a tailor and an unexpected gift for speechifying won him friends and influence, leading to his election as alderman, then mayor, of Greeneville.

Johnson proved an appealing candidate, serving in the Tennessee legislature, in the U.S. House of Representatives, as governor of Tennessee, and as a U.S. senator. With war imminent and other Southern states withdrawing from the Union, Johnson was steadfastly opposed to secession, choosing to remain in the Senate even after Tennessee joined the Confederacy. His principled constitutional stand was one reason that Lincoln chose Johnson as his running mate in 1864. Just six weeks after their swearing in, Johnson became the nation's seventeenth president after Lincoln's assassination.

The history of the Johnson Homestead, the home he inhabited in Greeneville for twenty-four years, bespeaks the paradox that was Johnson's presidency. On the one hand, the house was occupied by Confederate soldiers during the Civil War; in their view, Johnson was a traitor, and they defaced its walls with anti-Johnson graffiti that can be seen today. On the other hand, although Johnson acknowledged the need to carry out Lincoln's promise "to bind up the nation's wounds," his refusal to accede to the wishes of the Republican majority in Congress to grant political and civil rights to African Americans led to a series of confrontations, culminating in his impeachment by the House of Representatives in 1868. Though his Senate trial ended in acquittal by one vote, President Johnson pleased virtually no one. Succeeded in office by Secretary of War Ulysses Grant, he returned to his house on Main Street in Greeneville.

Seeking vindication for his political dismissal by the electorate, Johnson made repeated runs for office, but it wasn't until 1874 that he returned to Washington as the only former president to serve in the Senate. Fellow senators applauded him enthusiastically after his first speech, but he served only briefly, dying in 1875.

On view today at the Homestead are many of Johnson's furnishings and objects. The site is a worthy place to consider his rise from poverty (his tailor shop survives) to the presidency, along with what many historians regard as his signal failure to lead the nation through the difficult era that was Reconstruction.

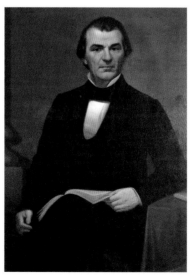

Senator Andrew Johnson, painted by Tennessee artist Samuel M. Shaver, about 1860. *Andrew Johnson National Historic Site / National Park Service*

The Johnson homestead, home to Andrew Johnson from 1851 until his death in 1875. *Andrew Johnson National Historic Site / National Park Service*

SPIEGEL GROVE
RUTHERFORD B. HAYES
(1877 – 1881)
FREMONT, OHIO

The namesake son never knew his father—the elder Hayes died ten weeks before the future president's birth—but Rutherford B. Hayes had the great good fortune to have a paternal stand-in, a wealthy and generous uncle (his mother's brother) named Sardis Birchard. A lifelong bachelor, Birchard contributed to the boy's education and, as Hayes (1822–1893) emerged as a powerful political figure in Ohio, built a fine house for his nephew and his family, the home known as Spiegel Grove.

By the time construction commenced in 1859, Hayes, a graduate of Harvard Law School, was a successful attorney with strong abolitionist leanings. He was Cincinnati's city solicitor when he volunteered for military service. The Civil War would delay progress on the four-thousand-square-foot brick house—it wouldn't be completed until 1863—and Hayes would return from war a much-honored soldier. Wounded four times, he rose to the rank of major general and, in absentia, was elected to Congress. In 1867, he would run for governor of Ohio.

Though Hayes had helped design his uncle's house and his family summered there, only in 1873 did Hayes, along with his wife, Lucy, and their children (four sons and a daughter would live to adulthood), occupy Spiegel Grove as his own. Hayes's reelection to the governorship in 1875 proved a step toward the presidency, as he was chosen the Republican nominee the following year. Ballots alone proved insufficient to decide the 1876 election—New York's governor, Democrat Samuel J. Tilden, won the popular vote—but disputed electoral votes in three Southern states required the creation of a special commission, which eventually declared Hayes the victor.

Hayes oversaw the close of Reconstruction and attempted to reform the civil service system, which for a generation had favored political connections over merit. Having pledged during the 1876 campaign to serve just one term, Hayes honored his promise and retired to Spiegel Grove in 1881.

Rutherford and Lucy Hayes would twice expand the home. In anticipation of his retirement they embarked on a major renovation, adding a library for the president's books, a great staircase, an elevator, gas lighting, and central heat. A second renovation in 1889 was interrupted by Lucy's unexpected death. Today the Rutherford B. Hayes Presidential Center is home to both the thirty-one-room mansion and the freestanding Hayes Library, which was the first presidential library in the nation when it opened in 1916.

President Rutherford B. Hayes, another of the nineteenth-century presidents too often remembered for their "gravely vacant and bewhiskered faces."
Hayes Presidential Center

As he considered renovating the house he inherited, Hayes confided in his diary, "The best part of the present house is the veranda. But I would enlarge it. I want a veranda with a house attached!"
Hayes Presidential Center

JAMES A. GARFIELD
NATIONAL HISTORIC SITE
JAMES A. GARFIELD
(1881)
MENTOR, OHIO

Neither rail stations nor college reunions are usually dangerous places, but James A. Garfield, awaiting a train to carry him north to his alma mater, Williams College, was shot twice on July 2, 1881, by a delusional office seeker. His doctors' unsterilized probing for the bullet lodged in his spine likely introduced the infections that killed him eighty days later.

James Garfield (1831–1881) had in his forty-nine years been a minister, teacher, college president, Army general, congressman, senator-elect, and president. Though he was shot just four months into his presidential tenure, his campaign style in attaining the office would have an impact on American politics. During the presidential race of 1880 he had respected the tradition of remaining at home, but only with reluctance; as he confided in his diary, "If I could but take the stump and bear a fighting share in the campaign."

The crowds that streamed to Mentor made a front-porch campaign possible. German Americans, ironworkers, Army veterans, Ohio neighbors, and other delegations stepped off the train onto the new platform at the stop known as Garfield Lane. Some seventeen thousand visited Mentor that summer and fall. Candidate Garfield delivered speeches almost daily to the crowds on the shaded green before his house, which was called Lawnfield.

During the campaign, a one-room structure to the rear of Lawnfield was recommissioned as Garfield's campaign office. Its tables piled with correspondence, this space was occupied constantly by clerks and a telegraph operator monitoring the dispatches arriving via the lines of the Atlantic and Pacific Telegraph Company.

Four years earlier James Garfield and his wife, Lucretia, had purchased the well-worn farmhouse surrounded by more than 120 acres. In the year of his presidential run, a renovation added eleven rooms, raising the roof to enclose three stories and subsuming the earlier structure. The house gained a new look, with decorative trusses in the gables, a deep-bracketed porch, and decorated dormers.

After her husband's demise, the Widow Garfield owned the home until her death thirty-seven years later. By then, the house had long since become a memorial to her husband. A "Memory Room" was at the center of a substantial stone addition built in 1885–1886 that included a library with a fireproof room for the late president's papers. Today the restored home, library, and campaign office at Lawnfield are very much in view, set back beyond the green on U.S. Route 20.

James A. Garfield photographed in the years before his presidency.
Library of Congress / Prints and Photographs

A nineteenth-century image of Lawnfield, site of the first "front-porch campaign."
Library of Congress / Prints and Photographs

GROVER CLEVELAND BIRTHPLACE

GROVER CLEVELAND

(1885 – 1889, 1893 – 1897)

CALDWELL, NEW JERSEY

In 1837, the Reverend Richard Falley Cleveland welcomed into the world a son named Stephen Grover. By the standards of the day, the pastor's residence was a plain place, suitable for a family of middling means. Though the family departed New Jersey in 1841, bound for western New York, the two-story house in Caldwell has for a century been a museum dedicated to the memory of the child who grew up to become president, by then known as Grover Cleveland (1837 – 1908).

Cleveland was just sixteen when his father died, and plans of college were set aside. At twenty-two he was admitted to the bar in Buffalo, which led to work as a district attorney during the Civil War and a sheriff in the early 1870s. As a prosperous and well-liked attorney in private practice, Cleveland was tapped in 1881 to run for mayor of Buffalo. His upset win was followed by election to governor of New York a year later; his corruption-busting record as governor in facing down Tammany Hall helped earn him the Democratic nomination for president in 1884.

Cleveland was admired for his work ethic and often remained at his desk in the White House until well past midnight. His polar principles were honesty and efficiency; though he initiated little legislation in his time in office, he is remembered as the "guardian president," a man who exercised the power of the veto as no president before had done.

His presidency is also remembered for family matters. A bachelor when elected, he married his twenty-one-year-old ward, Frances Folsom, during his first term. The much-admired "Frankie" would be the first first lady to give birth while in the White House.

Built in 1832, the Cleveland Birthplace remained the minister's manse for the First Presbyterian Church until friends and admirers purchased the home shortly after the death of the twenty-second and twenty-fourth president (*Grover Cleveland* is the answer to the riddle of how the United States has had just forty-three individuals serve but forty-four presidents, since he served two *nonconsecutive* terms). Today the collection at the Grover Cleveland Birthplace consists of a range of artifacts that suggest his financial and political success late in the century, but the house also has the Cleveland family cradle in which Ann and Richard's middle child slept after his birth in 1837.

Though just under six feet tall, Cleveland was a big man, broad-shouldered and portly, weighing in excess of 280 pounds.
Grover Cleveland Birthplace State Historic Site

The Grover Cleveland Birthplace, pictured on a snowy winter's day, is a two-story house with a kitchen ell to the east and a one-story lean-to attached to the rear.
Grover Cleveland Birthplace State Historic Site

SAXTON McKINLEY HOUSE
WILLIAM McKINLEY
(1897 – 1901)
CANTON, OHIO

The Saxton McKinley House is quite unlike other restored former presidential homes in one notable way: it celebrates a president, but he shares billing with first ladies in general and Ida Saxton McKinley in particular.

Though William McKinley (1843 – 1901) and his wife resided here off and on for twenty-eight years, the impressive house on Market Avenue belonged to his wife's family. The well-to-do Saxtons had schooled their daughter in Philadelphia and sent her on a European grand tour. When the young woman returned, she worked in her father's bank. Then, at age twenty-three, she married Major McKinley, another Canton native and an attorney and Civil War veteran.

McKinley would serve six terms in Congress and as governor of Ohio before running for president in 1896 against Williams Jennings Bryan in an election that was to be remembered for Bryan's rousing oratory and the deep pockets of McKinley's Republican Party. President McKinley took the nation into an international war, the first since Madison's War of 1812. With the victory over Spain in 1898, he was returned to the White House for a second term with a new running mate at his side, war hero and New York governor Theodore Roosevelt.

His private life in the intervening years had been filled with sadness. Ida had borne two daughters; one died in infancy, the other at three years of age. Chronic phlebitis and epilepsy left Ida an invalid, but her husband doted on her, accommodating her "fainting spells" by breaking White House protocol, seating her at his side at State Dinners. When McKinley was shot by an assassin in 1901, his first thoughts were of Ida. "My wife—be careful . . . ," he said to his secretary, "how you tell her—oh, be careful." He would die eight days later.

The brick Saxton McKinley home had been renovated in 1865, when the original gable-roofed house, constructed in 1841, was enlarged and gained a mansard roof. The result was an impressive three-story Second Empire–style mansion with a generous porch, elaborate cornice, and attic story highlighted by architectural embellishments. Today, public rooms have been restored to their Victorian appearance, and the study on the third floor looks much as it did when McKinley occupied it, with a rolltop desk, bookcases, and patterned wallpaper and carpet. The top-floor ballroom is lined with images of all the first ladies.

The Saxton McKinley House is a National Park Service site, operated by the National First Ladies' Library together with an education and research center nearby in a converted seven-story bank building.

William McKinley, looking confidently presidential, in 1896, the year of his election to the White House.
Library of Congress / Prints and Photographs

Note the hooded gable of the roof window, the keystone arches on the second floor, and the double-door entry to the Saxton McKinley House, all characteristic details of the Second Empire style.
Saxton McKinley House / National First Ladies' Library

WILLIAM HOWARD TAFT
NATIONAL HISTORIC SITE
WILLIAM HOWARD TAFT
(1909 – 1913)
CINCINNATI, OHIO

Some people grow up wanting to be president, but Alphonso and Louise Taft's son William wanted to be chief justice of the Supreme Court. In time, Will Taft would gain the unique distinction of holding the two highest offices in the nation, first as president, then, in 1921, as chief justice of the Supreme Court.

The Cincinnati-born Taft (1857 – 1930) grew up in a houseful of books and a family of high expectations. All of Alphonso's sons went to Yale; he himself served as a judge, founded the Ohio Republican Party, and was appointed by President Grant to the posts of attorney general and secretary of war.

A heavyset man known to many as "Big Bill," son William practiced law and served as an Ohio judge, then became a federal judge and solicitor general. Theodore Roosevelt made him secretary of war; the appointment emerged as part of a thinly veiled strategy to draft Taft as his successor in the White House. Even if Taft himself wasn't entirely sure about the office (reluctantly, he had twice turned down Roosevelt's offers of a Supreme Court seat,

influenced by his wife's ambitions for him to be president), the Ohioan won the 1908 presidential election easily.

As president, the less-aggressive Taft disappointed his friend Roosevelt, who then threw himself into the 1912 campaign, attempting to unseat Taft. In an unusual four-way race, Taft's Republican ticket outdid only Socialist Party candidate Eugene V. Debs, as Woodrow Wilson bested second-place Roosevelt's "Bull Moose" Progressives by a large margin. Taft's time in office had proved less than memorable, and today he is most often recalled for his support for income taxes and as the first president to throw the ceremonial first pitch on baseball's Opening Day. William Howard Taft was also an avid sportsman, enamored of golf (the game boomed in his era), and was the father of Robert Taft, later a powerful senator and himself a presidential candidate.

Built atop Mount Auburn north of Cincinnati's business district, the Taft house was one of a line of comfortable homes along Auburn Avenue, an area that was still largely agricultural. After purchasing the Greek Revival–style structure for $10,000, Alphonso Taft enlarged it, adding a brick ell to the rear. Today the first floor of the museum features five restored period rooms, one of which was the nursery where Will Taft was born. Upstairs are exhibits devoted to his life and accomplishments.

The combination of his great girth, waxed mustache, and intense gaze gave William Howard Taft an imposing appearance.
Library of Congress / Prints and Photographs

After a fire in 1878, the house assumed its present form, with a nearly flat roof and deep eaves that shade the home.
William Howard Taft National Historic Site / National Park Service

HARDING HOME
WARREN G. HARDING
(1921 – 1923)
MARION, OHIO

The man whose principal campaign pledge was "normalcy" lived in what appeared to be a quite average middle-class home in Marion, Ohio, a middle-American railroad town. In 1890, Harding (1865–1923) and his betrothed, Florence Kling DeWolfe, the daughter of a local banker, collaborated on the design of the Queen Anne–style house and, a year later, married at the foot of the front stairs. For three decades, it would be their home.

Harding had arrived in Marion at age seventeen. At nineteen, he and two partners acquired the *Marion Star,* a paper with such limited prospects that the price was $300. For Harding, however, the *Star,* which went from a four-page weekly to a daily with Harding as its publisher, proved to be his platform to local prominence. He would become a state senator, lieutenant governor, and U.S. senator. His campaign for president in 1920 was conducted from the front porch in the last campaign of its kind.

Just twenty-nine months into his presidency, Harding died of a heart attack while in San Francisco. Though his death occasioned an outpouring of sadness for the popular president, in the months afterward the attention of the nation would also be focused on the single greatest financial scandal in U.S. government history: the Teapot Dome affair, which would forever tarnish Harding's reputation and send his secretary of the interior to prison. Insinuations about Harding's private life also soon surfaced.

The Harding Home would have no other occupants: Mrs. Harding never returned after her husband's death, and following hers in 1924, the home became a museum to the late president. Today the collections consist almost entirely of objects that belonged to the Hardings, including gaslight fixtures, furniture, and clothing in the closets.

The amiable Harding (his secretary of state, Charles Evans Hughes, said of him in a eulogy, "He literally wore himself out in the endeavor to be friendly") is well remembered at the home and, fittingly, in the press headquarters, a small building behind the house. As a former newspaperman, Harding was perhaps the first president to appreciate the power of the press, advertising, and the media as political tools, as he explained to voters that "America's present need is not heroics, but healing; not nostrums, but normalcy."

President Warren G. Harding, as rendered by Hungarian artist Fülöp László in 1921.
Library of Congress / Prints and Photographs

A circa 1920 stereographic print of the Hardings' home in Marion, Ohio, visited that year by some 600,000 citizens who came to hear Harding declaim from his porch.
Library of Congress / Prints and Photographs

HERBERT HOOVER
NATIONAL HISTORIC SITE
HERBERT HOOVER
(1929 – 1933)
WEST BRANCH, IOWA

Herbert Hoover was at the helm when the nation's economy crashed on October 29, 1929, not quite eight months into his presidency. As a result, the enigmatic Hoover has traditionally borne much blame for the early years of the Great Depression, which ensued after "Black Tuesday." When viewed from another century, however, it is possible to see shades of gray between the stark contrast of the prosperity of Calvin Coolidge's years in office and the dark prospects that led to Hoover's return to private life when the electorate embraced Franklin Delano Roosevelt and his "New Deal" in 1932.

In West Branch, Iowa, the visitor is invited to consider the early life of Herbert Clark Hoover (1874–1964), the blacksmith's son who, orphaned at nine, would become the first president born west of the Mississippi. The child of Quaker parents, he arrived in a cramped frame house, just fourteen by twenty, which his father had built in 1871. Constructing even a small structure in the town on the west branch of the Wapsinonoc Creek meant bringing in foundation stones by wagon from the prairie; the timber arrived in Iowa via a raft, where it was cut into boards at a sawmill, then hauled some forty miles by ox team to the building site.

A chimney rises at the center of the Hoover birthplace, flanked by two rooms. The bedchamber contains a rope bed atop a smaller trundle bed that was pulled out at night for the children. The second room functioned as the kitchen, parlor, and dining room.

The restored cottage at West Branch today is part of a historic precinct at the Herbert Hoover National Historic Site that includes a blacksmith shop, Quaker meetinghouse, and schoolhouse. Also on the shared two-hundred-acre campus in West Branch is the Herbert Hoover Presidential Library and Museum. The museum contains exhibits exploring Hoover's post-Iowa life after his departure at age nine. He entered the newly founded college at Stanford, where he met his wife, Lou Henry Hoover, a fellow geologist and a woman of formidable accomplishments in her own right. As a mining engineer, businessman, and author, Hoover would make millions; in serving both Republican and Democratic presidents, before and after his own presidency, he would win national and international admiration for his relief work following both World Wars and for other humanitarian efforts. Yet his inability to devise a strategy to relieve economic distress during the early years of the Great Depression still defines his remembered legacy.

A studio portrait taken of candidate Herbert "Bert" Hoover in 1928.
Library of Congress / Prints and Photographs

The tiny board-and-batten cottage where Herbert Hoover was born.
Herbert Hoover National Historic Site

HARRY S TRUMAN
NATIONAL HISTORIC SITE
HARRY S. TRUMAN
(1945 – 1953)
INDEPENDENCE, MISSOURI

Former president Harry Truman described himself as a man "given to plain speaking." In very much the same spirit, he got behind the wheel of his own car when he left office in 1953 and, accompanied by wife Bess, headed home. He had no Secret Service protection and wanted none as he happily returned to private life in Independence, Missouri, the little city where he had spent virtually his entire adult life.

Today in Independence, Harry S. Truman (1884–1972) is recalled by visitors and townspeople alike as very much "the people's president." The fourteen-room Truman home looks much as it did when Harry and Bess took up residence with her parents after their 1919 honeymoon. Built by Bess's grandfather in 1885, the house has many touches on the exterior that enhance its Victorian character, including multiple rooflines, sawed and carved bargeboards, turned porch posts, and Queen Anne–style "picture windows" (sash with colored glass borders). Inside are tiled fireplaces and heavy mahog-

any furniture. Truman did little to the place over the years aside from adding carpeting and enlarging the back porch.

When Franklin Delano Roosevelt died on April 12, 1945, his vice president quite unexpectedly inherited the office of the president; by the time President Truman returned to Missouri in June of that year, welcomed by cheering townspeople, Independence had its own freshly painted white house on North Delaware Street. In his eight years in office, Truman would oversee the closing months of World War II and help shape the postwar world with the Truman Doctrine, the Marshall Plan, the Berlin Airlift, and the founding of the North Atlantic Treaty Organization. The former Missouri judge and U.S. senator is remembered today for protecting his predecessor's New Deal policies, making early steps in securing civil rights for African Americans, and establishing some basic principles in Soviet-American policy.

In his retirement years, Truman took a daily constitutional around the town. He raised funds for what would become the Harry S. Truman Library and Museum in Independence, and greeted visitors as if he were just an average resident of the town (in his characteristic manner, he titled the memoir he wrote in those years *Mr. Citizen*). The museum would contain an office for the former president, which today is preserved as it appeared at the time of his death.

This portrait of the thirty-third president, painted in 1945 by Jay Wesley Jacobs, hangs over the mantel at the home on North Delaware Street.
Harry S Truman National Historic Site

The Truman house is a rambling and generous six-bedroom home.
Harry S Truman National Historic Site

AFTERWORD

To write of the presidents has been a privilege. As a historian of the Revolutionary and early Federal eras, I came to the task of writing *Houses of the Presidents* well acquainted with the lives and times of the first four chief magistrates. Different as they were, George Washington, John Adams, Thomas Jefferson, and James Madison shared a common experience. To reapply Dean Acheson's pregnant phrase, they were present at the creation.

By contrast, the time span covered in this book is ever so much greater than the nation's first decades. The men in these pages have occupied the office throughout American constitutional history, the nearly two and a quarter centuries from George Washington's inauguration in 1789 to that of Barack Obama. I have had the singular honor to visit many of their domiciles in the course of the fifteen-thousand-plus miles traveled and the more than two years required to research and write this book. The challenge has been to understand each of these forty-three men in terms of their times and to place them, primarily, in their domestic contexts.

Given limitations of space, only so much of the vast material available could be incorporated into these pages; I would encourage the interested reader to learn more — there are satisfactions in the further investigation of these men, their houses, and their times. To advance that goal, you will find helpful information concerning travel to presidential sites in *Visitor Information* (see page 241) and, for armchair researchers, an annotated bibliography (see *For Further Reading,* page 248).

I brought to this project a mix of patriotism and curiosity, and a desire to understand the men — to date, alas, all have been men — who became president. Photographer Roger Straus and I have attempted to render onto the printed page evocative images of places and telling anecdotes of the presidents' lives. I hope that in the attempt we have illuminated something of the drama and tumult of American political life.

HUGH HOWARD
Hayes Hill, New York

VISITOR INFORMATION

GEORGE WASHINGTON'S MOUNT VERNON

President: George Washington (1789 – 1797)

Owner/Administrator: Mount Vernon Ladies' Association of the Union

Address: 3200 Mount Vernon Memorial Highway, Mount Vernon, VA 22309

Website: http://www.mountvernon.org

Phone: (703) 780-2000

Tours: Open daily

ADAMS NATIONAL HISTORICAL PARK

Presidents: John Adams (1797 – 1801) and John Quincy Adams (1825 – 1829)

Owner/Administrator: National Park Service, U.S. Department of the Interior

Address: 135 Adams Street, Quincy, MA 02169

Website: http://www.nps.gov/adam

Phone: (617) 770-1175

Tours: Open daily, April to November

MONTICELLO

President: Thomas Jefferson (1801 – 1809)

Owner/Administrator: Thomas Jefferson Foundation, Inc.

Address: 931 Thomas Jefferson Parkway, Charlottesville, VA 22902

Website: http://www.monticello.org

Phone: (434) 984-9822

Tours: Open daily, except Christmas Day

THOMAS JEFFERSON'S POPLAR FOREST

President: Thomas Jefferson (1801 – 1809)

Owner/Administrator: Corporation for Jefferson's Poplar Forest

Address: P.O. Box 419, 1542 Bateman Bridge Road, Forest, VA 24551

Website: http://poplarforest.org

Phone: (434) 525-1806

Tours: Open daily, March 15 to December 15, except Thanksgiving Day

JAMES MADISON'S MONTPELIER

President: James Madison (1809 – 1817)

Owner/Administrator: National Trust for Historic Preservation

Address: 11407 Constitution Highway, Montpelier Station, VA 22957

Website: http://montpelier.org

Phone: (540) 672-2728

Tours: Open daily, except Thanksgiving Day and Christmas Day

JAMES MONROE'S ASH LAWN-HIGHLAND

President: James Monroe (1817 – 1825)

Owner/Administrator: College of William and Mary

Address: 2050 James Monroe Parkway, Charlottesville, VA 22902

Website: http://www.ashlawnhighland.org

Phone: (434) 293-8000

Tours: Open daily, except Thanksgiving Day, Christmas Day, and New Year's Day

THE HERMITAGE, HOME OF PRESIDENT ANDREW JACKSON

President: Andrew Jackson (1829 – 1837)

Owner/Administrator: Ladies' Hermitage Association

Address: 4580 Rachel's Lane, Nashville, TN 37076

Website: http://www.thehermitage.com

Phone: (615) 889-2941

Tours: Open daily, except Thanksgiving Day, Christmas Day, and the
   third week in January

LINDENWALD

President: Martin Van Buren (1837 – 1841)

Owner/Administrator: National Park Service, U.S. Department
   of the Interior

Address: 1013 Old Post Road, Kinderhook, NY 12106

Website: http://www.nps.gov/mava

Phone: (518) 758-9689

Tours: Open daily, May to October

GROUSELAND

President: William Henry Harrison (1841)

Owner/Administrator: Grouseland Foundation, Inc.

Address: 3 West Scott Street, Vincennes, IN 47591

Website: http://www.grouseland.org

Phone: (812) 882-2096

Tours: Open Tuesday to Sunday in January and February; daily in
March to October, except Thanksgiving Day, Christmas Day,
and New Year's Day

BERKELEY PLANTATION

President: William Henry Harrison (1841)

Owner/Administrator: Berkeley Plantation

Address: 12602 Harrison Landing Road, Charles City, Virginia 23030

Website: http://www.berkeleyplantation.com

Phone: (804) 829-6018

Tours: Open daily, except Thanksgiving Day and Christmas Day

SHERWOOD FOREST,
HOME OF PRESIDENT JOHN TYLER

President: John Tyler (1841 – 1845)

Owner/Administrator: Sherwood Forest Plantation Foundation

Address: 14501 John Tyler Memorial Highway, Charles City, VA 23030

Website: http://www.sherwoodforest.org

Phone: (804) 829-5377

Tours: The grounds at Sherwood Forest are open daily; tours of the
interior of the house are by appointment only

JAMES K. POLK ANCESTRAL HOME

President: James K. Polk (1845 – 1849)

Owner/Administrator: James K. Polk Memorial Association

Address: 301 West 7th Street, Columbia, TN 38402

Website: http://www.jameskpolk.com

Phone: (931) 388-2354

Tours: Open daily

MILLARD FILLMORE HOUSE MUSEUM

President: Millard Fillmore (1850 – 1853)

Owner/Administrator: Aurora Historical Society

Address: 24 Shearer Avenue, East Aurora, NY 14052

Website: http://www.aurorahistoricalsociety.com

Phone: (716) 652-4735

Tours: Open Wednesday and weekends, June to October

FRANKLIN PIERCE HOMESTEAD

President: Franklin Pierce (1853 – 1857)

Owner/Administrator: State of New Hampshire / Hillsborough
Historical Society

Address: 301 2nd NH Turnpike, Hillsborough, NH 03244

Website: http://www.hillsboroughhistory.org/Franklin_Pierce_Homestead.html

Phone: (603) 478-3165

Tours: Open weekends, Memorial Day to Columbus Day

THE PIERCE MANSE

President: Franklin Pierce (1853 – 1857)

Owner/Administrator: Pierce Brigade

Address: 14 Horseshoe Pond Lane, Concord, NH 03301

Website: http://www.piercemanse.org

Phone: (603) 225-4555

Tours: Open mid-June to Labor Day, Tuesday to Saturday; September to
Columbus Day, Friday and Saturday

PRESIDENT JAMES BUCHANAN'S WHEATLAND

President: James Buchanan (1857 – 1861)

Owner/Administrator: LancasterHistory.org

Address: 230 North President Avenue, Lancaster, PA 17603

Website: http://www.lancasterhistory.org

Phone: (717) 392-8721

Tours: Open Monday to Saturday, April to October

LINCOLN HOME
NATIONAL HISTORIC SITE

President: Abraham Lincoln (1861 – 1865)

Owner/Administrator: National Park Service, U.S. Department of the Interior

Address: 426 South Seventh Street, Springfield, IL 62701

Website: http://www.nps.gov/liho

Phone: (217) 391-3226

Tours: Open daily, except Thanksgiving Day, Christmas Day, and New Year's Day

PRESIDENT LINCOLN'S COTTAGE
AT THE SOLDIERS' HOME

President: Abraham Lincoln (1861 – 1865)

Owner/Administrator: Armed Forces Retirement Home / National Trust for Historic Preservation

Address: Eagle Gate, intersection of Rock Creek Church Road NW and Upshur Street NW, Washington, D.C., 20011

Website: http://www.lincolncottage.org

Phone: (202) 829-0436

Tours: Open daily, except Thanksgiving Day, Christmas Day, and New Year's Day

ANDREW JOHNSON
NATIONAL HISTORIC SITE

President: Andrew Johnson (1865 – 1869)

Owner/Administrator: National Park Service, U.S. Department of the Interior

Address: 101 North College Street, Greeneville, TN 37743

Website: http://www.nps.gov/anjo

Phone: (423) 639-3711

Tours: Open daily, except Thanksgiving Day, Christmas Day, and New Year's Day

ULYSSES S. GRANT COTTAGE

President: Ulysses S. Grant (1869 – 1877)

Owner/Administrator: New York State Department of Parks, Recreation, and Historic Preservation / Friends of the Ulysses S. Grant Cottage

Address: Mount McGregor Road, Wilton, NY 12831

Website: http://grantcottage.org

Phone: (518) 584-4353

Tours: Open Wednesday to Sunday, Memorial Day to Labor Day; Saturdays and Sundays, Labor Day to Columbus Day

ULYSSES S. GRANT
NATIONAL HISTORIC SITE

President: Ulysses S. Grant (1869 – 1877)

Owner/Administrator: National Park Service, U.S. Department of the Interior

Address: 7400 Grant Road, St. Louis, MO 63123

Website: http://www.nps.gov/ulsg

Phone: (314) 842-1867

Tours: Open daily, except Thanksgiving Day, Christmas Day, and New Year's Day

ULYSSES S. GRANT HOME

President: Ulysses S. Grant (1869 – 1877)

Owner/Administrator: State of Illinois / Illinois Historic Preservation Agency

Address: 500 Bouthillier Street, Galena, IL 61036

Website: http://www.granthome.com

Phone: (815) 777-3310

Tours: Open Wednesday to Sunday, except Martin Luther King Day, Presidents' Day, Veterans Day, Election Day, Thanksgiving Day, Christmas Day, and New Year's Day

SPIEGEL GROVE

President: Rutherford B. Hayes (1877 – 1881)

Owner/Administrator: Ohio Historical Society / Rutherford B. Hayes Presidential Center

Address: Corner of Buckland and Hayes Avenues, Fremont, OH 43420

Website: http://www.rbhayes.org/hayes

Phone: (419) 332-2081

Tours: Open Tuesday to Sunday, except Easter, Thanksgiving Day, Christmas Day, and New Year's Day

JAMES A. GARFIELD
NATIONAL HISTORIC SITE

President: James A. Garfield (1881)

Owner/Administrator: National Park Service, U.S. Department of the Interior

Address: 8095 Mentor Avenue, Mentor, OH 44060

Website: http://www.nps.gov/jaga

Phone: (440) 255-8722

Tours: Open daily in May to October; weekends in November to April; closed Thanksgiving Day, Christmas Eve and Day, and New Year's Day

PRESIDENT CHESTER A. ARTHUR STATE HISTORIC SITE

President: Chester A. Arthur (1881 – 1885)

Owner/Administrator: Vermont Division for Historic Preservation

Address: 455 Chester Arthur Road, Fairfield, VT 05455

Website: http://www.historicvermont.org/sites/html/arthur.html

Phone: (802) 828-3051

Tours: Open weekends and Monday holidays, July to October

GROVER CLEVELAND BIRTHPLACE

President: Grover Cleveland (1885 – 1889, 1893 – 1897)

Owner/Administrator: New Jersey Department of Environmental Protection, Division of Parks and Forestry

Address: 207 Bloomfield Avenue, Caldwell, NJ 07006

Website: http://www.clevelandbirthplace.org

Phone: (973) 226-0001

Tours: Open Wednesday to Sunday, except state and federal holidays

BENJAMIN HARRISON PRESIDENTIAL SITE

President: Benjamin Harrison (1889 – 1893)

Owner/Administrator: Benjamin Harrison Presidential Site

Address: 1230 North Delaware Street, Indianapolis, IN 46202

Website: http://www.pbhh.org

Phone: (317) 631-1888

Tours: Open daily in June and July; Monday to Saturday in August to May, except the first three weeks in January, Memorial Day weekend, Labor Day, Thanksgiving Day, Christmas Eve and Christmas Day, and New Year's Day

SAXTON McKINLEY HOUSE

President: William McKinley (1897 – 1901)

Owner/Administrator: National Park Service/National First Ladies' Library

Address: 331 South Market Avenue, Canton, OH 44702

Website: http://www.firstladies.org/SaxtonMcKinleyHouse.aspx

Phone: (330) 452-0876, ext. 320

Tours: Open Tuesday to Sunday, June to August; Tuesday to Saturday, September to May, except Presidents' Day, Easter, Memorial Day, Independence Day, Labor Day, Thanksgiving Day and the day after, Christmas Day, New Year's Day, and during exhibit changes

SAGAMORE HILL NATIONAL HISTORIC SITE

President: Theodore Roosevelt (1901 – 1909)

Owner/Administrator: National Park Service, U.S. Department of the Interior

Address: 20 Sagamore Hill Road, Oyster Bay, NY 11771

Website: http://www.nps.gov/sahi

Phone: (516) 922-4788

Tours: The grounds are open daily, sunrise to sunset. The house is closed, however, until the completion of a rehabilitation project begun in spring 2012. The visitor center is open Wednesday through Sunday, except Thanksgiving Day, Christmas Day, and New Year's Day

WILLIAM HOWARD TAFT NATIONAL HISTORIC SITE

President: William Howard Taft (1909 – 1913)

Owner/Administrator: National Park Service, U.S. Department of the Interior

Address: 2038 Auburn Avenue, Cincinnati, OH 45219

Website: http://www.nps.gov/wiho

Phone: (513) 684-3262

Tours: Open daily, except Thanksgiving Day, Christmas Day, and New Year's Day

WOODROW WILSON HOUSE

President: Woodrow Wilson (1913 – 1921)

Owner/Administrator: National Trust for Historic Preservation

Address: 2340 S Street, NW, Washington, D.C., 20008

Website: http://www.woodrowwilsonhouse.org

Phone: (202) 387-4062

Tours: Open Tuesday to Sunday, except major holidays

WOODROW WILSON PRESIDENTIAL LIBRARY AND MUSEUM

President: Woodrow Wilson (1913 – 1921)

Owner/Administrator: Woodrow Wilson Presidential Library and Museum

Address: 20 North Coalter Street, Staunton, VA 24401

Website: http://www.woodrowwilson.org

Phone: (540) 885-0897

Tours: Open daily in March to November; Thursday to Sunday in the winter months, except major holidays

BOYHOOD HOME OF PRESIDENT WOODROW WILSON

President: Woodrow Wilson (1913 – 1921)

Owner/Administrator: Historic Augusta, Inc.

Address: 419 Seventh Street, Augusta, GA 30901

Website: http://www.wilsonboyhoodhome.org

Phone: (706) 722-9828

Tours: Open Tuesday to Saturday

WOODROW WILSON FAMILY HOME

President: Woodrow Wilson (1913 – 1921)

Owner/Administrator: Historic Columbia Foundation

Address: 1705 Hampton Street, Columbia, SC 29201

Website: http://www.woodrowwilsonhome.com

Phone: (802) 252-7742

Tours: At the time of this writing, the home is closed temporarily for restoration

HARDING HOME

President: Warren G. Harding (1921 – 1923)

Owner/Administrator: State of Ohio / Ohio Historical Society

Address: 380 Mount Vernon Avenue, Marion, OH

Website: http://hardinghome.org

Phone: (800) 600-6894

Tours: Open Memorial Day weekend and Wednesday to Sunday in June to September; Saturdays and Sundays in September and October; by appointment in November to May; closed Labor Day

PRESIDENT CALVIN COOLIDGE STATE HISTORIC SITE

President: Calvin Coolidge (1923 – 1929)

Owner/Administrator: Vermont Division for Historic Preservation

Address: 3780 Route 100A, Plymouth, VT 05056

Website: http://www.historicvermont.org/coolidge

Phone: (802) 672-3773

Tours: Open daily, May to October

HERBERT HOOVER NATIONAL HISTORIC SITE

President: Herbert Hoover (1929 – 1933)

Owner/Administrator: National Park Service, U.S. Department of the Interior

Address: 110 Parkside Drive, West Branch, IA 52358

Website: http://www.nps.gov/heho

Phone: (319) 643-2541

Tours: Open daily, except Thanksgiving Day, Christmas Day, and New Year's Day

HOME OF FRANKLIN D. ROOSEVELT NATIONAL HISTORIC SITE

President: Franklin Delano Roosevelt (1933 – 1945)

Owner/Administrator: National Park Service, U.S. Department of the Interior

Address: 4097 Albany Post Road, Hyde Park, NY 12538

Website: http://www.nps.gov/hofr

Phone: (800) 337-8474

Tours: Open daily, except Thanksgiving Day, Christmas Day, and New Year's Day

ROOSEVELT COTTAGE, ROOSEVELT CAMPOBELLO INTERNATIONAL PARK

President: Franklin Delano Roosevelt (1933 – 1945)

Owner/Administrator: Roosevelt Campobello International Park Commission

Address: Campobello Island, New Brunswick, Canada E5E 1A4

Website: http://www.fdr.net/roosevelt-cottage

Phone: (877) 851-6663

Tours: Open daily, June to November

ROOSEVELT'S LITTLE WHITE HOUSE HISTORIC SITE

President: Franklin Delano Roosevelt (1933 – 1945)

Owner/Administrator: Georgia Department of Historic Resources

Address: 401 Little White House Road, Warm Springs, GA 31830

Website: http://gastateparks.org/LittleWhiteHouse

Phone: (706) 655-5870

Tours: Open daily, except Thanksgiving Day, Christmas Day, and New Year's Day

HARRY S TRUMAN NATIONAL HISTORIC SITE

President: Harry S. Truman (1945 – 1953)

Owner/Administrator: National Park Service, U.S. Department of the Interior

Address: 232 North Main Street, Independence, MO 64050

Website: http://www.nps.gov/hstr

Phone: (816) 254-9929

Tours: Open daily, Memorial Day to November 1; closed Mondays the rest of the year

HARRY S. TRUMAN LITTLE WHITE HOUSE

President: Harry S. Truman (1945 – 1953)

Owner/Administrator: Key West Harry S. Truman Foundation

Address: 111 Front Street, Key West, FL 33040

Website: http://www.trumanlittlewhitehouse.com

Phone: (305) 294-9911

Tours: Open daily

TRUMAN FARM HOME

President: Harry S. Truman (1945 – 1953)

Owner/Administrator: National Park Service, U.S. Department of the Interior

Address: 12301 Blue Ridge Boulevard, Grandview, MO 64030

Website: http://www.nps.gov/hstr

Phone: (816) 254-9929

Tours: Open Friday, Saturday, and Sunday, Memorial Day to Labor Day

EISENHOWER NATIONAL HISTORIC SITE

President: Dwight D. Eisenhower (1953 – 1961)

Owner/Administrator: National Park Service, U.S. Department of the Interior

Address: 1195 Baltimore Pike, Suite 100, Gettysburg, PA 17325

Website: http://www.nps.gov/eise

Phone: (717) 338-9114

Tours: Open daily, except Thanksgiving Day, Christmas Day, and New Year's Day

EISENHOWER BIRTHPLACE STATE HISTORIC SITE

President: Dwight D. Eisenhower (1953 – 1961)

Owner/Administrator: Texas Historical Commission

Address: 609 South Lamar Avenue, Denison, TX 75021

Website: http://www.visiteisenhowerbirthplace.com

Phone: (512) 463-8908

Tours: Open Tuesday to Sunday, except Thanksgiving Day, Christmas Eve and Day, and New Year's Eve and Day

JOHN FITZGERALD KENNEDY NATIONAL HISTORIC SITE

President: John F. Kennedy (1961 – 1963)

Owner/Administrator: National Park Service, U.S. Department of the Interior

Address: 83 Beals Street, Brookine, MA 02446

Website: http://www.nps.gov/jofi

Phone: (617) 566-7937

Tours: Open Wednesday to Sunday, May to October

LYNDON B. JOHNSON NATIONAL HISTORICAL PARK

President: Lyndon Johnson (1963 – 1969)

Owner/Administrator: National Park Service, U.S. Department of the Interior

Address: Visitor Center and Boyhood Home: Johnson City, TX 78736; LBJ Ranch: Stonewall, TX 78621

Website: http://www.nps.gov/lyjo

Phone: (830) 868-7128

Tours: Open daily, except Thanksgiving Day, Christmas Day, and New Year's Day

NIXON PRESIDENTIAL LIBRARY AND MUSEUM

President: Richard M. Nixon (1969 – 1974)

Owner/Administrator: Richard Nixon Foundation; National Archives and Records Administration

Address: 18001 Yorba Linda Boulevard, Yorba Linda, CA 92886

Website: http://www.nixonlibrary.gov/themuseum/thebirthplace.php

Phone: (714) 983-9120

Tours: Open daily, except Thanksgiving Day, Christmas Day, and New Year's Day

JIMMY CARTER NATIONAL HISTORIC SITE

President: James Earl Carter (1977 – 1981)

Owner/Administrator: National Park Service, U.S. Department of the Interior

Address: 300 North Bond Street, Plains, GA 31780

Website: http://www.nps.gov/jica

Phone: (229) 824-4104

Tours: Open daily, except Thanksgiving Day, Christmas Day, and New Year's Day; the Carters' private residence and compound are not open to the public

RONALD REAGAN'S RANCHO DEL CIELO

President: Ronald Reagan (1981 – 1989)

Owner/Administrator: Young America's Foundation

Address: Ranch Center, 217 State Street, Santa Barbara, CA 93101

Website: http://www.yaf.org

Phone: (888) 872-1776

Tours: Open by appointment

RONALD REAGAN BOYHOOD HOME

President: Ronald Reagan (1981 – 1989)

Owner/Administrator: Ronald Reagan Boyhood Home

Address: 816 South Hennepin Avenue, Dixon, IL 61021

Website: http://reaganhome.org

Phone: (815) 288-5176

Tours: Open daily, April to November

PRESIDENT WILLIAM JEFFERSON CLINTON BIRTHPLACE HOME NATIONAL HISTORIC SITE

President: William Jefferson Clinton (1993 – 2001)

Owner/Administrator: National Park Service, U.S. Department of the Interior

Address: 117 South Hervey Street, Hope, AR 71801

Website: http://www.nps.gov//wicl

Phone: (870) 777-4455

Tours: Open daily, except Thanksgiving Day, Christmas Day, and New Year's Day

GEORGE W. BUSH CHILDHOOD HOME

President: George W. Bush (2001 – 2009)

Owner/Administrator: George W. Bush Childhood Home, Inc.

Address: 1412 West Ohio Avenue, Midland, TX 79701

Website: http://www.bushchildhoodhome.com

Phone: (432) 685-1112

Tours: Open Tuesday to Sunday, except Thanksgiving Day, Christmas Day, and New Year's Day

FOR FURTHER READING

For more than two centuries, uncounted scholars and writers have recorded, examined, and commented upon the U.S. presidents; their work constitutes a veritable library of life histories. Many of the presidents themselves are survived by papers that fill the presidential libraries devoted to them. In writing *Houses of the Presidents,* I have relied upon many primary sources (including diaries, journals, autobiographies, letters, official correspondence, and other documents), but as this work consists of brief biographies, architectural appraisals, and an array of dramatic stories, I have perused hundreds of secondary sources, including books, historic structure reports, articles, guidebooks, furnishing plans, pamphlets, monographs, obituaries, websites, and other printed materials. To the presidents and the authors who have gone before, then, my appreciation.

My thanks too to the librarians and archivists who helped me at the Library of Congress (special thanks to Kathy Woodrell and Emily Howie), the New York Public Library, the Boston Public Library, the New-York Historical Society, the Sterling and Francine Clark Art Institute Library in Williamstown, Massachusetts, the Sawyer Library at Williams College, and my local libraries, the Chatham Public Library in Chatham, New York, and the Milne Public Library in Williamstown, Massachusetts, as well as the collective resources of both the Mid-Hudson Library System and C/W MARS, the central and western Massachusetts library system.

To further investigate these men and places, see the list of suggested readings that follows, which represents a small sampling of the reference works drawn upon in researching this book.

1789 – 1797: GEORGE WASHINGTON

Undoubtedly more has been written on the general than about any other president, with two compendious twentieth-century biographies by James Thomas Flexner (*George Washington,* 4 vols., Little, Brown, 1965 – 1972) and Douglas Southall Freeman (*George Washington,* 7 vols., Scribner's, 1948 – 1957). While Washington's own papers and diaries fill many volumes, I would single out several secondary references on topics of particular interest—to wit: on architecture, *George Washington's Mount Vernon: At Home in Revolutionary America* by Robert F. Dalzell Jr. and Lee Baldwin Dalzell (Oxford, 1998); on his painted image, my own *The Painter's Chair* (Bloomsbury Press, 2009); and on slavery, Henry Wiencek's *An Imperfect*

God: George Washington, His Slaves, and the Creation of America (Farrar, Straus and Giroux, 2003). The full text of Joshua Brookes's commentary on his Mount Vernon visit, "A Dinner at Mount Vernon—1799," was reprinted in *New-York Historical Society Quarterly* XXXI, no. 2 (April 1947), 72 – 85. The official guidebook is *George Washington's Mount Vernon;* the website, http://www.mountvernon.org.

1797 – 1801: JOHN ADAMS;
1825 – 1829: JOHN QUINCY ADAMS

The most readable biographies are David McCullough's *John Adams* (Simon and Schuster, 2001) and Paul C. Nagel's *John Quincy Adams: A Public Life, a Private Life* (Alfred A. Knopf, 1997). The papers of father and son are invaluable resources; many are online at http://www.masshist.org/adams. For the architectural history, I drew upon the resources at the Adams National Historical Park, in particular Charles E. Peterson's reconnaissance report *The Adams Mansion* (National Park Service, 1963) and Helen Nelson Skeen's *Documentary Narrative of Buildings Shown on Historic Base Map of the Adams National Historic Site* (National Park Service, 1965, n.p.). In researching the opening anecdote concerning Gilbert Stuart, I learned from Andrew Oliver's *Portraits of John and Abigail Adams* (Harvard, 1967) and Carrie Rebora Barratt and Ellen G. Miles's *Gilbert Stuart* (Yale, 2004), and revisited *The Painter's Chair* (Bloomsbury, 2009). The website for the Adams National Historical Park is http://www.nps.gov/adam.

1801 – 1809: THOMAS JEFFERSON

The Jefferson literature is vast, beginning with Dumas Malone's six-volume *Jefferson and His Time* (1948 – 1981). Jack McLaughlin's *Jefferson and Monticello: The Biography of a Builder* (Henry Holt, 1988) is required reading for the student of Monticello. For Poplar Forest, the essential text is *Poplar Forest and Thomas Jefferson* by S. Allen Chambers Jr. (Corporation for Jefferson's Poplar Forest, 1993). The story of Monticello's second family is comprehensively told by Annette Gordon-Reed, in her closely argued *The Hemingses of Monticello* (Norton, 2008), though Lucia Stanton's *Free Some Day: The African-American Families of Monticello* (Thomas Jefferson Foundation, 2000) offers a broader view of African American life at Monticello. Both sites have very good guidebooks (*Monticello: A Guidebook* and *Thomas*

Jefferson's Poplar Forest: A Private Place); their websites are http://www .monticello.org and http://www.poplarforest.org.

1809-1817: JAMES MADISON

Irving Brant's six-volume *James Madison* (Bobbs-Merrill, 1941–1961) is the essential source for Madison; for Dolley, see Catherine Allgor's *A Perfect Union: Dolley Madison and the Creation of the American Nation* (Henry Holt, 2006). Much of the material for the opening vignette was drawn from Margaret Bayard Smith's letter to Anna Bayard Boyd, dated August 17, 1828, reprinted in Smith's *The First Forty Years of Washington Society* (Scribner's, 1906). Ralph Ketcham's *The Madisons at Montpelier: Reflections on the Founding Couple* (Virginia, 2009) is a brief and most readable look at the Madisons as framed by their lives in Central Virginia. The Montpelier guidebook *James Madison's Montpelier* offers a sound introduction to the site and, in particular, to its recent restoration; the website is http://www .montpelier.org.

1817-1825: JAMES MONROE

Biographical sources include Harry Ammon's *James Monroe: The Quest for National Identity* (McGraw-Hill, 1971) and Noble Cunningham's *The Presidency of James Monroe* (Kansas, 1996). A brisk recounting of the fifth president's long public life is to be found in *James Monroe* by Gary Hart (Times Books, 2005). Monroe's own papers are available in several incarnations, including *The Writings of James Monroe,* Stanislaus Murray Hamilton, ed. (1898–1903), and *The Papers of James Monroe,* Daniel Preston, ed. (Greenwood, 2003). The website for his home is http://www.ashlawn highland.org.

1825-1829: JOHN QUINCY ADAMS (SEE JOHN ADAMS, ABOVE)

1829-1837: ANDREW JACKSON

The essential Jackson scholar is Robert V. Remini, thanks to his voluminous writings on the seventh president, among them *Andrew Jackson and the Course of American Democracy, 1833–1845* (Harper, 1984). Jon Meacham's recent *American Lion* (Random House, 2008) is a most readable introduction to the presidential years. Jackson's collected six-volume *Correspondence of Andrew Jackson,* John Spencer Bassett, ed. (Carnegie Institution of Washington, 1926–1935), was an important resource for this chapter and makes surprisingly interesting reading. *The Hermitage: Home of Andrew Jackson* (the site guidebook) is a very useful introductory text in looking at the house and as an overview of Jackson's life. The website for the Ladies' Hermitage Association is http://www.thehermitage.com.

1837-1841: MARTIN VAN BUREN

As with Andrew Jackson, Robert V. Remini's scholarship is essential in considering Van Buren (in particular, see *Martin Van Buren and the Making of the Democratic Party,* Columbia, 1959). Also valuable is Donald B. Cole's biography *Martin Van Buren and the American Political System* (Princeton, 1984). The thirty-two-page monograph *Martin Van Buren* by Joseph G. Rayback (2006) is the de facto guidebook to the site, but the most essential document regarding Lindenwald is the National Park Service's historic resource study *A Return to His Native Town: Martin Van Buren's Life at Lindenwald, 1839–1862* (2006) by Leonard L. Richards, Marla R. Miller, and Erik Gilg (the full text of this resource study is available at Lindenwald's website, http://www.nps.gov/mava/index.htm).

1841: WILLIAM HENRY HARRISON

Though dated, the basic biography remains *Old Tippecanoe: William Henry Harrison and His Time* by Freeman Cleaves (Scribner's, 1939); a less sympathetic but more up-to-date examination of the man and his key role in the emergence of the Indiana territories is *Mr. Jefferson's Hammer* by Robert Owens (Oklahoma, 2007). Valuable primary sources are available online at http://www.archive.org/stream/messagesletters001harr#page/n13/ mode/2up. The Grouseland website is http://www.grouseland.org.

1841-1845: JOHN TYLER

John Tyler: The Accidental President by Edward P. Crapol (North Carolina, 2006) offers a measured view of Tyler; Oliver Perry Chitwood's *John Tyler: Champion of the Old South* (Appleton-Century, 1939) is slightly dated but more sympathetic. *And Tyler Too* by Robert Seager II (McGraw-Hill, 1963) looks more closely at John and Julia Gardiner Tyler's life together at Sherwood Forest. The website for the Charles City home is http://www .sherwoodforest.org.

1845-1849: JAMES K. POLK

Polk references include *The Presidency of James K. Polk* by Paul Bergeron (Kansas, 1987); Charles Sellers's readable and detailed two-volume recounting of the eleventh president's life, *James K. Polk, Jacksonian* (Princeton, 1957, 1966); and John Seigenthaler's briefer biography *James K. Polk* (Times Books, 2004). The guidebook to the site is *A Special House* by Betty Doak Elder (1980, 2004); on the Web, see http://www.jameskpolk.com.

1850 – 1853: MILLARD FILLMORE

The Fillmore literature is not extensive, but biographies include Robert J. Rayback's *Millard Fillmore: Biography of a President* (Buffalo Historical Society, 1959) and Benson Lee Grayson's *The Unknown President: The Administration of President Millard Fillmore* (University Press of America, 1981). The website for the Millard Fillmore House is http://www.aurorahistorical society.com.

1853 – 1857: FRANKLIN PIERCE

Peter Wallner's two-volume *Franklin Pierce* (Plaidswede, 2004, 2007) has become the standard biography. Regarding Pierce's presidency, see Larry Gara's *The Presidency of Franklin Pierce* (Kansas, 1991). Nathaniel Hawthorne's portrait of his friend's prepresidential years, *Life of Franklin Pierce* (1852), is an intriguing curiosity. The websites for the Pierce Manse and the Franklin Pierce Homestead are, respectively, http://www.piercemanse.org and http://www.hillsboroughhistory.org/Franklin_Pierce_Homestead.html.

1857 – 1861: JAMES BUCHANAN

Regarding Buchanan's home, the most valuable source is *The Story of Wheatland* by Philip Shriver Klein (Buchanan Foundation, 2003, originally published in 1936). Klein's biography *President James Buchanan* (Penn State, 1962) remains the standard. Jean H. Baker's *James Buchanan* (Times Books, 2004) offers a summary view of the man, while the dated but compendious two-volume *Life of James Buchanan* by George Ticknor Curtis (Harper, 1883) offers a flavor of the time. *Mr. Buchanan's Administration on the Eve of the Rebellion* (1866), written by Buchanan himself, is a carefully reasoned argument regarding his actions as the fifteenth president. See also http://www.lancasterhistory.org.

1861 – 1865: ABRAHAM LINCOLN

Dr. Wayne C. Temple's *By Square and Compass* (Mayhaven, 2001) offers an in-depth history of the Lincoln Home in Springfield and its builders and inhabitants; the monograph *Seventeen Years at Eighth and Jackson* by Thomas J. Dyba (IBC, 1982) provides a detailed look at life there. *Lincoln's Sanctuary: Abraham Lincoln and the Soldiers' Home* (Oxford, 2003) by Matthew Pinsker puts the Lincoln Cottage into a larger context. David Herbert Donald's *Lincoln* (Simon and Schuster, 1995) is a superior one-volume look at the life of the man; Doris Kearns Goodwin's *Team of Rivals* (Simon and Schuster, 2005) examines the Lincoln presidency. Among the many works on Mary Todd Lincoln, Jean H. Baker's biography (Norton, 1987) is a

good point of origin. The websites for both Lincoln sites offer much information: for the Lincoln Home, see http://www.nps.gov/liho/index .htm; for the Cottage, see http://www.lincolncottage.org.

1865 – 1869: ANDREW JOHNSON

Much of the Johnson bibliography is devoted to the 1868 impeachment trial and to his role in Reconstruction. For a more general look, see Hans Trefousse's readable and fair-minded biography *Andrew Johnson* (Norton, 1989); in her brief biography *Andrew Johnson,* Annette Gordon-Reed (Times Books, 2011) takes a much harsher view of both Johnson and his record as president. The website for the Andrew Johnson National Historic Site is http://www.nps.gov/anjo/index.htm.

1869 – 1877: ULYSSES S. GRANT

The Captain Departs by Thomas M. Pitkin (Southern Illinois, 1973) recounts the eventful last months; Mark Perry's *Grant and Twain* (Random House, 2004) tells of the two men's friendship. Josiah Bunting's brief life *Ulysses S. Grant* (Times Books, 2004) is a delight, erudite and steeped in military history. The *Personal Memoirs* of both Grant (Webster, 1894) and, in particular, wife Julia (Putnam, 1975) offer a look into the hearts and minds of the devoted couple. The website for the Grant Cottage is http://www.grantcottage.org.

1877 – 1881: RUTHERFORD B. HAYES

Hans Trefousse's brief biography *Rutherford B. Hayes* (Times Books, 2002) offers a current view of the man; more comprehensive is *Rutherford B. Hayes: Warrior and President* by Ari Hoogenboom (Kansas, 1995). Thanks to the Ohio Historical Society, Hayes's own words, as published in the five volumes of his diaries and letters, are online at http://www.ohiohistory .org/onlinedoc/hayes. The website for the Hayes Presidential Center is http://www.rbhayes.org.

1881: JAMES A. GARFIELD

Allan Peskin's *Garfield* (Kent State, 1978) remains the best life of the man. Ira Rutkow's *James A. Garfield* (Times Books, 2006) gives the life in short form; Rutkow, a professor of surgery, also takes a detailed look at the medical care Garfield received within its historical context. *The Diary of James A. Garfield* (Michigan State, 1967 – 1981) offers a chance to get acquainted with Garfield through his own words. The website for the James A. Garfield National Historic Site is http://www.nps.gov/jaga/index.htm.

1885–1889, 1893–1897: GROVER CLEVELAND

The best biography remains Allan Nevins's *Grover Cleveland: A Study in Courage* (Dodd, Mead, 1932). Richard E. Welch Jr.'s *The Presidencies of Grover Cleveland* (Kansas, 1988) examines his years in office; the most recent comprehensive biography, *Grover Cleveland: A Study in Character* by Alyn Brodsky (Truman Talley, 2000), takes a rather admiring look at the likable Cleveland. The website for the Grover Cleveland Birthplace State Historic Site is http://www.clevelandbirthplace.org.

1889–1893: BENJAMIN HARRISON

The Benjamin Harrison Presidential Site offers a brief history of the man and his house in its guidebook, which includes timelines and a brief overview of the twenty-third president's life as well as those of his family and key ancestors. For a broader look at Harrison, his military career, and his political life, the comprehensive choice is the three-volume *Benjamin Harrison* by Harry J. Sievers (1952–1968). At the other biographical extreme is Charles W. Calhoun's brief volume *Benjamin Harrison* (Times Books, 2005). The website for Harrison's Indianapolis home is http://www.presidentbenjaminharrison.org.

1897–1901: WILLIAM MCKINLEY

A monograph published by the National First Ladies' Library, Carl Sferrazza Anthony's *The President at Home* (2009), reviews the association of the twenty-fifth president with the Saxtons' house. Lewis L. Gould examines his time as chief executive in *The Presidency of William McKinley* (Kansas, 1980); Kevin Phillips takes a more bullish view of McKinley in his brief biography (Times Books, 2003). See also the National First Ladies' Library website, http://www.firstladies.org.

1901–1909: THEODORE ROOSEVELT

Sherman M. Craiger reported of Roosevelt's summer escape in "The President's Recreations at 'Sagamore Hill,'" *Town and Country* LXI, no. 24 (August 25, 1906); Charles Dawbarn's useful "Theodore Roosevelt, the Man and President: The Impressions of a Visitor to Oyster Bay" ran in the January 1909 issue of *Pall Mall Magazine*. Both were reprinted in *Selected Readings on Theodore Roosevelt and Sagamore Hill* (Sagamore Hill NHS, 1999). Various family memoirs recall the life of the place: Theodore Roosevelt Sr. and Jr. both wrote of it, as did daughter-in-law Eleanor B. Roosevelt in *Day Before Yesterday* (1959). For the full life, Edmund Morris's three-volume biography is unsurpassed (1979–2010). For a breezier look,

consult Louis Auchincloss's *Theodore Roosevelt* (Times Books, 2001), which offers an inside-society glimpse of the life through a novelist's eyes. The National Park Service website for Sagamore Hill is http://www.nps.gov/sahi/index.htm.

1909–1913: WILLIAM HOWARD TAFT

For an overview of the accomplishments of three generations of Tafts, see *An American Family* by Ishbel Ross (World, 1964). James Chace's *1912: Wilson, Roosevelt, Taft and Debs—The Election That Changed the Country* (Simon and Schuster, 2004) offers a balanced account of the election of 1912, in which Taft devolved to a supporting player. His letters to his wife during his presidential years, *My Dearest Nellie: The Letters of William Howard Taft to Helen Herron Taft, 1909–1912* (Lewis L. Gould, ed., Kansas, 2011), offer glimpses into both a marriage and the players in Washington at the time. The website for the Taft home is http://www.nps.gov/wiho/index.htm.

1913–1921: WOODROW WILSON

Several memoirs offer valuable recollections of the Kalorama house, not least the volumes by Wilson's widow, Edith (*My Memoir*, Bobbs-Merrill, 1939), and his physician, Rear Admiral Cary T. Grayson (*Woodrow Wilson: An Intimate Memoir*, Holt, 1960). Ray Stannard Baker's eight-volume *Woodrow Wilson: Life and Letters* (Doubleday, 1927–1939) is a basic resource. *When the Cheering Stopped* by Gene Smith (Morrow, 1964) is a moving and dramatic recounting of Wilson's late-life decline. Valuable for considering the National Historic Trust site is its summary brochure, *Woodrow Wilson House* (2008), and the forever-evolving website at http://www.woodrowwilsonhouse.org.

1921–1923: WARREN G. HARDING

The recent gossipy biography *Warren G. Harding* (Times Books, 2004), written by Nixon's White House counsel John Dean, is of interest; Dean brings insight to his subject, both as a child of Marion, Ohio, and for his triangulated views on the Harding administration's great scandal, Teapot Dome. Coauthors Eugene P. Trani and David L. Wilson examine Harding's twenty-nine months in office in *Presidency of Warren G. Harding* (Kansas, 1977). *The Rise of Warren Gamaliel Harding* by Randolph C. Downes (Ohio State, 1970) looks at his earlier life. The website for the home is http://hardinghome.org.

1923–1929: CALVIN COOLIDGE

The most current biography is Robert Sobel's *Coolidge: An American Enigma* (Regnery, 1998), but *Calvin Coolidge: The Man from Vermont* by Claude M. Fuess (Little, Brown, 1940) remains the most readable and comprehensive. Coolidge's *Autobiography* (Cosmopolitan, 1929) is, like the man himself, terse and occasionally wry but remains essential for the president's flashes of candor. Two organizations concerned with Coolidge and the village and farm at the "Notch" have useful websites. One, under the auspices of Vermont State Historic Sites, is http://www.historicvermont.org/coolidge; the other, that of Calvin Coolidge Memorial Foundation, is http://calvin-coolidge.org.

1929–1933: HERBERT HOOVER

In his long life—Hoover lived to age ninety—he wrote many books, including the two-volume *Memoirs of Herbert Hoover* (Macmillan, 1951–1952). A brief and thoughtful appraisal of the life is to be found in William E. Leuchtenburg's *Herbert Hoover* (Times Books, 2009); Richard Norton Smith examines Hoover's postpresidential years in *An Uncommon Man* (Simon and Schuster, 1984). The websites for the Herbert Hoover National Historic Site and the Herbert Hoover Presidential Library and Museum are, respectively, http://www.nps.gov/heho and http://hoover.nara.gov.

1933–1945: FRANKLIN DELANO ROOSEVELT

The young FDR comes alive in the pages of Geoffrey Ward's *Before the Trumpet* (Harper, 1985). Kenneth Davis's biography recounts the life in five very readable volumes, beginning with *FDR: The Beckoning of Destiny* (Putnam, 1972). The war years as experienced by both Eleanor and Franklin are explicated by Doris Kearns Goodwin in her much admired *No Ordinary Time* (Simon and Schuster, 1994). Eleanor left reams of writings, not least her book *This I Remember* (Harper, 1949). The National Park Service website for Springwood is http://www.nps.gov/hofr/index.htm.

1945–1953: HARRY S. TRUMAN

For Truman in his own words, see *Mr. Citizen* (Bernard Geis, 1960); for more vintage Truman via the work of writer Merle Miller, see the classic *Plain Speaking* (Berkley, 1974). Two traditional biographies are David McCullough's Pulitzer Prize–winning *Truman* (Simon and Schuster, 1992) and Alonzo Hamby's *Man of the People: A Life of Harry S. Truman* (Oxford, 1998). The respective websites for the Harry S Truman National Historic Site and the Harry S. Truman Library and Museum, both of which are located in Independence, are http://www.nps.gov/hstr and http://www.trumanlibrary.org.

1953–1961: DWIGHT D. EISENHOWER

Eisenhower's memoir, *At Ease* (Doubleday, 1967), is a thoughtful look at a life, with valuable material concerning the Pennsylvania farm; his *Letters to Mamie* (Doubleday, 1978) are a prism on the war years and Ike and Mamie's marriage. Michael Korda's *Ike* (HarperCollins, 2007) is a breezy biography. With respect to the Eisenhower home in Gettysburg, two publications offer some insight, namely the folksy *Ike: Gettysburg's Gentleman Farmer* by Stanley R. Wolf and Audrey (Wolf) Weiland (2008) and the collection of photographs that is *The Eisenhowers: Gettysburg's First Family* by Stan Cohen (Pictorial Histories, 1986). The National Park Service website for the Eisenhower National Historic Site is http://www.nps.gov/eise.

1961–1963: JOHN F. KENNEDY

Just as she played *the* central role in the restoration, Rose Kennedy's memoir, *Times to Remember* (Doubleday, 1974), is a key resource in seeking to understand the Kennedy birthplace. Doris Kearns Goodwin's *The Fitzgeralds and the Kennedys* (Simon and Schuster, 1987) puts the early players in a larger historical context, while Robert Dallek's more recent biography *An Unfinished Life* (Little, Brown, 2003) offers a measured view of President Kennedy. An invaluable document in considering the birthplace is the National Park Service historic resource study *John F. Kennedy's Birthplace: A Presidential Home in History and Memory* (2004), available online at www.nps.gov/history/history/online_books/jofi/birthplace.pdf. The National Park Service website for the John Fitzgerald Kennedy National Historic Site is www.nps.gov/jofi.

1963–1969: LYNDON JOHNSON

When it comes to straight biographies, Robert Caro's much admired and compendious three-volume life, *The Years of Lyndon Johnson* (Knopf, 1982–2002), tends to take a harsh view of the thirty-sixth president; Robert Dallek's two-volume life, *Lone Star Rising* and *Flawed Giant* (Oxford, 1991 and 1998), is perhaps kinder, though hardly partisan. Before his death, Johnson provided unique personal access to Doris Kearns Goodwin, then a presidential aide and Harvard graduate student; as she helped prepare his memoirs, he offered his recollections, and two books resulted. One, Goodwin's *Lyndon Johnson and the American Dream* (Harper, 1976), has the eerie reality of a late-night confessional as recorded by a Freudian;

Johnson's *The Vantage Point: Perspectives of the Presidency, 1963–1969* (Holt, 1971), despite occasional flickers of Johnson's warmth, is largely a cool and careful exercise in justification. Regarding the Johnson domiciles, *LBJ's Texas White House* by Hal K. Rothman (Texas A&M, 2001) is invaluable. The National Park Service website for the Lyndon B. Johnson National Historical Park is http://www.nps.gov/lyjo/index.htm.

1969–1974: RICHARD M. NIXON

Nixon's own autobiography, *RN: The Memoirs of Richard Nixon* (Grosset and Dunlap, 1978), provides a personal perspective on the author's childhood years. Many historians have taken aim at Nixon, among them Stephen E. Ambrose in his three-volume *Nixon* (Simon and Schuster, 1987–1991) and former *New York Times* columnist Tom Wicker, who offers a more sympathetic perspective in *One of Us: Richard Nixon and the American Dream* (Random House, 1991). Yet the elusive figure that was Nixon has yet to be rendered onto the page in a definitive way. The website for the Richard Nixon Foundation is http://nixonfoundation.org; for the Presidential Library and Museum, see http://www.nixonlibrary.gov.

1977–1981: JAMES EARL CARTER

The former president himself is perhaps the best source regarding life in Plains, Georgia. *An Hour Before Daylight* (Simon and Schuster, 2001), Carter's memoir of his childhood (and the complex racial culture that was Georgia in the years before World War II), is moving and vivid. His *White House Diary* (Farrar, Straus and Giroux, 2010) is an invaluable document. Rosalynn Carter's memoir, *First Lady from Plains* (Houghton Mifflin, 1984), suggests much of her gracious and candid manner. Oddly, not a little of the biographical literature is already dated, but among more recent works are a brief biography, *Jimmy Carter,* by Julian Zelizer (Times Books, 2010) and *The Unfinished Presidency* by Douglas G. Brinkley (Viking, 1998), devoted to his postpresidential years. The website for the Carter Center is http://www.cartercenter.org/index.html; for the Jimmy Carter National Historic Site, visit http://www.nps.gov/jica/index.htm.

1981–1989: RONALD REAGAN

The presidential *Reagan Diaries* (Harper, 2007) and Reagan's own memoir (*An American Life,* Simon and Schuster, 1990), as well as Nancy Reagan's *My Turn: The Memoirs of Nancy Reagan* (Random House, 1989), tell their life stories in their own words. The tandem of Edmund Morris's *Dutch* (Random House, 1999) and Lou Cannon's *President Reagan: The Role of a*

Lifetime (Simon and Schuster, 1993) offer complementary perspectives on the notoriously elusive man in question. Former Secret Service agent John Barletta's *Riding with Reagan* (Citadel, 2005) takes a from-the-saddle view of Reagan; the story of the ranch is recounted in detail in Peter Hannaford's *Ronald Reagan and His Ranch* (2002). The Young America's Foundation website has many pages dedicated to Rancho del Cielo at http://www.yaf.org/TheReaganRanch.aspx.

1989–1993: GEORGE H. W. BUSH
(SEE GEORGE W. BUSH, BELOW)

1993–2001: WILLIAM JEFFERSON CLINTON

Both the former president and his mother published memoirs in which life at the house at 117 South Hervey Street is warmly described; Clinton's book is *My Life* (Knopf, 2004), and Virginia Kelley's, cowritten with James Morgan, is *Leading with My Heart* (Simon and Schuster, 1994). The Clinton biographical literature is immense, and most authors mention, at least in passing, the house on Hervey Street. Many also seek to explain the complex psychodynamics of Billy Blythe and his two mothers (that is, his strict grandmother and his free-spirited mother). Psychologist John Gartner's *In Search of Bill Clinton* (St. Martin's, 2008) is particularly thorough, if somewhat speculative, in this regard. Two useful online sources of information include the website of the organization that purchased and restored the house as a museum at http://www.clintonchildhoodhomemuseum.com and the site of the present owner and operator, the National Park Service, at http://www.nps.gov/wicl.

1989–1993: GEORGE H. W. BUSH;
2001–2009: GEORGE W. BUSH

Memoirs by father (*Looking Forward,* with Victor Gold, Doubleday, 1987), mother (*Barbara Bush: A Memoir,* Scribner's, 1994), and son (*Decision Points,* Crown, 2010) tell the story of 1950s life in Midland, Texas. Two distinctly different approaches to the so-called Bush dynasty are apparent in *The Bushes* by Peter and Rochelle Schweizer (Doubleday, 2004) and *American Dynasty* by Kevin Phillips (Viking, 2004). The website for the George W. Bush Childhood Home is http://www.bushchildhoodhome.com.

ACKNOWLEDGMENTS

The memory keepers made this book possible, the men and women who restore, maintain, and operate these houses. We are indebted to a vast range of directors, curators, site managers, researchers, librarians, educators, archivists, owners, docents, and others. Thus, first and foremost, thanks must go to those who were our guides to the architectural past of the presidents.

At the individual presidential sites, then, listed in the order of the presidents we are remembering, the following are the people who were our most essential sources for individual chapters. At Mount Vernon, Carol Borchert Cadou, Dawn Bonner, Mary V. Thompson, and James Rees; the Old House, Kelly Cobble and Patty Smith; Monticello, Justin Sarafin, Robert Self, Susan Stein, Lisa Stites, Leah Stearns, and Leslie Greene Bowman; Poplar Forest, Travis McDonald, Octavia Starbuck, Lynn A. Beebe; Montpelier, Michael Quinn, Sean T. O'Brien, Lynne Hastings, Jeni Spencer, Ellen Wessel, and Peggy Vaughn; and David Mattern at the Papers of James Madison Project.

At Ash Lawn-Highland, we consulted Carolyn Holmes; at The Hermitage, Marsha Mullin; Lindenwald, Jim McKay, Patricia West, and Mike Wasko; Grouseland, Daniel B. Sarell; Sherwood Forest, Kay Tyler; James K. Polk State Historic Site, John Holtzapple and Thomas Price; Millard Fillmore House Museum, Robb Mair and Kathy Frost; the Pierce Manse, Michael Reopel and Jean Keckley Gannon; Wheatland, Patrick Clarke; Lincoln Home, David Wachtveitl, John Popolis, Rodney Naylor, and Susan Haake; President Lincoln's Cottage, Erin Carlson Mast, Alison Mitchell, and Richard Moe.

Kendra Hinkle was most helpful at the Andrew Johnson National Historic Site, as were Timothy Welch, Cindy Finger, Dave Hubbard, and especially Steve Trimm at the Ulysses S. Grant Cottage; thanks also to Tom Culbertson and Nan Card at Spiegel Grove; Todd Arrington at the James A. Garfield National Historic Site; John Dumville at the Chester A. Arthur State Historic Site; Sharon Farrell at the Grover Cleveland Birthplace; Jennifer Capps and Phyllis Geeslin, Benjamin Harrison Presidential Site; Patricia Krider, Saxton McKinley House / National First Ladies' Library; Mark Koziol, Susan Sarna, and Sherry Justus at Sagamore Hill; E. Ray Henderson, William Howard Taft National Historic Site; Frank Aucella and John Powell at the Woodrow Wilson House (Washington, D.C.); William Browning, Barbara Wimble, and Peggy Dillard at the Woodrow Wilson Presidential Library and Museum (Staunton, Virginia); Erick Montgomery, Boyhood Home of President Woodrow Wilson; Sherry Hall at the Harding Home; William W. Jenney at the Calvin Coolidge State Historic Site and Paul Carnahan, Vermont Historical Society; Cary Wiesner at the Herbert Hoover National Historic Site; Kevin R. Thomas and Scott Rector at Springwood and Robert Clark at the Franklin Delano Roosevelt Library; Mike T. Ryan at the Harry S Truman National Historic Site; John Joyce and Carol Hegeman at the Eisenhower National Historic Site; Jim Roberts, Desiree Taylor, Sara Patton, Myra Harrison, and Malka Benjamin of the John Fitzgerald Kennedy National Historic Site; Cynthia Dorminey at the Boyhood Home and Jonathan Penman-Brotzman at the Ranch, as well as Russ Whitlock and Rosa Lara, Lyndon B. Johnson National Historical Park; Robert Lyons of the Richard Nixon Foundation and Olivia Anastasiadis and Jonathan Movroydis at the Nixon Presidential Library and Museum.

At the Jimmy Carter National Historic Site, our thanks to Gary Ingram, as well as to Melissa Montgomery, Peggy Carson, Mary Prince, and most of all Rosalynn and Jimmy Carter for opening their home. Danielle Fowler was our guide at Ronald Reagan's Rancho del Cielo —our thanks to her and Marilyn Fisher, both at the Young America's Foundation; thanks as well to Laura A. Miller at the President William Jefferson Clinton Birthplace Home National Historic Site, and Martha Berryman at the Clinton Birthplace Foundation, Inc.; and finally our appreciation to Paul St. Hilaire, George W. Bush Childhood Home.

We are indebted too to our editor, Michael Sand, who has brought insight and enthusiasm, as well as patience, to the complex process of making this book. Thanks to Melissa Caminneci; Karen Landry, for finding our literary lapses; designer Jean Wilcox; and Elizabeth Garriga, publicist. Our heartfelt thanks, as always, to friend and agent Gail Hochman, for helping us negotiate our way around the ever-trickier world of publishing. Traveling companions Wayne Walker, Sarah Howard, Elizabeth Lawrence Howard, and Elizabeth Anne Howard offered valuable insights, as did many new and old friends encountered along the way—among them were Bruce Boucher, Christina Corsiglia, Jan and Jim Day, Michael Koortbojian, Jody Lahendro, Jane Lawrence, Pope Lawrence, Mark Magowan, Lynn Waggoner, and Glenn Williams. Our thanks to all.

INDEX

Italic page numbers refer to photos and their captions on the same or adjacent pages.

Little, Brown and Company

Hachette Book Group

237 Park Avenue, New York, NY 10017

littlebrown.com

First Edition: November 2012

Little, Brown and Company is a division of Hachette Book Group, Inc., and is celebrating its 175th anniversary in 2012. The Little, Brown name and logo are trademarks of Hachette Book Group, Inc.

The publisher is not responsible for websites (or their content) that are not owned by the publisher.

The Hachette Speakers Bureau provides a wide range of authors for speaking events. To find out more, go to hachettespeakersbureau.com or call (866) 376-6591.

The images that open the book; appear on its title page; and face the epigraph were taken, respectively, at the Adams National Historical Park; the President Calvin Coolidge State Historic Site; and James Madison's Montpelier.

Library of Congress Cataloging-in-Publication Data

Howard, Hugh

   Houses of the presidents : childhood homes, family dwellings, private escapes, and grand estates / Hugh Howard ; original photography by Roger Straus III.—1st ed.

      p. cm.

   Includes bibliographical references and index.

   ISBN 978-0-316-13327-2

   1. Presidents—Homes and haunts—United States. 2. Presidents—United States—Biography. 3. Dwellings—United States. 4. Historic buildings—United States. 5. Architecture, Domestic—United States. 6. United States—History, Local. I. Straus, Roger. II. Title.

   E176.1.H835 2012

   973.09'9—dc23

   [B]   2011051326

10 9 8 7 6 5 4 3 2 1

SC

Designed by Jean Wilcox, Wilcox Design

Printed in China